## Praise for Harold Senk

In an age of antichristian, antichurch, and anticlerical rhetoric, daring to enter the service of pastoral ministry is not just a noble task. It is a perilous one. Fightings within and fears without, the young man seeking to serve in word-and-sacrament ministry dares not walk alone. *Take Courage* is not just a tribute to a pastor's pastor who has dedicated some of the best years of his life to picking up fallen comrades along the way, binding their wounds and pressing them on. It is also a tool for young pastors and lay elders alike, a study guide for the challenges that face us, and an admirable contribution to the task at hand. *Be strong . . . all you who wait for the LORD!*

Rev. Jonathan Fisk
Author of *Broken, Echo,* and *Without Flesh*
St. Paul's Lutheran Church, Rockford, Illinois

*Take Courage,* the Festschrift in honor of Pastor Harold Senkbeil's long and fruitful ministry, delivers that which the title bids. Whether debunking the missional church paradigm by confessing the church as family, exposing the misguided mantra of pastor as leader with the true identity of pastor as a servant, or unpacking the gifts of confessing Christ's ascension for the pastoral ministry, these essays offer both timely and practical help. As the reflection on Jesus' parable of the Good Samaritan reminds us to be first served by Christ before we attempt to show mercy to others, this collection reflects how that truth has transformed the heart of Pastor Senkbeil and those blessed by his life.

Rev. Paul F. Becker, S.T.M.
Concordia Lutheran Church, Kingsport, Tennessee

This book is aptly titled: *Take Courage.* The essays contained herein cover the vast spectrum of pastoral care and practice. Each accomplishes what is intended by this book, that is, to encourage and strengthen pastors in their work of preaching the word and administering the sacraments rightly. The essay "Ten Reasons to Leave the Ministry and One Reason to Stay" alone is worth the price of this volume. Enjoy!

Rev. Bill Metzger
Holy Cross Lutheran Church, Cary, Illinois

All praise and thanks to God for the life and ministry of Harold Senkbeil! This festschrift is a fitting doxology to the Lord for the blessing that Rev. Senkbeil has been to so many.

His work through *DOXOLOGY: The Lutheran Center for Spiritual Care and Counsel* has been a tremendous blessing to pastors in helping them to grow in caring for the souls of others and for their own. Rev. Senkbeil's efforts have also benefited many lay people and congregations as they serve together with their pastors. Praise God from Whom all blessings flow!

Rev. Jon Rathjen<br>Trinity Lutheran Church, Auburn, Nebraska

This treasure of essays is a must-read for any pastor who feels his own failures in this office. You will find courage to be a faithful under-shepherd as you learn the habit of sitting at the feet of the Chief Shepherd. His leading makes this otherwise impossible office possible for you.

Rev. Matthew Wurm<br>DOXOLOGY Collegium Fellow<br>Mt. Calvary Lutheran Church, Brookings, South Dakota

What a great book! It reminds us that we need a pastor who is a shepherd and will point us in turn to the Good Shepherd. We should all, pastors and laity alike, read this book.

Rev. Benjamin Pollock

"Collegiality" has been a gift exhibited by Harold Senkbeil throughout his ministry. In him beats a desire both to know and to show a deep pastoral concern for his brothers in the ministry—brothers he has served for decades with characteristic deep humility. The essays found in *Take Courage* fittingly build upon and extend the legacy of Senkbeil's efforts on behalf of the glory of God and the good of his church.

Rev. Robert C. Zick, S.T.M.<br>2nd Vice President, South Wisconsin District

In our day and age, the Christian church often, and tragically, fulfills Forest Gump's famous words, "Mama always said, life is like a box of chocolates; you never know what you're going to get." Sadly, pastors are viewed as CEO's, life-coaches, or hired hands; and the church is somehow expected to be a spiritual 24-Hour Fitness, a Fortune 500 company, and more entertaining than Disney.

Thankfully, here is a collection of essays that buck these trends in favor of an older, more biblical view of church and ministry; in a word, *Seelsorge*, the care of souls. This is the pastor's vocation; this is the church's marching orders from Jesus in the Scriptures. Teach. Preach. Baptize. "Feed my sheep," Jesus says.

Harold Senkbeil has done this in the classroom and the pulpit for nearly half a century. In his work with DOXOLOGY he continues to be a pastor to pastors, teaching the art of caring for souls and instilling in undershepherds the love and mercy of their Good Shepherd. Here in this tome you will find refreshment for your soul, rest in the promises of Jesus in your vocation as pastor, and courage in Christ crucified for you. Happy reading!

Rev. Samuel Schuldheisz
Beautiful Savior Lutheran Church, Milton, Washington

A collection of essays centered on the gospel, *Take Courage* honors a pastor and professor who dedicated his life to proclaim the very same gospel. Harold Senkbeil knows firsthand the work of tending to the Lord's sheep with the staff of God's word. Nothing could honor such a pastor in a better way than a book which magnifies the Lord's work through that word to bring the comfort of the gospel to terrified consciences. This book does just that and is a joy for anyone to read.

Rev. Evan Goeglein
Host of Table Talk Radio
Faith Lutheran Church, Rogue River, Oregon

Hal first came to my attention via his first book, *Sanctification: Christ in Action*, and then soon after with *Dying to Live*. We were all struggling with how to make heads or tails of the Church Growth Movement, and especially its consequences for worship. We had been studying rubrics at the seminary but not really delving very deeply into the theology of worship overall. Kurt Marquart's dogmatics courses and the wonderful liturgical life at Kramer chapel were very influential. Hal's books really helped me put the practical side of Lutheranism in place. How is this Lutheran life lived corporately and individually? What joy I had as I raced through page after page of Law-Gospel clarity, and this written by a well-seasoned pastor who had tried the methods he now was critiquing! His service to the church has blossomed in amazing ways. His teaching career was stellar. The founding of DOXOLOGY, which has been such a positive force for good in the lives of pastors and their spouses and families, is the *coup de grâce*. Here's to you, my friend and father in Christ!

Rev. Dr. Matthew C. Harrison
President, The Lutheran Church—Missouri Synod

In this and every age, Christ's sheep and lambs become tangled in thickets of sin, despair, and cultural godlessness. *Take Courage* offers inspirational pastoral responses from seasoned voices, rich with biblical wisdom and rooted in the extravagant grace and love of God in Christ Jesus. These timely essays offer thought-provoking analyses and applications of soul-care practice and principles which will benefit any pastor who endeavors to serve the souls entrusted to his care. Happily, the Festschrift honors Senkbeil's 45 years of faithful pastoral work by inviting his "brothers and sons" in ministry to examine the necessity, the tools, the art, and the gift of spiritual care. You'll want this book on your desk; it's that good!

Dr. Beverly Yahnke
Executive Director for Christian Counsel
*DOXOLOGY: The Lutheran Center for Spiritual Care and Counsel*

# Take Courage

# Take Courage

ESSAYS IN HONOR OF
HAROLD L. SENKBEIL

*Edited by:*
**Timothy J. Pauls & Mark A. Pierson**

*Take Courage*

© 2016 New Reformation Publications

Published by:
New Reformation Publications
PO Box 54032
Irvine, CA 92619–4032

Publisher's Cataloging-In-Publication Data
(Prepared by The Donohue Group, Inc.)

Names: Pauls, Tim, 1967- editor. | Pierson, Mark A., 1976- editor.
Title: Take courage : essays in honor of Harold L. Senkbeil / Rev. Timothy J. Pauls and Rev. Mark A. Pierson, editors.
Description: Irvine, CA : NRP Books, New Reformation Publications, [2016] | Includes bibliographical references.
Identifiers: ISBN 9781945500572 (hard cover) | ISBN 9781945500589 (soft cover) | ISBN 9781945500596 (ebook)
Subjects: LCSH: Lutheran Church—Clergy. | Pastoral care. | Clergy— Counseling of. | Essays. | Senkbeil, Harold L.—Influence. | LCGFT: Essays. | Festschriften.
Classification: LCC BX8071 .T35 2016 (print) | LCC BX8071 (ebook) | DDC 284.1—dc23

Printed in the United States of America

Cover art by Ed Riojas

NRP Books, an imprint of New Reformation Publications, is committed to packaging and promoting the finest content for fueling a new Lutheran Reformation. We promote the defense of the Christian faith, confessional Lutheran theology, vocation and civil courage.

# Contents

# Tribute

*Fratrem cordis mei . . .*

"The saying is trustworthy: If anyone aspires to the office of over-seer, he desires a noble task" (1 Tim 3:1). Since St. Paul wrote these words to young pastor Timothy, countless other men have taken up the mantle of that noble task. Called and ordained into the office of overseer in the church, such men are yoked to Christ, to his unend-ing love, and to all for whom he shed his precious blood.

The occasion for this writing is the celebration of one who aspired to this noble task and, by God's grace, has now entered into his forty-fifth year of service to our Lord. I count it a high honor to mark this milestone in the life and service of my dear friend, Harold L. Senkbeil.

He is a *Seelsorger* of the highest order, passionately taking to heart our Lord's command to feed his lambs and nourish his sheep. For four-and-one-half decades, Hal has faithfully shepherded and fervently delivered the gifts of Christ's forgiveness, life, and salvation to those entrusted to his care. To this day he remains infatuated with the care of souls. Most recently for him, this means caring for the souls of pastors (and their wives) who enroll in *DOXOLOGY: The Lutheran Center for Spiritual Care and Counsel*, which is a unique advanced pastoral training program cofounded by Hal and his fel-low Executive Director, Dr. Beverly Yahnke. The program has gone global and his passion for the treatment of souls is beginning to be felt worldwide.

In fact, as Paul was to Timothy, so Hal is to many countless brothers and sons in the ministry. Dear to his heart are the souls placed into the office of overseer. As a DOXOLOGY Fellow, I

regularly see it and hear it first-hand, and have myself been tremen-
dously blessed by the great compassion and care this man offers in
the name and stead of Christ.

We first became acquainted with one another through the
shared joy of this noble task of ministry. At the time, he was a vet-
eran pastor and professor at Concordia Theological Seminary, Fort
Wayne, and I was a young pastor seeking to better myself with
an advanced degree. Soon after my classes ended, I enrolled in
DOXOLOGY where I grew even better acquainted with him, and
our bond of friendship flourished over our mutual pastoral passions.
As life would have it, our relationship deepened permanently with
the shared grief of similar tragic family losses.

Since then, we have grown to enjoy a deep fraternal bond that
is not very common these days. Perhaps it can be best expressed
by the bond shared between the elder Augustine and the younger
Alypius. They were confidants, peers, and intellectual sparring part-
ners, but they also provided mutual care and conversation to one
another. In his *Confessions*, Augustine referred to Alypius as *fratrem
cordis mei* (my heart's brother), and that phrase exemplifies the relationship we share today.

Of course, behind every good man there is often also a good
woman. Hal would be the first to tell you that he is what he is today
because of his wonderful wife, Jane. I have the privilege of calling her
a dear friend as well. (In fact, Hal and Jane are baptismal sponsors to
our youngest daughter, Soteria.) He would like nothing better than
that you know the tremendous woman, wife, mother, and grandmother that Jane is and how she has been endlessly supportive of
him through all of these years. The countless number of pastors and
parishioners who have been helped and healed by Hal in the name
of the Lord are a tribute to her selfless giving and sharing of this man
with all of us. Thank you, Jane!

The essays contained in this volume demonstrate the width
and breadth of the pastors and scholars that have been impacted
by the life and work of this man. We thank our Lord Jesus Christ
for giving us an undershepherd with the stature and grace of
Harold L. Senkbeil. He is beloved by many, but most especially
by our Lord, who shed his blood for Hal and who, 45 years ago,

charged Hal with the noble task to feed and tend his sheep. The voices heard within this book write in honor of this undershepherd and his life's service to Christ and his church.

Rev. Lucas V. Woodford, D.Min.
Zion Lutheran Church
Mayer, Minnesota
Twelfth Sunday After Pentecost, 2016

# Biographical Foreword

## Harold Leigh Senkbeil

*1945—(2020)*

Harold L. Senkbeil has earned the noteworthy reputation for being a pastor to pastors. His legacy includes providing colleagues with enrichment, encouragement, valuable resources, and personal pastoral care. Indeed, he has a penchant for reminding his brothers and sons in the ministry that the gospel is for them, too. To me, however, he is simply known as "Dad."

My personal memories as a pastor's kid verify what all who know him can attest: his vocation is a life of service to others. As children, my brother (Timothy), sister (Katherine), and I saw the same examples of sacrifice and service at home that members of the church received. I vividly remember, for instance, a visit to the playground in Morris, Minnesota, when I was seven years old and my sister was five. Kate was riding on the merry-go-round but lost her grip and slipped off. Dad quickly threw himself into her path and wrapped his arms around her to take the brunt of the fall. Undoubtedly, any loving parent would have done the same thing in that situation; but when you witness your own father doing it, it reinforces the comforting truth that you can always count on Dad.

Whether a pastor, author, or professor, he never lost sight of his calling to serve as the head of our household. An incident recalled by his good friend Lucas illustrates this well:

> Hal's daughter, Kate, tells the story of how she remembers meeting some young college pre-seminary guys who found out "who she is."

(I think she was in high school or early college at the time.) They excitedly began to fawn over what a great writer and theologian Pastor Senkbeil is, and how privileged they felt to meet his daughter. They even asked if perhaps, just maybe, she would be so kind as to help them meet *the* Pastor Senkbeil. Unimpressed by their banter, Kate simply replied, "Guys, he's my dad," implying that's a far better thing than any of the stuff they were saying about him.

Kate told me this once in front of Hal, and Hal simply smiled and said something like, "That's right. You're my girl. A father first, then a pastor." I remember thinking how important it is for pastors to hear that, especially coming from him.

Dad's devotion to our family began when he married our mother, Jane Frances Nesset, in 1971. They have been together for 49 years, which is as long as he has been in the ministry. Having raised his three children well, he now spends time with his four grandchildren who all live in the area of Waukesha, Wisconsin, where he currently resides.

When his busy schedule permits, Dad enjoys gardening and time outdoors. He has never lost his love of the farm life, having been born on March 6, 1945, in the farming community of Bellingham in western Minnesota. His parents, Harold and Enid Senkbeil, had him baptized and confirmed at Trinity Lutheran Church in Walter Township, and raised him with a strong work ethic. This upbringing served him well as he went on to complete undergraduate work at Concordia Senior College in Fort Wayne, Indiana (1967), as well as his Masters of Divinity (1971) at Concordia Theological Seminary in Springfield, Illinois, and his Masters of Sacred Theology (1986) from the same institution after it moved to Fort Wayne, Indiana.

My father served as a parish pastor in the Lutheran Church—Missouri Synod (LCMS) for 31 years. He began his ministry in the established parishes of Bethlehem Lutheran Church in Mahnomen, Minnesota, then Zion Lutheran Church in Morris, Minnesota, before taking a mission call in 1980 to Madison, Wisconsin. Seven years later he accepted what would become his longest call to Elm Grove Evangelical Lutheran Church in Elm Grove, Wisconsin, where he served until 2002. That same year, Dad began training others for the office of the ministry when he joined the faculty of Concordia

Theological Seminary as Associate Professor of Pastoral Ministry and Missions. He taught there full-time until 2008 and remained an adjunct professor for some years thereafter.

One of Dad's biggest passions is sharing his years of parish ministry experience when helping develop the skills of pastors. That is why he happily accepted the call in 2008 to serve as the Executive Director for Spiritual Care at DOXOLOGY, a Recognized Service Organization of the LCMS. This has allowed him to impart his wisdom and, especially, the gospel to those who are called to shepherd Christ's sheep. Though he has many treasured memories of his service to the church, I believe Dad finds it especially fulfilling to build a legacy of care for his fellow pastors through his work at DOXOLOGY.

He has enjoyed various honors, accomplishments, and responsibilities along the way as well. In 1988 he was given the *Servus Ecclesiae Christi* Award for his outstanding service to the LCMS. Although a fairly prolific writer, the books Dad is perhaps best known for are *Sanctification: Christ in Action* (1989) and *Dying to Live: the Power of Forgiveness* (1994), as well as his recent *The Care of Souls: Cultivating a Pastor's Heart* (2019). Somehow, he also found time to serve as an elected member of the Commission on Theology and Church Relations from 1988–2002. My father was greatly honored by Concordia Seminary, St. Louis, in 2001 in the bestowing of the degree of Doctor of Divinity, *honoris causa*, and was elected to the Board of Regents of that same institution in 2010. He continues to contribute to the academic growth and practical wisdom of the church, frequently addressing the cultural challenges of our times.

Despite his vocations and achievements over the years, however, I still only see him as Dad. His genuine care and selfless love for others begins and ends with his family. As another example of this, I will conclude with one of our favorite memories. During a family trip to an ocean-side beach, Dad, who has never been a strong swimmer, waded out with us kids. We swam around a while, but then noticed that the steady tide had taken Dad out to sea a few hundred yards. He began to panic and swim harder, but without much success. After struggling to keep his head above water, the waves pulled him under and he realized he was probably not going to make it. As Dad recalls it, there was nothing like a near-death experience where his life flashed before his eyes, and no specific memory came to mind.

Instead, having resigned himself to drowning, his only thought was the horrible inconvenience he was causing his family by dying *so far away from home*. "How in the world," he wondered, "is Jane ever going to get my body back there?" Concerned, as always, with taking care of everything for us, Dad had completely forgotten that him dying would be the bigger issue! Eventually Kate and I managed to rescue him, which made for a rare occasion when he was dependent on our help instead of the other way around. We laugh about the whole thing now, but deep down we are thankful beyond words that God saw fit to preserve the life of this amazing husband and father.

Michael L. Senkbeil
January 28, 2020

# Editorial Introduction

Any attempt to assess the results of a faithful pastor's work will invariably fall short, not least when that pastor is Harold "Hal" L. Senkbeil. Whether through books, articles, lectures, presentations, or word and sacrament ministry in the parish, Hal has provided care and cure for countless souls. His deft diagnosis and treatment of their sinful condition has enabled many to take courage in the sufficient work and comforting presence of Christ Jesus. Often times, the recipients of such healing have been pastors themselves. This, coupled with Hal's formation of future pastors at seminary, has allowed his remedial influence and restorative techniques to extend exponentially beyond himself. While he would be the first to insist that he has done nothing extraordinary, nothing more than what his calling requires—namely, performing the rudimentary task of delivering Christ and the forgiveness of sins and teaching others to do likewise—those who have benefited from and admired Hal's service can scarcely express their gratitude enough. Accordingly, this book is meant to honor his legacy and express a modicum of thanks for all his work as *Seelsorger*.

The editors would like to express heartfelt appreciation for the numerous people who helped make this project possible. Our biggest thanks go to the contributors whose essays provide various and helpful perspectives on pastoral care in the twenty-first century in the context of our Lutheran heritage. Collectively, they managed to meet our request that their work not be overly academic but appeal to a wide readership. It should be noted that additional students and colleagues of Hal were willing to participate, but were unable to do so for a number of reasons. One such reason was the demanding deadline we imposed to ensure this volume could be presented at a celebration in honor of the forty-fifth anniversary of his ordination. Although this tribute was initially conceived a few years prior in hopes of recognizing Hal on his seventieth birthday, it was postponed mainly due to several health problems suffered by Lucas Woodford. Lucas began as a co-editor, but begrudgingly stepped down when he realized his ailments would prove too much of a hindrance in completing the task. Nonetheless, he was involved every step of the way, for which we are grateful. And, thanks be to God, Lucas's condition has improved such that he returned to full-time parish ministry and has since been elected president of the Southern Minnesota District of the Lutheran Church—Missouri Synod.

Once the project was up and running again, we were guided by Beverly Yahnke's optimism and persistent encouragement that a collection of essays *could* be put together in six month's time. To meet this pressing goal, we received assistance with proofreading which proved invaluable. This small army of helpers includes Jason Braaten, Adriane Heins, Katie Hill, Sarah Ludwig, Jeni Miller, Dana Niemi, Gretchen Roberts, and Rebecca Thompson. Although the hurried version initially presented at Hal's anniversary celebration was expected to be penultimate, various events—both personal and professional—delayed the final publication further. We gratefully acknowledge Hal's patience, as well as that of the contributors, in the intervening time.

Greatly appreciated are the artists who have honored Hal with their remarkable talents. Edward Riojas kindly agreed to have his magnificent painting, "The Great Shepherd," grace the cover of this volume. Stephen P. Starke and Phillip Magness have composed a forceful yet beautiful hymn for just this occasion. It is from "Take Courage, Brothers, in the Lord" that the present tome receives its title.

Lastly, we are indebted to the generosity, flexibility, and kindness of NRP Books who made this publication possible. It is their hope and ours that the contents of these pages will both pay tribute to Harold L. Senkbeil and serve as a helpful resource for any would-be physician of the soul.

Rev. Timothy J. Pauls
Good Shepherd Lutheran Church
Boise, Idaho
DOXOLOGY Collegium Fellow

Rev. Mark A. Pierson
St. Paul's Lutheran Church
Long Beach, California
Ph.D. Candidate

# Abbreviations

| | |
|---|---|
| *ANF* | *The Ante-Nicene Fathers*, eds. Alexander Roberts and James Donaldson, 1885–1887, 10 vols. (reprint; Peabody, Mass.: Hendrickson, 1994). |
| **BDAG** | *A Greek-English Lexicon of the New Testament and Other Early Christian Literature*, eds. W. Bauer, F. W. Danker, W. F. Arndt, and F. W. Gingrich, 3rd ed. (Chicago: University of Chicago Press, 2000). |
| *JSNTSup* | *Journal for the Study of the New Testament: Supplement Series.* |
| **Kolb-Wengert** | *The Book of Concord: The Confessions of the Evangelical Lutheran Church*, eds. Robert Kolb and Timothy J. Wengert, trans. Charles P. Arand et al. (Minneapolis: Fortress Press, 2000). |
| *LW* | *Luther's Works*, American Edition: eds. Jaroslav Pelikan and Helmut Lehmann, vols. 1–55 (St. Louis: Concordia; Philadelphia: Fortress, 1955–1986); eds. Christopher Boyd Brown and Benjamin T. G. Mayes, vols. 56–82 (St. Louis: Concordia, 2009–). |
| *PG* | *Patrologia graeca* [= *Patrologiae cursus completus: Series graeca*], ed. J.-P. Migne, 162 vols. (Paris, 1857–1886). |
| **Tappert** | *The Book of Concord: The Confessions of the Evangelical Lutheran Church*, ed. and trans. Theodore G. Tappert (Minneapolis: Augsburg Fortress, 1959). |

| | |
|---|---|
| **TDNT** | *Theological Dictionary of the New Testament*, eds. G. Kittel and G. Friedrich, trans. G. W. Bromiley, 10 vols. (Grand Rapids: Eerdmans, 1964–1976). |
| **Triglotta** | *Triglot Concordia: The Symbolic Books of the Evangelical Lutheran Church*, ed. F. Bente (St. Louis: Concordia, 1921). |
| **WA** | *D. Martin Luthers Werke: Kritische Gesamtausgabe*, 73 vols. (Weimar: H. Böhlau, 1883–2009). |
| **WABr** | *D. Martin Luthers Werke: Briefweschel*, 18 vols. (Weimar: H. Böhlau, 1930–1985). |
| **WA DB** | *D. Martin Luthers Werke: Deutsche Bibel*, 12 vols. (Weimar: H. Böhlau, 1906–1960). |
| **WUNT** | Wissenschaftliche Untersuchungen zum Neuen Testament. |

## References to the Book of Concord:

| | |
|---|---|
| **AC** | Augsburg Confession |
| **Ap** | Apology of the Augsburg Confession |
| **Ep** | Epitome of the Formula of Concord |
| **FC** | Formula of Concord |
| **LC** | Large Catechism |
| **SA** | Smalcald Articles |
| **SC** | Small Catechism |
| **SD** | Solid Declaration |
| **Tr** | Treatise on the Power and Primacy of the Pope |
| **RN** | Rule and Norm of the Formula of Concord |

# Hebrews on Liturgical Leadership

## John W. Kleinig

"Leadership" has become a buzzword and trendy topic for the last few decades both in the world and in the church.[1] As is usually the case with any similar intellectual fashion, the popularity of a topic shows our lack of good leaders and how confused we are about the true definition of leadership. Worse, discussion about the characteristics of good leaders in the church seldom appreciates how spiritual leadership differs from secular or political leadership. Though church leaders may have the same set of skills as other leaders, they differ in their authorization and the way they exercise authority. God appoints leaders in the church and authorizes them to act on his behalf as his ministers. He equips them with his word to work with him in the administration of his grace. Thus in Hebrews 13:7 the author reminds the church of all ages that its leaders lead by speaking God's word. And the better they speak his word, the better they lead the church.

That definition may seem far too simple to cover the knowledge and expertise needed to lead a congregation, let alone a denomination. Yet the task of speaking God's word is far more complex and demanding than it appears at first glance. It goes way beyond biblical knowledge and theological understanding. Any pastor who teaches

---

[1]See, for example, the two influential handbooks of Stephen R. Covey: *The Seven Habits of Highly Effective People: Restoring the Character Ethic* (New York: Simon & Schuster, 1989); and *Principle-Centered Leadership* (London: Simon & Schuster, 1992).

God's word must do much more than just tell what the Bible says and explain what the church confesses. A good pastor does everything with the word and teaches in the process. He enacts God's word for God's people aptly in the divine service and in the pastoral care of their souls. He does the work of God by saying what God is saying and giving what God is giving to them; he offers God's grace to people pastorally as "timely help" (Heb 4:16). He does not offer the whole Bible to people all at once, but speaks the right word from it that meets their need. No one can learn that from a textbook. It is a matter of wisdom that is gained from experience and given as needed.

Like a good physician who is equally skilled in the diagnosis and treatment of his patients, a wise church leader knows what to say, to whom, when, where, and how, so that the word has the right effect on its hearers. For that to be done well, three things are required. First, the church leader needs to steep himself in God's word in meditation and prayer, so that as it speaks to his own conscience, he himself is fed and led by it. Second, he needs to use God's word to diagnose the spiritual state of his people, the state of their souls as is evident from the behavior of their conscience in reaction to God's word. Third, guided by God's own diagnosis of his people, he needs to speak the relevant word of God as law or gospel to their conscience. That requires much spiritual skill, the expertise that God's Spirit provides from case to case and situation to situation.

The letter to the Hebrews shows us how the complexity of leading God's people with God's word is done. Here we have a good pastor, a wise leader, who uses God's word to lead his people in worship and holy living. He leads them pastorally and winsomely from the pulpit in the divine service. Despite his erudition and eloquence, the most remarkable thing about him is his self-effacement. He deliberately encourages the congregation to join with him in listening to the voice of God rather than his own voice (2:1). He does not share his own views, but has his flock hear what God is saying to them, there and then, from his word. He adopts this stance because God himself gives them a good conscience and ushers them into his presence in the heavenly sanctuary through his word. He leads them with God's word as he himself is led by it. He leads them in their reception of God's heavenly gifts, "the better things that belong to their salvation" (6:9).[2]

My dear friend, soul mate, and brother in ministry, Hal Senkbeil, has been such a leader. While he has eschewed high office as a district president or church official, he has shown wise pastoral leadership to the members of the congregations whom he has served, students whom he has taught at Concordia Theological Seminary, and pastors whom he has mentored so ably through DOXOLOGY. He has used God's word to diagnose their spiritual maladies and provide healing for their souls. He has used it liturgically to deliver a good conscience and usher them from earth to heaven in the divine service. He has led God's people with God's word.

On the anniversary of his ordination, I am very pleased to present this essay on preaching in Hebrews to honor Dr. Senkbeil for leading so many people wisely and well with God's word. It is my thank offering to God the Father through his Son for Hal's ministry and his fraternal friendship. He has led God's people by speaking God's timely word to them and me in season and out of season. I can offer no higher praise than that!

## Hebrews as a Written Sermon

In 13:22, the author of Hebrews describes his letter as "a word of encouragement."[3] While this description indicates the purpose of this written discourse, it also designates its genre. It is now commonly agreed that Hebrews is a written sermon, a homily to an unnamed

---

[2]The Son is the first of twelve "better gifts" that belong to the eschatological inheritance of the congregation (1:4). Since God's Son has purified the heavenly things with the blood from "better sacrifices" than in the old covenant (9:23), he is much "better" than the angels (1:4) and Abraham (7:7). He is the mediator of a "better covenant" (7:22; 8:6), ordained by "better promises" (8:6) which offer "the better things that belong to salvation" (6:9) and the "better hope" (7:19) for a "better resurrection" (11:23) and a "better possession" (10:34) in a "better fatherland" (11:16). In this new covenant the Son speaks "something better" than the blood of Abel (12:24), "the better thing" that God has foreseen for the congregation (11:40).

[3]Much of what follows comes from the introduction to my commentary, *Hebrews* (Concordia Commentary; St. Louis: Concordia, 2017).

congregation.[4] The same term is used in Acts 13:15 to describe Paul's address to the assembled congregation in the synagogue on the Sabbath at Pisidian Antioch.[5] Both this noun and its verbal stem are used elsewhere in the New Testament for expository preaching that culminates in an appeal to the congregation for an appropriate response to what has been said (Acts 2:40; Rom 12:8; 1 Tim 4:13; 6:2; 2 Tim 4:2; Tit 1:9; 2:15). Hebrews is, in fact, "the only example in the New Testament of a homily that has come down to us in its entirety."[6]

This word of encouragement was most likely meant to be read out aloud, in place of the usual sermon, to a congregation who had assembled for the divine service. Its liturgical character is evident in the inclusion of a formal benediction and doxology at the end of the main discourse in 13:20–21. The covering note in the final verses shows that the sermon was sent as a letter to the congregation. As it

---

[4]See the following: William L. Lane, *Hebrews* (2 vols.; *Word Biblical Commentary 47A–B*; Dallas: Word, 1991), lxxiv–lxxv; Victor C. Pfitzner, *Hebrews* (*Abingdon New Testament Commentaries*; Nashville: Abingdon Press, 1997), 20; David A. deSilva, *Perseverance in Gratitude: A Socio-Rhetorical Commentary on the Epistle "to the Hebrews"* (Grand Rapids: Eerdmans, 2000), 57–58; Craig R. Koester, *Hebrews: A New Translation with Introduction and Commentary* (Anchor Bible 36; New York: Doubleday, 2001), 80–81; Luke Timothy Johnson, *Hebrews: A Commentary* (*The New Testament Library*; Louisville: Westminster John Knox, 2006), 10–11; Ben Witherington III, *Letters and Homilies for Jewish Christians: A Socio-Rhetorical Commentary on Hebrews, James and Jude* (Downers Grove, Ill.: InterVarsity Press, 2007), 20–21; Peter T. O'Brien, *The Letter to the Hebrews* (*The Pillar New Testament Commentary*; Grand Rapids: Eerdmans, 2010), 20–21; Gareth Lee Cockerill, *The Epistle to the Hebrews* (*The New International Commentary on the New Testament*; Grand Rapids: Eerdmans, 2012), 12–14; and Albert Vanhoye, *The Letter to the Hebrews: A New Commentary* (trans. Leo Arnold; New York / Mahwah, N.J.: Paulist Press, 2015), 1–2. Other commentators, such as Simon J. Kistemaker, *The Exposition of the Epistle to the Hebrews* (*Baker New Testament Commentary; Grand Rapids: Baker, 1984*), 3–4, and Paul Ellingworth, *The Epistle to the Hebrews* (The New International Greek New Testament Commentary; Grand Rapids: Eerdmans, 1993), 59–62, regard Hebrews as a letter with homiletical characteristics.

[5]This kind of preaching assumes that God gives hopeful encouragement to his people through the Scriptures (1 Macc 12:9; Rom 15:4).

[6]Vanhoye, *Letter to the Hebrews*, 238.

was read in the assembly, the author addressed his hearers directly as if he were himself present with them both as a member of that community and as its teacher.[7]

Over the last sixty years the work of some scholars has set this thesis on much more certain foundations than ever before. Building on their studies, others have also drawn out the far-reaching implications of this understanding of Hebrews as a written sermon.

The first scholar to investigate how Hebrews resembled the homilies given in the synagogues of the Jewish Hellenistic diaspora was Hartwig Thyen in 1955.[8] He noted the following similarities: the direct address of the audience as "you" in its plural form as well as with the inclusive "we," the citation of texts from the Septuagint as the foundation for the discourse, the use of inferential particles to mark the flow of the argument, and the frequent recourse to admonition.[9]

After a lapse of thirty years, Lawrence Wills corroborated, deepened, and extended Thyen's analysis.[10] Wills argued that Hebrews adapted a three-part pattern commonly used in Jewish Hellenistic and early Christian liturgical discourses. This pattern uses authoritative examples from the Old Testament with biblical quotations and their exposition to provide the foundation for its argument, explains their present relevance to those who are addressed, and culminates in an exhortation based on the conclusions of its exposition.

Thus, Hebrews is a sermon addressed by an unnamed teacher to an unnamed congregation. Even though it has been turned into a letter by the covering note in 13:22–25, the final benediction with its doxology in 13:20–2 shows that it, like Paul's ecclesiastical letters,[11] was obviously meant to be read as a sermon in the liturgical assembly

---

[7]See O'Brien, *Letter to the Hebrews*, 21.

[8]Hartwig Thyen, *Der Stil der Jüdisch-Hellenistischen Homilie* (*Forschungen zur Religion und Literatur des Alten und Neuen Testaments*, n.s. 47; Göttingen: Vandenhoeck & Ruprecht, 1955).

[9]James Swetnam has summarized and assessed this groundbreaking research in "On the Literary Genre of the 'Epistle' to the Hebrews," *Novum Testamentum* 11 (Oct. 1969): 261–69.

[10]Lawrence Wills, "The Form of the Sermon in Hellenistic Judaism and Early Christianity," *Harvard Theological Review* 77 (Oct. 1984): 277–99.

[11]See Thomas M. Winger, *Ephesians (Concordia Commentary*; St. Louis: Concordia, 2014), 10–12, 53–54.

of the community to whom it was sent. Hebrews therefore functions primarily as an oral communication meant to be read out aloud in an assembly and heard by its audience in its liturgical context.[12]

## Preaching Encouragement

In Hebrews, the verb παρακαλέω, "encourage" or "comfort," and its noun παράκλησις, which means both "encouragement" and "comfort," derive their meaning and function from the Septuagint. There, the term is key in prophecies about God's final judgment and the role of the Messiah in the last times.

The term first takes on an eschatological nuance in the prophetic Song of Moses in Deuteronomy 32:1–43, whose use in the Greek-speaking synagogues led to its inclusion as the second of the Odes in the Septuagint. The author of Hebrews and his congregation seem to be so familiar with this song that it is quoted in Hebrews 1:6 and 10:30 as something that they both "know" (10:30). In Deuteronomy 32:36, Moses speaks about God's day of judgment when he would vindicate his people and "encourage" them by taking vengeance on his enemies.[13] Their encouragement comes from God's vindication of them, his justification of them.

That promise of eschatological encouragement for God's people is developed by the prophecies of Isaiah, where it takes on the extra nuance of comfort in grief and pain. In Isaiah, God's grief-stricken people are comforted by a word or act that alleviates their pain by dealing with its cause, such as death, destruction, and captivity. Encouragement provides a wide range of emotional comfort apart from vindication and restoration, such as consolation in bereavement and freedom from guilt, cheer in unhappiness and relief from pain, solace in discomfort and release from anxiety, courage in weakness,

---

[12]See Witherington, *Letters and Homilies for Jewish Christians*, 38; Albert Vanhoye, *Structure and Message of the Epistle to the Hebrews* (*Subsidia Biblica 12*; Rome: Pontifical Biblical Institute, 1989), 40; and Arthur A. Just, Jr., "Entering Holiness: Christology and Eucharist in Hebrews," *Concordia Theological Quarterly* 69 (Jan. 2005): 78.

[13]The Septuagint translates the Hithpael form יתנחם in Deuteronomy 32:36 with a future passive: "He will gain comfort for his servants."

and liberation from despair. The result of encouragement is a change of emotional state, a change of mood, from sadness to joy, from fear to hope, from grief to jubilation, from uncertainty to confidence. Its purpose is peace (Isa 57:18–19).

That note of comforting encouragement is first sounded in the great prophecy of Isaiah 35, part of which is paraphrased in Hebrews 12:12. After promising that God's people would see the Lord's glory in the city of Zion in Isaiah 35:1–2, the Septuagint introduces the theme of encouragement in its translation of 35:3–4:

> Be strong, you listless hands and weakened knees!
> Give encouragement, you faint-minded people:
> "Be strong! Don't be afraid!
> See your God renders justice and he will render it.
> He will come to save you."

The Septuagint therefore construes 35:4 as the word of encouragement that is to be spoken by the demoralized citizens of Zion to each other, a word that announces God will come to vindicate and save them. On that day of salvation they will be healed, so they will be no longer blind and deaf to God, no longer lame and dumb. Rather, redeemed and purified, they will rejoice as they walk on the holy way into God's presence in Zion, a city now transformed from a desert into a fertile oasis by God's glorious presence in it.

That theme of comforting encouragement reappears in Isaiah 40:1–11. There in the Septuagint, God himself thrice gives the command to "encourage" his people and their city Jerusalem,[14] because their time of humiliation is over and their sin has been undone. While the Hebrew text does not say who should speak that word, the Septuagint addresses it to the priests or to God's people as priests. God commissions them to speak his message of encouragement to his people. This prophecy adds two things to what has already been promised. On the one hand, the holy way that in Isaiah 35:8–10 had been depicted as the route by which God's people would return to

---

[14]The Septuagint translates the Hebrew imperative phrase "Cry to her" as "Comfort her."

him in Zion, is now described as the way by which the Lord would come to reveal his glory and salvation to all people on earth. On the other hand, the message of good news that announces the Lord's return with his people to Zion includes the promise in Isaiah 40:11 that, like a shepherd who carries the lambs in his arms and cares for the pregnant ewes, he would "encourage" them by bringing them back with him.

The subsequent prophecies of Isaiah expand on the "comforting encouragement" theme in four ways. First, God is the only one who "comforts" his people in captivity (51:12). The comfort that they speak to each other comes from him. In 41:27, the Septuagint reinforces this point by construing God's promise of good news—his gospel to Jerusalem—as his comforting encouragement of her on her journey back to God.[15]

Second, the prophecies explain the nature of God's comfort. In Isaiah 49:10 and 13, God promises to "comfort" his people by gathering them from distant places, traveling with them on their return from exile, and providing for them on their journey. In 57:18–19 God makes this promise to each penitent person:

> I have seen his ways and I will heal him;
> I will comfort him and give him true comfort,
> peace upon peace to those who are far and near . . .
> I will heal them.

Even though his people have grieved him by their sin, he pledges to provide true comfort for them by healing them and granting them ever-increasing peace.

Third, God promises to rebuild Zion, the holy city, and make it a place for comfort. Thus in Isaiah 51:3 we have his word that he would "comfort" Zion by turning the ruined city into his garden, a new garden of Eden, a place of joy and gladness, thanksgiving and praise.[16] And more than that! In 66:10–13, he declares that in his new creation he would use Zion, like a mother nursing her child at her

---

[15]The Septuagint gives this translation of 41:27: "I will give Zion a beginning and comfort Jerusalem for the journey."

[16]See also Jer 31:13; Zech 1:17.

comforting breast and holding it on her lap, to "comfort" those who mourn over her desolation.

Fourth, God would commission the Messiah, his anointed servant, to comfort his mourning people in Zion. The first allusion to this commission is in Isaiah 49:7–11, where God promises to comfort his people by appointing his servant to free the people from captivity and restore their inheritance from him in the land. That theme is developed more fully in 61:1–3, the Song of the Messiah. In that song, the Messiah himself declares that he was anointed and sent to "comfort" those who mourn over Zion by announcing God's amnesty to his people, their release from captivity (cf. Heb 9:22; 10:18).

Given the nature and extent of these prophecies of eschatological comfort, it is no wonder that the hope for the consolation of Zion figured so prominently in the expectation of the Messiah. Thus Luke does not need to explain what he means when he notes that Simeon was waiting in Jerusalem for the "consolation of Israel" at the coming of the Messiah (Luke 2:25–26). Likewise, Jesus assumes that his audience is familiar with that hope when he declares, "Blessed are those who mourn, for they shall be comforted" (Matt 5:4).

The fulfillment of those prophecies by Jesus led to a new kind of preaching in the early church, a way of teaching that expounded the Septuagint in terms of its fulfillment by Christ and used it to encourage the congregation as an eschatological community who already now in faith enjoys the blessings of the age to come.[17] Thus when Paul addressed the synagogue in Antioch, Luke describes it as "a word of encouragement" (Acts 13:15).

The letter to the Hebrews builds on that new tradition in two ways: with the author calling his sermon "a word of encouragement" (13:23) and then developing that theme in his sermon. Most significantly, in 6:18 he teaches that through God's sworn promises the congregation "has strong encouragement" to take hold of what they hope for—namely, their entry into the inner shrine in the heavenly sanctuary together with Jesus as their high priest. Already now, by faith, they can approach the throne of grace with freedom and confidence to receive God's mercy and grace (4:16). That encouragement, that

---

[17]See 1 Tim 4:13; 6:2; 2 Tim 4:2; and Tit 1:9 for use of this verb and its noun for that kind of preaching.

comfort, is an eschatological gift that they already now possess. Like a father with his sons, God provides "a word of encouragement" for his royal sons (12:5) so they may share in his holiness and produce the harvest of peace as they are healed by him (12:7–13). Since they have that comfort, the author instructs them to "encourage" each other to hear God's voice (3:13) and to gather together to provide mutual encouragement to live together as a holy, heavenly community on earth (10:24). He himself also "encourages" the congregation to bear with what he says (13:22) and pray for his reunion with them (13:19). So the author speaks his message of comfort and encouragement in a liturgical context. There they receive God's eschatological comfort as they participate in the divine service.

## The Liturgical Context of Hebrews: The Service of God

While there has been an ongoing and inconclusive debate on whether Hebrews either mentions or alludes to the Lord's Supper,[18] little attention has been given to its nature and purpose as a sermon in its liturgical context. Ben Witherington sums up this issue well:

> Since this homily is meant to be read in the context of worship, we should evaluate it in that light. In worship we praise God for what he has done and is, and we draw near to him, as the letter exhorts us to do, but in worship we also hear and learn what we must go forth and do. Hebrews then is a vehicle for worship that leads to the right sort of service.[19]

It is, however, hard to follow his advice because we are so severely hampered by disagreement on the nature, content, and purpose of worship, both then for that congregation in the ancient world and now in our modern ecumenical context.

While the sermon speaks only about the "worship" of the angels in the sense of their prostration before the exalted Lord Jesus in 1:6, it

---

[18]The following seven passages most likely allude to the participation of the congregation in the Lord's Supper: Heb 6:4–5; 9:20; 10:19–22, 29; 12:24; 13:9–12, 15.

[19]Witherington, *Letters and Homilies for Jewish Christians*, 38.

lays great weight on the "service" of the congregation (9:9, 14; 12:28) in contrast with the "service" of God's people in the old covenant (8:5; 9:1, 6; 10:2; 13:10). In fact, the sermon sets out to encourage the congregation to "serve" the living God in a well-pleasing way with a clean conscience (9:14; 12:28). In their service, they are, by faith, able to "come near" to God, in order to present their offerings to him and receive gifts from him (4:16; 7:19, 25; 10:1, 22; 11:6; 12:22). Thus this sermon promotes the faithful service of God in the divine service.

The liturgical character of the sermon corresponds with the theological purpose of the service. It revolves around the presence of Christ Jesus as their great high priest and their possession of him (4:14; 8:1; 10:21). He is available and accessible to them in their service. Through him they have access to God's presence in heaven (10:19–22). Because they "have" him as their high priest, they "have" the other eschatological gifts that come from God: strong encouragement to enter God's presence (6:18) and free-speaking access to God (10:19), the hope of God's blessing (6:19) and a great reward (10:35), a cloud of witnesses all around them (12:1), God's grace (12:26), and an altar that provides them with heavenly food (13:10).

He, their great high priest, serves the congregation as its mediator (8:6; 9:15; 12:24). Jesus is faithful in serving God and merciful in ministering to them (2:17). As their liturgical minister he, like the priests in the old covenant, brings them to God and God to them (8:2, 6). On the one hand, he now appears on their behalf with his blood before God in heaven (9:11–12, 24). There he stands in for them and intercedes for them (7:25). There he presents them with himself to God (2:13). Through him they come near to God and present their offerings to him (7:25; 13:15). On the other hand, Jesus also now speaks God's word to them on earth (1:2; 12:25). He proclaims God's name to them as he sings God's praises (2:10). He pardons their sins (2:17); he purifies them (9:14) and makes them holy (2:11; 13:12). Through his sprinkled blood, he offers them the better things that come from God (12:24), the better things that belong to their salvation (6:9). As they listen to him, they receive grace and mercy from God (4:16). Through Jesus, the great high priest, God equips them with every good thing for them to do what pleases him (13:21).

What, then, is the liturgical context of this liturgical homily? Was it a charismatic service in which the gifts of the Spirit were distributed and exercised? Yes, but that occurred as they heard the message of salvation (2:1–4) and shared a holy meal (6:4–5)! Was it a service of prayer and praise? Yes, but that was done in connection with hearing God's word (4:12–16) and eating the holy food that came from the Lord's altar (13:8–15)! Was it a service of the word with readings from the Septuagint and teaching, much like what happened in the Greek-speaking synagogues of the Jewish diaspora? Yes, but that service of the word was associated with the celebration of the Lord's Supper as a communal meal!

While we do not know exactly what was done, in what order, or how, the service most likely had the following components:

- Leaders who spoke God's word to the congregation (13:7, 17)
- The confession of faith in Jesus as the Christ, God's Son, and Lord (3:1; 4:14; 10:23)
- The presentation of psalms and hymns of praise together with the angels as a thank offering to God through Jesus (2:11–12; 12:22; 13:15)
- Readings from the Old Testament by which God spoke to the congregation through the prophets and by his Son (1:1–2)
- The exposition and application of the readings from the Old Testament by a teacher in a word of encouragement to the congregation (13:22)
- The presentation of offerings (13:16)
- Petitions for help from God (4:16; cf. 7:25)
- Intercessions for others (4:16; 13:18)
- Reception of Christ's body and blood in a sacrificial meal (13:9–12)
- The performance of a benediction (13:20–21)
- The performance of doxology to Jesus (13:21)
- A liturgical greeting for the bestowal of God's grace (13:25)

Thus Vanhoye accurately sketches out the liturgical context of Hebrews:

The Priestly Sermon (Heb 1:1–13:31) has been composed to be read aloud before a Christian assembly, doubtless like the one which St. Luke describes in Acts 20:7–8 or St. Paul in 1 Cor 14:26. The

Christians have come together to hear the word of God, to sing, to pray, and also, quite likely, to celebrate the Eucharist (cf. Acts 20:7; 1 Cor 11:20).[20]

It is therefore most likely that Hebrews was meant to be read as a sermon in the context of a service that began with the reading of the Old Testament and culminated in the celebration of the Lord's Supper. If that is so, then its liturgical setting is, in fact, much more significant for its interpretation than the social, cultural, and political context of the congregation.

The liturgical setting of this sermon colors how it is heard and understood both in its original context and in its present context. For example, if the congregation heard the words of Christ in the Lord's Supper, "This cup is the new covenant in my blood, which is poured out for you," this would, no doubt, have influenced how it understood the mention of "the new covenant" (8:8; 9:15; 12:24), the phrase "in the blood" (10:19; 13:20), and other similar references to the blood of Jesus (9:12, 14; 10:29; 12:24; 13:12). Likewise, the mention of attention to what had been heard in 2:1 and tasting the heavenly gift in 6:6 would also have been considered by the congregation in the light of its liturgical context. Thus, Art Just rightly notes that the issue for debate is not whether Hebrews refers, explicitly or implicitly, to the Lord's Supper in a few isolated verses, but whether this homily was addressed to a congregation who regularly celebrated the Lord's Supper. He argues that the latter was most likely the case, and therefore concludes:

> As a homily, Hebrews . . . is intended to be preached as a performative word in the context of a worshipping assembly where Christ is present bodily as he comes to the hearers in their ears through the word and in their mouths through the Lord's Supper.[21]

The liturgical context of the sermon determines how it is heard by the congregation.

---

[20]Vanhoye, *Structure and Message of the Epistle to the Hebrews*, 40.
[21]Just, "Entering Holiness," 78.

## The Liturgical Purpose of Hebrews: Communal Access to God

The issue of liturgical context is closely connected with the liturgical purpose of the sermon. If the hearing of this sermon prepared the congregation for the reception of the Lord's Supper, and if the risen Lord Jesus was regarded as the priestly host of that celebration, that context colors how the congregation considered its involvement with Jesus in the divine service and its approach of God through him. So too the exhortations in this sermon to hold onto its confession, to serve the living God, and to present their offering of praise to God through him![22]

The teaching on God's provision of access to himself through Jesus shows us the sermon's liturgical purpose,[23] which the author of Hebrews clearly regards as a communal undertaking, done publicly and corporately (4:15; 7:19, 25; 10:19–22; 12:22–24). Scott Mackie therefore rightly critiques those who, like John Scholer in *Proleptic Priests*,[24] hold that it is a subjective spiritual experience rather than a communal activity, a provisional anticipation of our eventual participation in the eschatological heavenly *cultus*.[25] He argues that "the author's entry exhortations must reflect the actual experience

---

[22]See the twelve inclusive hortatory appeals in 4:1, 11, 14, 16; 6:1; 10:22, 23, 24; 12:1, 28; 13:13, 15.

[23]See Marie E. Isaacs, *Sacred Space: An Approach to the Theology of the Epistle to the Hebrews* (*JSNTSup* 73; Sheffield: JSOT Press, 1992) for a careful examination of this theme in Hebrews.

[24]John M. Scholer, *Proleptic Priests: Priesthood in the Epistle to the Hebrews*, *JSNTSup* 49 (Sheffield: JSOT Press, 1991). See his stress on the inner spiritual service of God in prayer (11, 108, 142, 149). In a similar vein, Lane maintains that access to the heavenly realm is available in prayer (*Hebrews 1–8*, 115) and in an act of faith and commitment (*Hebrews 9–13*, 307–8), while for David G. Peterson in *Hebrews and Perfection: An Examination of the Concept of Perfection in the Epistle to the Hebrews* (Society for New Testament Studies Monograph Series 47; Cambridge: Cambridge University Press, 1982), 160–61, and O'Brien in *Letter to the Hebrews*, 184–85, 249, it is given by a new personal relationship with God.

[25]Scott D. Mackie, *Eschatology and Exhortation in the Epistle to the Hebrews* (WUNT II/223; Tübingen: Mohr Siebeck, 2007), 201–11.

of unhindered, substantial, and life-changing access to God and his Son."[26]

Well, how can that be? Hebrews, says Mackie, is an eschatological exhortation for those upon whom the end of the ages has come through the sacrificial self-offering and manifestation of Jesus as high priest in the heavenly sanctuary (9:26). There he provides them with access to God by interceding for them (7:25), cleansing (9:14), consecrating (2:11; 10:10, 29; 13:12), and perfecting them as members of God's household, which is the new sacral sphere (10:14). Through Jesus they enjoy the heavenly gift of the Spirit and the powers of the age to come for their earthly existence (6:4–5). So the teaching of Hebrews about the provision of access to God through Jesus as the great high priest culminates in exhortation to "come near" to God and his throne of grace (4:16; 10:19–22; 12:22–24; cf. 7:25).

Two answers have been given on how the congregation has access to God in the heavenly realm. The first is that this access refers to a mystical, visionary experience.[27] Mackie and Barnard, for example, hold that the author is a mystagogue who leads the congregation into a mystical encounter with the exalted Lord Jesus. His sermon stems from his own visionary meditation on certain key passages from the Old Testament, by which he engages the congregation imaginatively to produce a similar mystical experience. Yet despite its commendable attention to the importance of vision in Hebrews, this interpretation rests on uncertain foundations. Its main problem is that visionary experiences, such as Paul's revelation in 2 Corinthians 12:1–10, are not public and communal, but intensely private and personal. In contrast, Hebrews presupposes that the congregation shares a common vision of Jesus as their exalted priest and king (2:9; 3:1; 12:2).

---

[26]Scholer, *Proleptic Priests*, 208.

[27]See Scott D. Mackie, "*Heavenly Sanctuary Mysticism in the Epistle to the Hebrews*," *Journal of Theological Studies* 62 (Apr. 2011): 77–117; and Jody A. Barnard, *The Mysticism of Hebrews: Exploring the Role of Jewish Apocalyptic Mysticism in the Epistle to the Hebrews* (WUNT II/331; Tübingen: Mohr Siebeck, 2012). Both of these scholars hold that Hebrews was profoundly influenced by Jewish apocalyptic mysticism.

The second and more traditional interpretation is that communal access to God is given liturgically in the divine service.[28] There the whole congregation participates in Christ and his priestly activity (3:14). Access to God comes from the common involvement of the congregation in the liturgical ministry of Jesus as their high priest (8:2, 6). As they hear the voice of God and Jesus and the Holy Spirit, the members of the congregation become enlightened, so that, like Moses (11:27), they all see what is otherwise unseen and hidden from human sight (6:4; 10:32).[29] As they hear God's word, they, by faith, "see" Jesus as God's Son and themselves as his holy brothers (2:9–13; 3:1; 12:1–2).

Thus the sermon in Hebrews teaches a kind of sacramental, liturgical "mysticism." It discloses the presence of Christ, divinely anointed Priest and King, with his brothers in the divine service. Communal access to God occurs in the congregation by way of a liturgical theophany (12:22–25). As the congregation participates in the divine service in heavenly Jerusalem, it experiences the new theophany of God, his gracious manifestation to his people, just as the Israelites had once experienced his theophany at Mount Sinai. In the divine service they hear Jesus "speaking" God's word to them from heaven (12:25).[30] There God the Father speaks to them (1:6–12; 5:6); there Jesus speaks to them (2:12; 10:5–7); there the Holy Spirit

---

[28]See Brooke Foss Westcott, *The Epistle to the Hebrews* (3d ed.; London: Macmillan, 1903), 415; N. A. Dahl, "A New and Living Way: The Approach to God according to Hebrews 10:19–25," *Interpretation* 5 (Oct. 1951): 408–11; O. Michel, *Der Brief an die Hebräer* (12th ed.; Göttingen: Vandenhoeck und Ruprecht, 1966), 461; Harald Hegermann, *Der Brief an die Hebräer* (*Theologischer Handkommentar zum Neuen Testament* 16; Berlin: Evangelischer Verlagsanstalt, 1988), 258; Ellingworth, *Epistle to the Hebrews*, 678; and Pfitzner, *Hebrews*, 187.

[29]For a discussion on the role of vision in Hebrews see Daniel J. Treier, "Speech Acts, Hearing Hearts, and Other Senses: The Doctrine of Scripture Practiced in Hebrews" in *The Epistle to the Hebrews and Christian Theology* (ed. Richard Bauckham et al.; Grand Rapids: Eerdmans, 2009), 337–50 and Mackie, "Heavenly Sanctuary Mysticism in the Epistle to the Hebrews," 104–17.

[30]While "him who speaks" could refer to the Lord God, the mention of the sprinkled blood of Jesus in the previous verse indicates that this is Jesus.

speaks to them (3:7; cf. 10:15–17).[31] There they hear the voice of God "today" (3:7, 13, 15; 4:7).

In the divine service, God's glory is revealed to the congregation in and through Jesus (1:1–4), just as it was manifest to the congregation of Israel at the tabernacle in the daily services (Lev 9:6, 23–24).[32] He is the radiance of God's glory (1:3). There and then, those who confess Jesus as Lord have access to the heavenly realm and the heavenly gifts by faith in God's word. His word shows them what they cannot otherwise see. Yet they do not merely hope for what will be given on the last day; they already now receive what they hope for from God. By faith they perceive what is otherwise unseen (11:1); they "see" what will be visibly shown to them only in the final theophany of our Lord (9:28).

Yet these heavenly gifts are already now given and disclosed verbally through God's word in the divine service as an unusual kind of theophany. In its worship, the earthly congregation straddles two worlds. As it participates in Christ, he involves the congregation in his priestly ministry. He engages the congregation in the service that is both earthly and heavenly, the service in which he officiates as high priest and is himself the radiance of God's glory (1:3). It is also in the service that God the Father speaks to the congregation in his Son, thus disclosing his glorious presence and delivering his heavenly gifts to his enlightened people.

In sum: the sermon in Hebrews is an example of liturgical preaching and teaching. In it, and by it, the teacher aims to lead his congregation into deeper and fuller participation in the divine service as he himself is led by God (6:1).

## Conclusion: Speaking What Is Heard

The author of Hebrews begins his written sermon by claiming that God "has spoken to us by his Son" (1:2). That "us" can be taken in

---

[31]Tellingly, the author uses the prophetic present tense "he says," as in 8:8–10, to introduce a divine oracle from the Old Testament as a word that God now speaks to his people.

[32]See John W. Kleinig, *Leviticus* (Concordia Commentary; St Louis: Concordia, 2003), 217–22.

two ways. On the one hand, it functions as an inclusive pronoun that refers to the whole congregation and the whole people of God in the new age. Thus as the author of Hebrews teaches, he stands with all those who hear what God has to say to them in his Son. That hearing stance is reinforced in 2:1 by his claim that "we must pay much closer attention to what we have heard." His identification with them continues for the duration of his sermon (1:3; 2:3; 4:13; 6:20; 7:14, 26; 9:14; 10:15, 20, 26; 11:40; 12:1, 9, 25; 13:21, 23). On the other hand, the pronoun "we" also functions as an exclusive pronoun that refers to all other teachers of God's word (2:5; 5:11; 6:9, 11; 8:1; 9:5; 13:18, 23). He therefore also stands with other pastors who have likewise received the message of salvation from the apostles (2:3).

It is often said that a good leader is a good listener, a person who uses both ears to pay equal attention to both points of view in a discussion or dispute. That description applies even more to pastors as leaders in the church. Yet church leaders differ from secular leaders in distinct ways. They do not stand at the head of a community of people here on earth; they stand before God the judge of all and Jesus the mediator together with all the people of God in the heavenly assembly (Heb 12:22–24). They speak God's word as they hear it from him; they pass on the good things that they receive from him; they do what he gives them to do. They also listen as their people react and respond to his word.

As pastors hear, so they speak. The better they hear, the better they speak God's word. The better they speak God's word, the better they lead their people who, as they come near to the throne of grace with free-speaking confidence, may receive God's mercy and find his grace that provides timely help for them (Heb 4:16).

# The Grammar of Absolution

*James Arne Nestingen*

In a classical treatment of Article V of the Augsburg Confession, Robert W. Jenson made a fruitful distinction between two different grammatical forms of the phrase "ministry of word and sacrament." The first is the subjective genitive, in which the word "of" functions to describe the ministry carried out through the preached word and the administered sacrament. The second is the objective genitive, in which the word "of" becomes "to." Ministry to the word and sacrament is a particular calling of the pastor, he argued, in which the pastor serves the "vivacity and authenticity" of the word and sacraments in the life of the congregation.[1]

Although preaching, baptism, and the Lord's Supper all call out for this second dimension of ministry, absolution is in particular need of service. Like the Son of Man himself, confession and absolution commonly has no place to lay its head. Congregations in a hurry pass over it altogether, keeping the sacred hour of worship in bounds; theologians dismiss it as the preoccupation of introspective consciences or, on the other hand, argue that people no longer see any need for it. Pastors seeking relevance paraphrase according to contemporary social standards, turning confession into a political statement. Christ's death for our sins has apparently become superfluous for many of his middle-class churches.

---

[1]Eric W. Gritsch and Robert W. Jenson, *Lutheranism: The Theological Movement and its Confessional Writings* (Philadelphia: Fortress, 1976), 117–19.

Given the necessity of ministry to word and sacrament and the contemporary confusion, there are compelling reasons for slowing down and taking a closer look at the practice of absolution. The purpose of this paper—written in tribute to a dear friend, a wise and faithful pastor—is to do just that: make a fundamental distinction and then examine the grammar involved in speaking this word.

## Therapeutic or Eschatological?

Some years ago, there was opportunity for conversation about this topic with Tuomo Mannermaa, the great Finnish theologian. The conversation began with a distinction between therapeutic and what might be called eschatological absolution. Mannermaa was convinced that for whatever significance forgiveness might have for healing, its real import is Christological and for the future that Christ is bringing to realization, that is, eschatological.

Therapeutic absolution involves people who have lost themselves inappropriately. The loss may be as apparently minor as the morning after the night before, when memories of excess bring embarrassment. More substantially, the loss may involve a marriage, a relationship with a parent, son, or daughter, or it might concern matters of vocation. Such memories have a way of taking on a life of their own, escalating into bondage. Circling ever more tightly into the self, they evoke continuing rehearsals of the relationships gone wrong and the consequent regrets. They may, while on the other side of the loss, include visions of retaliation or revenge accompanied by cycles of resolutions, all of them reflecting the ongoing failure. Beset in this way, a person gets lost in ever-increasing sorrow, helplessly carried along. In such circumstances, which are as common as country music, the absolution can literally restore the lost self so that a person can move forward in hope, gaining some new purchase on daily life and relationships. That is when its therapeutic character becomes apparent.

Because therapeutic forgiveness involves restoration, the participation of the self is critical to the process. The person forgiven must acknowledge the offense or the problem, and recognize the implication of the self in the situation. So, too, there must be a demonstrable willingness to make amends. Otherwise, the predicament prevails and the circling starts up all over again. Martin Luther defined repentance in just such terms: sorrow over sin along with a good resolve to seek the better.

As straightforward as this definition is, however, in its actual workings matters can get complicated. For example, as Luther pointed out in the Antinomian Disputations, repentance is often accompanied by confusion. There is a vague, uneasy sense that something has gone wrong, that relationships have changed for the worse. It appears that things are closing down, but it never focuses. This is something like what Franz Kafka described in *The Trial*. Mr. K, the protagonist, lives with a constant sense of accusation that never resolves into an indictment. The heart (or, in Luther's terms, the conscience), the sense of standing in relationship, circles through a variety of possibilities, trying to pin down the source of the difficulty but is never quite sure of what it might be.

In the anomie of contemporary culture, which effaces historic moral and ethical standards, leaving people rootless, this is a common problem. When the church neglects the Decalogue, whether by legalism or license, the confusion gets compounded. Penance is constant, but it does not become repentance—not without both the law and the gospel.

In a similar way, the therapeutic character of forgiveness can undermine it. Once again, in alcoholism for example, relationships circle up. Abuse feeds on itself. In the words of a great old pastor and therapist, Phil Hanson, a person gets sick and tired of being sick and tired. Instead of ending it, words of forgiveness prematurely spoken give life to the cycle, numbing instead of killing. There is neither resolution nor repentance—the bondage compounds itself.

Because of these and countless other permutations, Jesus joins the authority to absolve with the authority to retain (John 20:22–23; Matt 16:19). Retention of sins does not automatically equate with exclusion. Instead, it indicates that the person or people whose sins have been retained are not in a position to make faithful use of forgiveness at that point. By the same token, it involves a commitment to stay with those under retention until the timing is right so that absolution can be spoken with finality.

Gerhard Forde liked to say that the reasoning of the means of grace is flood logic. By its very nature, the grace of Christ Jesus rises

above the boundaries and limits generally imposed. At his coming,
every knee shall bow and every tongue confess that Jesus Christ is
Lord to the glory of God the Father. Absolution cannot be bound to
a particular office or chain of command. It can and should be spoken
by every baptized believer and even by some who are not. "He who
hears you, hears me," Jesus said (Luke 10:16).

At the same time, the therapeutic use of absolution requires
pastoral discernment. Hardly anything brings more assurance than
watching a faithful father and mother absolve their children. It is
like listening in on eternity to hear a dying spouse and the survivor
letting one another go in the promise of forgiveness. But genuine
*Seelsorge*, real service of the conscience, requires careful theological and pastoral discipline. Someone, who is grounded in the word
and has extended experience ministering to the conscience, needs
to be around to spot the tricks and traps of the old Adam and to
show the way to use the promise appropriately. In the examples mentioned, a conscientious pastor can see through the confusion and
name the specifics, which can be a great help. Genuinely repentant
people commonly do not know what is happening to them and hear
the specifics with relief. By the same token, a pastor, close enough to
hear but distant enough to see the topography of the narrative, can
recognize the point where a repetitive sinner is beginning to see the
self's implication in the predicament.

Eschatological forgiveness differs from the therapeutic version
on a couple of counts. It shifts the focus from the beneficiary to the
benefactor, from the one forgiven to the one who is so graciously
working out his purposes. As such, considered eschatologically,
absolution requires no qualifications from its recipients but depends
solely on the merit of Christ. Further, its purpose is not the restoration of the self but the genuine self-loss of faith. Its primary reference,
therefore, is not to the past but to the future Christ Jesus creates.

In New Testament stories of forgiveness, Jesus passes right
over the qualifications of those he so blesses. In Mark 2:4–12, for
example, Jesus' sermon is interrupted by a commotion on the roof
of the house. Four men carrying a paralytic have climbed the thatch
and removed enough of it to lower their friend into the room in
front of Jesus. Jesus ignores altogether any question of the paralytic's
religious fitness. He sees their faith—that is, the faith of the friends

carrying the stretcher—and absolves the paralytic. It is a sovereign act of grace.

This brings to the surface the real issue: Jesus' authority to forgive. The Pharisees strike at it immediately, asking, "Who can forgive sins but God alone?" apparently convinced that the question answers itself. In response, Jesus plays with them. He returns their question with an apparently nonsensical one of his own. Which is easier to say, the absolution or words of healing? Then, "that they may know that the Son of Man has authority on earth to forgive sins," he turns to the paralytic and puts him on his feet.

Everything turns here. Others in positions of responsibility gain their standing from precedent, appealing to prior practice, or from their position in a chain of authority. Just so, such people are dependent on the cooperation or submission of those to whom they speak. Jesus speaks "as one with authority." His word is complete unto itself. He does not require prior human authorization. Neither does he require the cooperation of the human will to complete what he has done. Like the words of the Creator, his speech does what he says.

His purpose becomes clear shortly after this incident in Mark's Gospel. He is "binding the strong man" so that he can "plunder his goods" (Mark 3:27). All of the different aspects of Jesus' ministry—his preaching and teaching, his exorcisms and healings, his willing submission to the cross and death, and his resurrection—share this common purpose. He is taking on the powers of deceit, death, and the devil that demean and destroy, that bind and capture creaturely life.

This makes the forgiveness of sins an all-out frontal attack on the bondage of the will that encloses us within ourselves. In this context, the endless discussions of who gets to say the absolving word or the quality of the response of those who hear it is just more evidence of sin's dominion. At this point, such questions are not only beside the point but more of the old Adam's diversions. It becomes clear in both the context and the declarations of the "keys" passage in John 20 that the forgiveness of sins is the contemporary equivalent of the resurrection of the dead. Jesus breaks the power of sin, one believer at a time in the whole community of the Christian church across the face of the earth, because, having been raised from the dead, he now has the last word. He is restoring Adam and Eve to the point from which they fell, clearing the chaos to renew the creation and make it a garden again.

Thus, the real force of confession and absolution is not for the past but rather the future. As Luther said in the Small Catechism, "Where there is forgiveness of sins, there is also life and salvation." A new future opens in the absolution, one in which the past no longer grips like grim fate, always threatening to catch up. Christ Jesus has taken up all of the indictments, real and imagined, into himself; he has broken the paralysis so that sinners can stand up and walk into a gracious future in which he makes and shapes the decisive turns of the day. Thus, for Luther, forgiveness is a synonym for freedom. Christ has opened the door and freed the captives.

Gustaf Wingren, whose major work was *Luther on Vocation*, often noted Jesus' common address to those he had healed or freed from the demonic.[2] There was the regular reference to the "messianic secret"—they were told to keep quiet about what happened. But then he also told such people to go home, to go about their business. This is where we generally die the daily death of repentance, signified by Holy Baptism. The jostlings of the self-seeking, the competitive rub of alternative futures in the making, the "hindering and defeating" of evil counsels that Luther referred to in the explanation of the third petition of the Lord's Prayer, all happen here, at home and at work. But the resurrection to newness of life, also signified by Holy Baptism, happens in just the same context. In the forgiveness of sins, it is possible to go home again and to be of some service.

So while among sinners the absolution has therapeutic implications and gifts to bestow, its real character is for the future: the immediate that unfolds a day at a time, but also the eschatological future when Christ will have completed his work. Jenson once called baptism "the last judgment let out ahead of time," and said the judgment is "unconditionally affirmative."[3] In the joyful redundancy of the means of grace, the same can be said of absolution.

---

[2] Gustaf Wingren, *Luther on Vocation* (trans. Carl C. Rasmussen; Eugene, Ore.: Wipf & Stock, 2004).

[3] Robert W. Jenson, "Christian Initiation: Ethics and Eschatology," *Institute of Liturgical Studies Occasional Papers*, Paper 14 (1981): 60.

## The Grammar

Lutherans whose ancestors immigrated to the United States and Canada from the Scandinavian churches, especially Norway, have had a long-standing conflict about public absolution. In the folk churches, both in northern Europe and in their approximations here, citizenship and church membership are the same. This has its disadvantages. Those who perceive themselves as devout always have to deal with sinners not so eager to join "the awakened." But for those who have claimed conversion, this has been a real annoyance. Proclaiming the absolution publicly obscures the difference, the argument goes, so that instead of being released, public sinners are being confirmed in their sinfulness.

Luther addressed a somewhat similar concern in the order for private confession and absolution he later included in the Small Catechism. He was convinced, on both biblical and pastoral grounds, that faith is necessary to the appropriation of the sacraments. So he wrote in the Large Catechism that "our faith does not constitute baptism but receives it" (LC IV, 53). This is the essential point. Like the sacraments themselves, absolution is Christ's work. Faith receives it, not as a legal qualification, but in using the benefits. So in the order for private confession, the pastor asks, "Do you believe that the words I am about to speak are God's word?" The question is down-to-earth and practical. Can you use this word? Can you hear what Christ is saying and cling to it? Faith, like prayer itself, is as simple as asking. If a sinner does not want Christ's benefits, there is no point in proceeding.

Scandinavian Lutherans in America went another way. For some, it was a breaking point in church union. The Church of the Lutheran Brethren split from the other Norwegian Americans who had gathered or who were just coming together in what eventually became the Evangelical Lutheran Church. Not surprisingly, the heirs of this protest—though they generally do not identify themselves as such—are among the most outspoken, if not vituperative, in attacking public absolution. They commonly also find issues with private confession and absolution. It appears sometimes that the real problem is forgiveness itself.

In the *Service Book and Hymnal* (*SBH*) of 1958, produced for the churches that came together in the American Lutheran Church thereafter, the problem of public absolution was solved to the satisfaction of the remaining protesters by making a distinction. The absolution opened with a generic statement about forgiveness, with no direct statement of the "for you." Following confession, the pastor said, "Almighty God, our heavenly Father, hath had mercy on us, and hath given his only Son to die for us, and for his sake forgiveth us all our sins."[4] With this, instead of moving to the "for you," the statement shifts into the third person. "To them that believe on his Name, he giveth power to become the sons of God and bestoweth upon them his Holy Spirit. He that believeth and is baptized shall be saved. Grant this, O Lord, unto us all."

The problems are evident. The generic statement of forgiveness has no address; it never comes home. Who are the "us"? For a sinner, caught in the confusion of repentance, the answer is bound to be "the others," an answer confirmed by the use of the third person. "They" are forgiven, "they" receive the gifts of the Spirit—but poor, miserable sinners are excluded. In fact, not coincidentally it appears, such a statement comforts the comfortable, convinced of their own righteousness, and afflicts the afflicted, struggling with themselves.

After further conflict, the *Lutheran Book of Worship* (*LBW*) of 1978, originally planned by a commission that included representatives of the Lutheran Church—Missouri Synod (LCMS), cleaned up some of the problems. The traditional protesters were given an out—an alternative form that maintained the generic. Such political concessions led wags to call the green hymnal the "Lutheran Book of Options." But this time around, the common service included a much more direct statement of absolution.

The first alternative opens with the generic statement familiar from the *SBH*. But in the *LBW*, it immediately turns more specific. There was a political compromise involved—in order to get a fuller, more direct statement of forgiveness, it was agreed to make it conditional on the office of the pastor. So the first form of the absolution reads, "As a called and ordained minister of the Church of Christ, and by his authority, I therefore declare to you the entire forgiveness of all your sins in the name of the Father, and of the Son, and of the Holy Spirit."[5]

---

[4]*Service Book and Hymnal* (Minneapolis: Augsburg, 1958), 1.
[5]*Lutheran Book of Worship* (Minneapolis: Augsburg, 1978), 56.

The second form of absolution in the *LBW* also bears the marks of compromise. This time around, it starts out specifically, "In the mercy of Almighty God, Jesus Christ was given to die for you, and for his sake God forgives you all your sins."[6] But what one hand gives the other takes away. Following the specifics, the absolution shifts back to the third person familiar from the *SBH*.

More difficult to predict is *Evangelical Lutheran Worship* (*ELW*), the hymnal of the Evangelical Lutheran Church in America (ELCA), released in 2006. The politicization of worship has resulted in 11 options for the common service. Apparently, you can get whatever you want, except of course, political incorrectness. But in fact, the language of the first alternative in the *LBW* is maintained in *ELW*, still with a more generic alternative.

Against the background of earlier ELCA hymnals, the *Lutheran Service Book* (*LSB*)—also from 2006—is surprisingly familiar, perhaps reflecting LCMS participation in the drafting of the *LBW*. In fact, *LSB* also presents two alternative forms of absolution, the first one almost identical to the absolution conditional on the pastoral office. But there is a critical difference. Having invoked the office and Christ's authority, the pastor says, "I therefore forgive you all your sins, in the name of the Father and of the Son and of the Holy Spirit," with a citation to John 20:19–23.[7] A declaration retreats one step from direct address, leaving the hearer to wonder about personal qualifications. *LSB* has closed the gap so that the old Adam cannot mess around: "I therefore forgive you." The alternative form of *LSB* retreats again, suggesting that Missouri can also find pietists in their ancestry. In this alternative, the more general statement is joined with a prayer: "May the Lord, who has begun this good work in us, bring it to completion in the day of our Lord Jesus Christ." If the absolution has been taken up into generalities, at least the community is joining the sinner in hope.

As complicated as the worship wars become, the grammar of absolution is as simple as the statement. Christ is the subject of the verb. If the pastor speaks "in his name and in his stead" to say "I forgive you," clearly the pastor is merely a stand-in for the one who has

---

[6]*Lutheran Book of Worship*, 56.

[7]*Lutheran Service Book* (St. Louis: Concordia, 2006), 151.

done, is doing, and will complete the work. If anyone else becomes the subject of the verbs in absolution, one of two things happen: either the self-confident set themselves at a distance from the sinners, or the certainty of the promise is undermined. The sinner turns back to the self rather than to Christ Jesus, and ends up mired down in uncertainty. When Christ remains in the center as speaker, the hearer is the direct object, the recipient or beneficiary. There is no substitute for the personal pronoun: I forgive you. Finally, a conditional absolution is no absolution at all. Any sinner worth his salt sees right through it and recognizes that the pious are playing games. Everybody loses.

# He Gave Gifts to Men

## The Ascension of Christ and the Office of the Holy Ministry

*Bryan Wolfmueller*

> *Jesus didn't just die for you; Jesus didn't just rise from the dead for you; He also ascended for you. That's why we celebrate this evening a joy that has no end. That's why we, like the disciples before us, can return to our homes tonight with great joy. We haven't lost someone we love even though we can see Him no more with these eyeballs of ours. He Himself promised: "Lo, I am with you till the close of the age."*
>
> —Harold Senkbeil, Ascension Sermon, 2007[1]

There are ten facts about Jesus confessed in the Apostles' Creed. Eight are about the past (his incarnation, birth, suffering, crucifixion,

---

[1]As long as I have known Dr. Senkbeil—first as a student at Concordia Theological Seminary in Fort Wayne, Ind., then as a colleague in DOXOLOGY, now through the DOXOLOGY Collegium, and especially as a friend—he has been concerned with the "right now" life of the church. This includes the life of her pastors, families, and individuals, for it is the life that Jesus continues to serve his people from the font, pulpit, and altar. This concern is good and godly; in fact, it is Jesus' own concern. He was raised to "shepherd his flock in the strength of the Lord" (Mic 5:4).

death, burial, descent into hell, and ascension) while one pertains to the future (his second coming). But there is also a sentence that speaks of how things are now, the present reality: "He sits at the right hand of God the Father Almighty." The ascension of Jesus has to do with the "right now" life of the church, which is why she confesses this line with joy and clarity.

Jesus ascended into heaven to take his place at the Father's right hand, to sit in his appointed place, to rule and reign over the entire cosmos as the one who was crucified for sinners. This is pictured beautifully in the revelation that Jesus gave to John. In the midst of the throne in heaven is the Lamb who was slain (Rev 5:6; 7:17). He is enthroned with divine power and receives worship, yet he still has the wounds of his cross. So the crucifixion and the ascension are bound up together. The glory of the cross is extended into heaven. The blood that speaks better things than the blood of Abel (Heb 12:24) is carried as evidence into the heavenly courtroom, and now we have an advocate with the Father, Jesus Christ the righteous one (1 John 2:1–2).[2]

Jesus enters the heavenly holy of holies, but unlike the priests of the old covenant who *stood* in the temple to offer sacrifices perpetually, Jesus *sits*—a testimony that he offered one sacrifice for all time (Heb 10:11–13). The work of atonement for the sins of the world is accomplished. Death is destroyed. The devil is bound. The cry from the cross, "It is finished" (John 19:30), is proven true as Jesus takes his place at the Father's right hand.

The ascension of Jesus, then, is the defining confession of the current reality of the church, a bold declaration that the one who died for us now rules and reigns over the entire cosmos for us. God the Father, Paul tells us,

---

[2]First, note that the Greek word *paraklete* (παράκλητος) used in 1 John 2:1 to describe Jesus' role in the heavenly court is also used by Jesus as a title of the Holy Spirit in John 14:16; 15:26; 16:7. Just as Jesus brings the testimony of his blood into the heavenly court, so the Holy Spirit brings both the testimony of Jesus' blood and our declared righteousness into our hearts and consciences. Second, the advocacy of Jesus is contrasted with the accusing of the devil. ("Satan" is the Hebrew word for "accuser.") Revelation 12 gives a beautiful and comforting picture of the expulsion of the devil from the heavenly court. The devil's accusations end where the advocacy of Christ begins.

> seated him [Jesus] at his right hand in the heavenly places, far above all rule and authority and power and dominion, and above every name that is named, not only in this age but also in the one to come. And he put all things under his feet and gave him as head over all things to the church (Eph 1:20–22).

Our confidence in this life comes from knowing that, by his ascension, Jesus is keeping his promises, protecting his church, never leaving us nor forsaking us, and working all things together for those who love him and are called according to his purpose.

But while the fact and the confession of Christ's ascension are foundational for the life of the church and of every Christian, it is a mostly neglected theological topic. First, then, the scriptural discussion of the ascension will be considered; the demonstration of the centrality of this event in the minds of the authors should help create for the reader a similarly high regard. Second, a closer look at Psalm 68 and Ephesians 4 will show the profound connection between the ascension and the office of holy ministry. A few practical conclusions from this relationship will be offered, especially for the comfort of those who have been given the office of pastor.

## The Significance of the Ascension

### Historical Event

Matthew and John have no mention of the ascension. Mark's account is straightforward: "So then the Lord Jesus, after he had spoken to them, was taken up into heaven and sat down at the right hand of God" (Mark 16:19). It is this simple teaching that we confess in the Creed: "He ascended into heaven and sits at the right hand of God the Father Almighty."

The fullest picture of what occurred comes from Luke. First his Gospel gives an abbreviated account:

> Then he led them out as far as Bethany, and lifting up his hands he blessed them. While he blessed them, he parted from them and was carried up into heaven. And they worshiped him and returned to

Jerusalem with great joy, and were continually in the temple blessing God (Luke 24:50–53).

Then Luke expanded this event in more detail in Acts 1:6–11:

> So when they had come together, they asked him, "Lord, will you at this time restore the kingdom to Israel?" He said to them, "It is not for you to know times or seasons that the Father has fixed by his own authority. But you will receive power when the Holy Spirit has come upon you, and you will be my witnesses in Jerusalem and in all Judea and Samaria, and to the end of the earth." And when he had said these things, as they were looking on, he was lifted up, and a cloud took him out of their sight. And while they were gazing into heaven as he went, behold, two men stood by them in white robes, and said, "Men of Galilee, why do you stand looking into heaven? This Jesus, who was taken up from you into heaven, will come in the same way as you saw him go into heaven."

Note the conversation that serves as the prelude to the ascension: the disciples ask Jesus about the timing of the inauguration of the kingdom. Many commenters understand this question to be an extension of the false Messianic expectation of the Pharisees, that the disciples were still expecting Jesus to establish an earthly kingdom. Understood this way, the answer of Jesus is a rebuke: "None of your business." But a careful reading of the conversation reveals something more regarding the nature of the coming kingdom, as well as the meaning of the ascension.

"It is not for you to know times or seasons that the Father has fixed by his own authority." The timing of the kingdom's coming is not for the disciples; they are to look for other signs. They will know the coming of the kingdom not through the clock and calendar, but by something else. "But you will receive power when the Holy Spirit has come upon you, and you will be my witnesses in Jerusalem and in all Judea and Samaria, and to the end of the earth." The kingdom will come when the Holy Spirit comes. And the result will be the preaching of the gospel to the world.

This text may well have been in Luther's mind when he taught the second petition of the Lord's Prayer.

> *How does God's kingdom come?* God's kingdom comes when our heavenly Father gives us His Holy Spirit, so that by His grace we believe His holy Word and lead godly lives here in time and there in eternity (SC III, 2).

The marks of the kingdom are the Spirit and the word. That is what the apostles were to look for; these are what the Christian prays for in the Lord's Prayer; this is what Jesus establishes in his ascension. He went to his throne, and his kingdom is now extended through the world by the Holy Spirit through the apostles—namely, by their baptizing and teaching (Matt 28:18–20).

There is also the report in Acts 1:11 of two angels who question the apostles' astonishment: "Men of Galilee, why do you stand looking into heaven? This Jesus, who was taken up from you into heaven, will come in the same way as you saw him go into heaven."

## Theological Import

So far the history, but there are a number of theological insights in the Scriptures regarding the ascension. We will survey these under five headings: (1) The Throne; (2) Advocate; (3) Priest; (4) Sender; (5) The Exaltation.

**The Throne.** Jesus is not ascending *from* something, but *to* something. He goes to the heavenly throne, to the right hand of God the Father. The question of what "God's right hand" means played a major role in the sacramental controversies of the Reformation. Is this referring to a place or to an office? Here is Luther on the matter:

> In the first place, we take up the article that Christ sits at the right hand of God, which the fanatics maintain makes it impossible for Christ's body also to be in the Supper. Now if we ask how they interpret God's "right hand" where Christ sits, I suppose they will dream up for us, as one does for the children, an imaginary heaven in which a golden throne stands, and Christ sits beside the Father in a cowl and golden crown, the way artists paint it. For if they did not have such childish, fleshly ideas of the right hand of God, they surely would not allow the idea of Christ's bodily presence in the Supper to vex them so. . . .

The Scriptures teach us, however, that the right hand of God
is not a specific place in which a body must or may be, such as on a
golden throne, but is the almighty power of God, which at one and
the same time can be nowhere and yet must be everywhere. It cannot be at any one place, I say. For if it were at some specific place, it
would have to be there in a circumscribed and determinate manner,
as everything which is at one place must be at that place determi-
nately and measurably, so that it cannot meanwhile be at any other
place. But the power of God cannot be so determined and measured,
for it is uncircumscribed and immeasurable, beyond and above all
that is or may be (*LW* 37:55, 57).

Luther further believed that the union of the humanity and divinity
of Christ means there are no limits to where and in what manner he
can be present:

If God and man are one person and the two natures are so united
that they belong together more intimately than body and soul, then
Christ must also be man wherever he is God. If he is both God and
man at one place, why should he not also be both man and God at a
second place? (*LW* 37:229).

And more, the union of the two natures in the one person of
Christ means that the divine attributes are communicated to the
human nature, and at the ascension Jesus took up the full and free
exercise of these divine attributes. Here is the extended but indispensable assertion of the Formula of Concord:

Hence also the human nature, after the resurrection from the dead,
has its exaltation above all creatures in heaven and on earth; which is
nothing else than that He entirely laid aside the form of a servant, and
yet did not lay aside His human nature, but retains it to eternity,
and is put in the full possession and use of the divine majesty according to His assumed human nature. However, this majesty He had
immediately at His conception, even in His mother's womb, but, as
the apostle testifies (Philippians 2:7), laid it aside; and, as Dr. Luther
explains, He kept it concealed in the state of His humiliation, and did
not employ it always, but only when He wished.

But now He does, since He has ascended, not merely as any other saint, to heaven, but, as the apostle testifies (Ephesians 4:10), above all heavens, and also truly fills all things, and being everywhere present, not only as God, but also as man has dominion and rules from sea to sea and to the ends of the earth; as the prophets predict, Psalm 8:1, 6; Psalm 93:1f; Zechariah 9:10, and the apostles testify, Mark 16:20, that He everywhere wrought with them and confirmed their word with signs following. Yet this occurred not in an earthly way, but, as Dr. Luther explains, according to the manner of the right hand of God, which is no fixed place in heaven, as the Sacramentarians assert without any ground in the Holy Scriptures, but nothing else than the almighty power of God, which fills heaven and earth, in possession of which Christ is installed according to His humanity, *realiter*, that is, in deed and truth, *sine confusione et exaequatione naturarum*, that is, without confusion and equalizing of the two natures in their essence and essential properties; by this communicated divine power, according to the words of His testament, He can be and truly is present with His body and blood in the Holy Supper, to which He has directed us by His Word; this is possible to no other man, because no man is in such a way united with the divine nature, and installed in such divine almighty majesty and power through and in the personal union of the two natures in Christ, as Jesus, the Son of Mary. For in Him the divine and the human nature are personally united with one another, so that in Christ dwelleth all the fullness of the Godhead bodily, Colossians 2:9, and in this personal union have such a sublime, intimate, ineffable communion that even the angels are astonished at it, and, as St. Peter testifies, have their delight and joy in looking into it (1 Peter 1:12) (FC SD 8.26–30; *Triglotta*).

To the divine Son of God belongs all authority from eternity, but in the ascension Jesus received this authority as a gift to his person which now and eternally includes his human nature. "All authority in heaven and on earth has been given to me" (Matt 28:18). Psalm 110:1 is fulfilled as Jesus sits at the right hand and the Father makes his enemies his footstool.[3]

---

[3]Psalm 110, which consists of a mere seven verses, is one of the most often quoted Old Testament passages in the New Testament. The frequent use of verse 1, especially, shows the importance of this prophecy in the thinking of

The one who sits on the throne of heaven, as noted above, is
"the Lamb who was slain" (Rev 5:6). The rule of Christ is an extension of his sacrifice; his love for the church that drove him to the
cross is the same love that he brings to his throne. It is this friend
of sinners, our Savior, who handed himself over to suffering in our
place, who is seated at God's right hand.

Paul filled the hearts of the Ephesians with joy by telling them
how Jesus' present reign is for their benefit:

> [God the Father] seated [Jesus] at his right hand in the heavenly
> places, far above all rule and authority and power and dominion, and
> above every name that is named, not only in this age but also in the
> one to come. And he put all things under his feet and gave him as
> head over all things to the church, which is his body, the fullness of
> him who fills all in all (Eph 1:20–23).

Similarly, as Jesus takes his place at the Father's right hand in
Revelation 5:14, he stands at the center of the heavenly worship.

**Advocate.** St. John gives confidence to repentant sinners by
preaching, "But if anyone does sin, we have an advocate with the
Father, Jesus Christ the righteous one" (1 John 2:1). The advocate is
a legal role, a defender in the courtroom of God. This means Jesus
pleads our case in heaven. "Christ Jesus is the one who died—more
than that, who was raised—who is at the right hand of God, who
indeed is interceding for us" (Rom 8:34). He brings before the throne
of God the evidence of his blood (see Heb 9:11–14, 23–25).

The result of all of this is that the devil is removed from his seat
in heaven, expelled from the heavenly court. The first two chapters
of Job and Zechariah 3:1–5 remind us that Satan has a place to stand
before God's judgment throne. He is "the accuser of our brothers . . .
who accuses them day and night before our God" (Rev 12:10). In
spite of this fact, Revelation 12 gives us the dramatic results of the
victory of Jesus' death and resurrection being carried into the heavenly court.

---

the apostles and evangelists (see Matt 22:44; Mark 12:36; Luke 20:42; Acts 2:34;
Heb 1:13; cf. Mark 16:19; 1 Cor 15:25; Eph 1:22; Col 3:1).

> Now war arose in heaven, Michael and his angels fighting against the dragon. And the dragon and his angels fought back, but he was defeated, and there was no longer any place for them in heaven. And the great dragon was thrown down, that ancient serpent, who is called the devil and Satan, the deceiver of the whole world—he was thrown down to the earth, and his angels were thrown down with him. And I heard a loud voice in heaven, saying, "Now the salvation and the power and the kingdom of our God and the authority of his Christ have come, for the accuser of our brothers has been thrown down, who accuses them day and night before our God. And they have conquered him by the blood of the Lamb and by the word of their testimony, for they loved not their lives even unto death" (Rev 12:7–11).

The judicial language of the Scriptures, especially regarding the justification of the sinner before God by faith, is not a mere metaphor or image; rather, it is an expression of the reality of the heavenly court and the judgment throne of God.

The ascension of Jesus, and the resultant expulsion of Satan from before God's face, is the background to Paul's crescendo of comfort.

> What then shall we say to these things? If God is for us, who can be against us? He who did not spare his own Son but gave him up for us all, how will he not also with him graciously give us all things? Who shall bring any charge against God's elect? It is God who justifies. Who is to condemn? Christ Jesus is the one who died—more than that, who was raised—who is at the right hand of God, who indeed is interceding for us (Rom 8:31–34).

Jesus' office of advocate binds up the ascension to the doctrine of justification. The declaration of our righteousness is the result of Jesus' advocacy before the Father, the outcome of his blood and testimony in the heavenly court. Jesus is the one who is able "to present you blameless before the presence of his glory with great joy" (Jude 24). It is through his death on the cross that Jesus has gone to "prepare a place for us" (John 14:3).

**Priest.** Psalm 110 unites Jesus' sitting at the right hand of God with his priestly office. There are two verses in the Psalm that reveal the conversation from the Father to the Son: "Sit at my right hand, until I make your enemies your footstool" (v. 1); "You are a priest forever after the order of Melchizedek" (v. 4). This Psalm answers the ancient riddle as to how the Messiah could be both a Davidic king from the tribe of Judah and a priest from the tribe of Levi: Jesus' priesthood is not Levitical but Melchizedekian, and is exercised in the ascension. Indeed, Hebrews compares Jesus' ascension to the high priest entering into the holy of holies:

> We have this as a sure and steadfast anchor of the soul, a hope that enters into the inner place behind the curtain, where Jesus has gone as a forerunner on our behalf, having become a high priest forever after the order of Melchizedek (Heb 6:19–20).
>
> Now the point in what we are saying is this: we have such a high priest, one who is seated at the right hand of the throne of the Majesty in heaven, a minister in the holy places, in the true tent that the Lord set up, not man (Heb 8:1–2).

Jesus' actions as our heavenly high priest are explained further: he appears in the presence of God for us (Heb 9:24); he carries his own blood into the heavenly holy of holies (Heb 9:11–14); he has finished the work of redemption, as indicated by his "sitting down" (Heb 10:11–12); he is perfecting those who are being sanctified (Heb 10:14); he intercedes for us (Heb 7:25); he gives us both a clean conscience and the boldness to enter into the holy place ourselves (Heb 10:19–22). The entire discussion of Hebrews 7 also centers on Jesus as the sinless high priest who offered himself as the superlative sacrifice and who remains a priest forever, after the order of Melchizedek.

One of the stipulations for the Jewish high priest was to bless the people (Num 6:22–27). This Jesus did at his ascension: "Then he led them out as far as Bethany, and lifting up his hands he blessed them. While he blessed them, he parted from them and was carried up into heaven" (Luke 24:50–51). Jesus our high priest ascends to the right hand of the Father to bless us, and, as the angels said, he "will come in the same way" (Acts 1:11). This provides great comfort for all who have Christ as their great high priest: he will return with hands raised in blessing.

**Sender**. Jesus sends forth from his throne blessings for his people. He sends, chiefly, the Holy Spirit. "It is to your advantage that I go away, for if I do not go away, the Helper will not come to you. But if I go, I will send him to you" (John 16:7).[4] And not only does Jesus send forth the Holy Spirit, but also the apostles. "Peace be with you. As the Father has sent me, even so I am sending you" (John 20:21). This introduces the text upon which we will dwell in the second half of this essay, Ephesians 4:7–11:

> But grace was given to each one of us according to the measure of Christ's gift. Therefore it says, "When he ascended on high he led a host of captives, and he gave gifts to men." (In saying, "He ascended," what does it mean but that he had also descended into the lower regions, the earth? He who descended is the one who also ascended far above all the heavens, that he might fill all things.) And he gave the apostles, the prophets, the evangelists, the shepherds and teachers. . . .

Shepherds—that is, pastors—are sent from the ascended Jesus. It can be a humbling experience to find "pastor" on a list that includes the apostles and prophets, but there it is. In this way, Jesus gives gifts not only to the whole church by providing shepherds, but also to pastors themselves by placing them in this office.

**The Exaltation.** We note finally that Jesus is worshiped when seated at the right hand of God. This is one of the simplest and most convincing arguments that Jesus is divine: he was worshiped. This devotion occurred when he was a child, as an adult, and immediately upon rising from the dead (Matt 2:11; 14:33; 28:9). Most significant, however, is the worship of the ascended Jesus by the earliest Christians, since they paid tribute to him in a manner reserved only for God himself.[5]

When Jesus ascends to the Father's right hand we know that the state of humiliation is finished. He takes up the full use of his divine nature according to his person, and, in fact, the attributes of the divine nature are communicated to the human nature. The Lutheran fathers called this the "majestic genus," or *genus maiestaticum*. The Formula of Concord states:

---

[4]See also John 7:39: "Now this he said about the Spirit, whom those who believed in him were to receive, for as yet the Spirit had not been given, because Jesus was not yet glorified."

[5]This point is forcefully made by Larry W. Hurtado, *Lord Jesus Christ: Devotion to Jesus in Earliest Christianity* (Grand Rapids: Eerdmans, 2003), 134–53.

> We believe, teach, and confess also that the assumed human nature
> in Christ not only has and retains its natural, essential properties,
> but that over and above these, through the personal union with the
> Deity, and afterwards through glorification, it has been exalted to
> the right hand of majesty, power, and might, over everything that can
> be named, not only in this world, but also in that which is to come
> (Ephesians 1:21) (FC SD 8.12; *Triglotta*).

This theological point was not only helpful for understanding the
Scriptures—as with the phrase, "him who fills all in all" (Eph 1:23)—
but also served as the backdrop to the Lutheran assertion that the
body and blood of Jesus are truly present in the Lord's Supper. If
the body of Jesus is omnipresent, then it can easily be on the altar
while also at God's right hand.

The confessors of the Formula could not help, then, but preach
the comfort of Christ's ascension.

> But we hold that by these words the majesty of the man Christ is
> declared, which Christ has received, according to His humanity, at the
> right hand of the majesty and power of God, namely, that also accord-
> ing to His assumed human nature and with the same, He can be,
> and also is, present where He will, and especially that in His Church
> and congregation on earth He is present as Mediator, Head, King, and
> High Priest, not in part, or one-half of Him only, but the entire per-
> son of Christ is present, to which both natures belong, the divine and
> the human; not only according to His divinity, but also according to,
> and with, His assumed human nature, according to which He is our
> Brother, and we are flesh of His flesh and bone of His bone. Even as
> He has instituted His Holy Supper for the certain assurance and con-
> firmation of this, that also according to that nature according to which
> He has flesh and blood He will be with us, and dwell, work, and be
> efficacious in us (FC SD 8.78–79; *Triglotta*).

Having considered the ascension of Christ in summary, we now take
up Psalm 68 and Ephesians 4, considering how Christ's ascension
and the office of the ministry are bound up with one another.

## The Ascension and the Office of Holy Ministry

Psalm 68 is a poem and prayer of King David. The occasion is unknown and perhaps indiscernible, but the theme is clear: YHWH stands as King at the head of an army for the benefit of his people. Luther, in his commentary on Psalm 68, gave it the title, "About Easter, Ascension, and Pentecost," because he interpreted it as applying directly to Christ's death, resurrection, ascension, and the life of the church (*LW* 13:13). Verse 18 in particular was seen as the crux of the whole Psalm, which reads: "You ascended on high, leading a host of captives in your train and receiving gifts among men, even among the rebellious, that the Lord God may dwell there." In Luther's words,

> This is the cardinal verse of the entire psalm. St. Paul quotes it in Ephesians 4:8. The psalmist here refers to the festivals of Ascension and Pentecost. This is the import of his words: "All the miracles foretold here of the Gospel and Christendom are traceable to Thine ascent into heaven. For there Thou didst receive all power and didst send the Holy Spirit to the earth with His gifts, by means of which the Gospel was proclaimed, the world converted, and all that was predicted fulfilled" (*LW* 13:20).

This is the precise point made by St. Paul about the ascension:

> But grace was given to each one of us according to the measure of Christ's gift. Therefore it says, "When he ascended on high he led a host of captives, and he gave gifts to men." (In saying, "He ascended," what does it mean but that he had also descended into the lower regions, the earth? He who descended is the one who also ascended far above all the heavens, that he might fill all things.) And he gave the apostles, the prophets, the evangelists, the shepherds and teachers, to equip the saints for the work of ministry, for building up the body of Christ, until we all attain to the unity of the faith and of the knowledge of the Son of God, to mature manhood, to the measure of the stature of the fullness of Christ, so that we may no longer be children, tossed to and fro by the waves and carried about by every wind of doctrine, by human cunning, by craftiness in deceitful schemes (Eph 4:7–14).

St. Paul made the ascension a theme of the letter to the Ephesians. In the first chapter, Jesus' sitting at the Father's right hand provides hope, it places Jesus above all earthly and demonic powers, and his exaltation is for the sake of the church (Eph 1:21–23). Shortly thereafter, Paul reminds us that God "raised us up with him and seated us with him in the heavenly places in Christ" (Eph 2:6). This is a mystery, yet one that comforts us. (It is similar to the apostle saying our lives are "hidden with Christ in God" [Col 3:3].) Paul, then, is building a foundation for faith, love, and hope on the fact of Christ's ascension so that we are ready when he makes this event the basis of the church's hope in Ephesians 4.

The picture of the ascension in both Psalm 68 and Ephesians 4 is of a king taking up his throne when returning victorious from a battle. In the prophecy, "He led captivity captive," David speaks of Christ like a king coming home from war with the spoils following behind him. Through his death on the cross and his resurrection from the grave, Jesus overcame sin, death, and the devil. He brought to an end the threats and condemnation of the law because he suffered in our place the profound wrath of God due to sinners. His death is our rescue, our life, our only hope.

Luther especially preached of the victory of Christ over the condemnation of the law:

Where then can we find help in this sore distress? Hear once more what the Holy Spirit says through the prophet in [Psalm 68]: "He, Christ, has ascended on high and has led captivity captive;" that is: He wrenched from the law, which, whether we feel it now, or not till death, was our greatest enemy, all its authority and power over us. The law exhausted itself when it sinned so wretchedly against Christ, its own Master, when it condemned Him as the greatest blasphemer and rebel to die upon the cross, and declared Him accursed . . . But now and for ever the law lies prostrate under the feet of Christ; it is bound, condemned, and executed, yea, it has lost every vestige of power over those who believe in Him; its curse is removed from these, and they also, through their faith, have it under their feet.[6]

[6]Martin Luther, "Ascension Day Sermon" in *Dr. Martin Luther's House-Postil, or, Sermons on the Gospels for the Sundays and Principal Festivals of the Church-Year* (trans. E. Schmid and D. M. Martens; 3 vols; Columbus, Ohio: Schulze & Gassmann, 1869–1884), II: 393–94.

Life, salvation, and the forgiveness of sins are the spoils of the Lord's victory. Now that sin, death, the devil, and the condemnation of the law have been overcome, these gifts are dispersed.

There is a noteworthy discrepancy between the Psalm and its quotation by Paul. Psalm 68 reads, "receiving gifts among men," yet Ephesians reads, "he gave gifts to men." The inconsistency cannot be solved by comparing the Septuagint with Paul's rendition:

ἀνέβης εἰς ὕψος, ᾐχμαλώτευσας αἰχμαλωσίαν, ἔλαβες δόματα ἐν ἀνθρώπῳ (LXX Ps 67:19);

Ἀναβὰς εἰς ὕψος ᾐχμαλώτευσεν αἰχμαλωσίαν, ἔδωκεν δόματα τοῖς ἀνθρώποις (Eph 4:8).

Instead, Paul is interpreting the Psalm to indicate that the gifts received by the Messiah when he was taken up are for the sake of serving his people. Jesus' ascension, like his descent, was not for his own benefit, but for ours. So Luther says:

> The psalmist does not say: "Thou hast given mankind gifts," but "Thou hast received gifts among men." This may be construed to mean, as St. Peter says [in] Acts 2:33, that He has received such gifts from the Father to relay to men. For He has not received them only for Himself and into Himself, but they were bestowed on Him to infuse into men. This outpouring of gifts came to pass at Pentecost and repeatedly thereafter (*LW* 13:21).

The triumph of Jesus on the cross wins a people and a kingdom for him, and for us it wins a Savior.

Then comes the catalogue of gifts: "he gave the apostles, the prophets, the evangelists, the shepherds and teachers" (Eph 4:11). Like emissaries and messengers sent from the palace to announce the king's victory, Jesus sends out preachers to proclaim his victory. This reveals the character of his kingdom: it is brought about through preaching because it is a kingdom of the word, established by the Lord's commands and promises, and built up in truth.

Jesus does not send forth warriors, intellectuals, or tycoons. He sends preachers. "It pleased God through the folly of what we preach to save those who believe" (1 Cor 1:21). Seated at the Father's right hand, Jesus has been given "all authority in heaven and on earth." How does he exercise this authority? In part, by sending others in his stead: "Go therefore and make disciples of all nations, baptizing them in the name of the Father and of the Son and of the Holy Spirit, teaching them to observe all that I have commanded you" (Matt 28:19–20).

The ascension reminds us that Jesus' kingdom is not of this world but is a different sort of kingdom, and that his authority is found not in power and riches but in the humility of the word, in baptism, in his Supper. Again, Luther:

> The ascension of Christ, His going upwards, indicates first of all, and beyond all doubt, that He will have nothing to do with this world and its kingdoms; else He would have remained here, wielding the power of earthly kings and potentates. . . . By this He teaches us what His kingdom is and how we should regard it; that it is not of this world, . . . but [is] a spiritual, eternal kingdom, in which He distributes spiritual blessings, to all who are His subjects.[7]

That the cloud took Jesus "out of their sight" (Acts 1:9) means that his kingdom will not be a visible kingdom like the kingdoms of this world. Luther, whose entire commentary on Psalm 110 is worth consulting, noted:

> This is really an extraordinary kingdom. This King sits above at the right hand of God, where He is invisible, an eternal, immortal Person; but His people are here below on earth in this miserable, mortal condition, subjected to death and any kind of mishap which a man may meet on earth, so that everyone is buried and becomes ashes. Still we have here great praise for the authority and the eternal, almighty power of this King, even though everywhere it appears as nothing because men cannot see it (*LW* 13:240).

The ascension, then, gives shape to the pastoral office. Jesus sits. The work is finished. Sin, death, and the devil have been carried

---

[7]Luther, "Ascension Day Sermon," 386.

away captive. The kingdom is established. There is no more work to be done, there is only news to spread, words to teach, promises to be announced.

The work of the apostles, prophets, evangelists, pastors and teachers are given by Jesus, Paul says,

> to equip the saints, for the work of ministry, for building up the body of Christ, until we all attain to the unity of the faith and of the knowledge of the Son of God, to mature manhood, to the measure of the stature of the fullness of Christ, so that we may no longer be children, tossed to and fro by the waves and carried about by every wind of doctrine, by human cunning, by craftiness in deceitful schemes (Eph 4:12–14).[8]

The kingdom of Christ is a kingdom built on truth—the truth of the death and resurrection of Jesus, and the truth of sin forgiven. The "unity of the faith" and the "knowledge of the Son of God" are the pillars and bulwark of this kingdom. It is a kingdom and church established only on and by the word. Accordingly, the humble work

---

[8]There has been quite a debate over the first comma in verse 12. The question is this: who does the work of the ministry? The traditional reading of the passage sees the "work of the ministry" as one of the three things given to the apostles and pastors. This was the understanding of Philip Melanchthon: "For wherever the Church is, there is the authority [command] to administer the Gospel. Therefore it is necessary for the Church to retain the authority to call, elect, and ordain ministers. And this authority is a gift which in reality is given to the Church, which no human power can wrest from the Church, as Paul also testifies to the Ephesians when he says, Eph 4:8: He ascended, He gave gifts to men. And he enumerates among the gifts specially belonging to the Church pastors and teachers, and adds that such are given for the ministry, for the edifying of the body of Christ" (Tr 67; *Triglotta*). More recently the Church Growth Movement has made it a pillar of their ideology that the work of the pastor is to equip the saints (that is, the laity) to do the work of the ministry. This is a misreading of the text, made worse by the fact that the Church Growth Movement has a completely different definition of "ministry" than can be found in Scripture. Paul states in Ephesians 4 that the ministry consists of teaching, resisting false doctrine, and coming to the unity of the faith. Accordingly, the first comma has been added to the English Standard Version.

of preaching and teaching, baptizing, absolving, and handing out the Lord's body and blood can seem to be of little effect, but hidden under the weakness of the word is the power of God. As Luther said, "It is the achievement of the Christian faith to learn something of which no other faith or doctrine knows: that this God is both supremely weak and alone almighty" (*LW* 13:254).

What is true of God is true of his word: it is both supremely weak and alone almighty. The preaching of the gospel is everywhere despised and rejected, but it alone is the power of God unto salvation (Rom 1:16). The ascension of Jesus sets this weak and powerful preaching in place. Preachers are sent with this feeble yet robust word, and hidden in their work is the Holy Spirit who calls, gathers, enlightens, and sanctifies for himself a people who will inherit life.

## The Correction and Comfort of the Ascension for Pastors

When, then, a pastor is tempted to worry and despair, the words "He ascended into heaven" prevent it. Jesus still sits on the throne.

When a pastor is tempted to pride, to thinking that he causes God's kingdom to come, that his vision and leadership bring life, the words "He ascended into heaven" prevent it and cast down the haughty. The pastor is put in the proper place of being a servant to the ascended Lord. Jesus declared, "I will build my church . . ." (Matt 16:18). The church belongs not to pastors, but to him who still sits on the throne.

When a pastor is tempted to doubt the power of God's word, to add something to it in hopes of making it more effective, to think that the growth of the church is something that he must bring about, the words "He ascended into heaven" prevent it. Jesus still sits on the throne. All authority belongs to Christ, not to us. His word is our confidence.

When a pastor is tempted to think that all is lost, that the devil has won the day in the world and in the church, the words "He ascended into heaven" prevent it. Jesus has led captivity captive. The devil is bound. We are set free from bondage and fear (see Hebrews 2:14).

When a pastor is tempted to timidity and fear, especially in the face of the world and its power, the words "He ascended into heaven" prevent it. The church, Luther reminded us, is "defiant." It is our Lord who sits on the heavenly throne.

> All Christendom, from the beginning until this day, has based its comfort and defiance on this verse [Psalm 110:1]. This is what protected and preserved it. No human or physical power or might has protected and maintained Christendom until this day. On the contrary, in the greatest weakness and frailty, against all the devils and the wrath and rage of all the world, it was protected and maintained only through faith and by defiance in the name of this Lord, to whom was said this שֵׁב לִימִינִי, "Sit at My right hand" (*LW* 13:245–46).

When the pastor is tempted to gloom, to sorrow and misery in this life of trouble, the words "He ascended into heaven" prevent it. Jesus still sits on the throne.

> But this Lord Christ sits above at the right hand of God, having a kingdom of life, peace, joy, and redemption from all evil, not a kingdom of death, sorrow, and misery. Therefore it must follow that His own will not remain subject to death, anxiety, fear, spiritual conflict, and suffering (*LW* 13:240).

The confession "He ascended into heaven" gives clarity and confidence to the pastor and to every Christian—confidence that the one who loved us enough to die for us is the one who rules and reigns over all things for us. The ascension gives us hope in these last days, and it gives us joy in life and death. May God grant us this hope and joy for Christ's sake. Amen.

> You might be happy or sad tonight; I don't know. You can't always be happy, that's for sure. Happiness comes and goes in this world. But I can tell you this: there's enough joy here tonight to last you a lifetime. Joy that your sins, which are many, are gone forever; blotted out in Jesus' blood. Joy that your Savior died and rose in your place; that He has gone on ahead of you, ascended up on high at the right hand of the Father, where He always lives to make intercession for you. Joy that He has gone to heaven to prepare a place for you. Joy that He will come again to take you to Himself. But above all this, joy that He is

with you still today, right here and now, this very night, to lighten up your load, to carry all your sorrows, to bring you the kind of peace that passes all human understanding. This night Jesus Christ invites you to share in His eternal joy. And that's a joy that no one can take away; not now, not in the future, not ever.

—Harold Senkbeil, Ascension Sermon, 2007

# Luther's Reading of Psalm 90

## The Eschatology of Pastoral Theology

### John T. Pless[1]

Writing in 1952, Hermann Sasse stated,

> In our day the Biblical doctrine of the Last Things has come alive for
> us as a gift given in the midst of what the church has had to endure. At
> the beginning of this century a complacent church regarded the Last
> Things as an element of the first Christian proclamation which more
> or less belonged to that first period, a form of the Gospel, which was
> for us only of historical interest. Or, alternately, it was thought of
> as something that might be of significance for the future, at the end
> of our lives, or at the end of the world, something we needed to study
> only in preparation for such an end. That there is for the church no
> more vitally relevant doctrine than that of the Last Things was brought
> home to Christians in Europe by all they were called upon to endure.[2]

---

[1] I am pleased to contribute this essay in honor of my friend and former
neighbor and colleague at Concordia Theological Seminary, Dr. Harold
Senkbeil, who has assisted me and countless other pastors in understand-
ing death and dying in light of God's law and gospel. One fine example of
Dr. Senkbeil's work on this theme that I have used in my classes in pastoral
theology is "Through the Shadowlands: A Christian Handbook on Death and
Life" in *A Reader in Pastoral Theology* (ed. John T. Pless; Fort Wayne, Ind.:
Concordia Theological Seminary Press, 2001), 143–45.

[2] Hermann Sasse, "Last Things: Church and Antichrist" in *We Confess the
Church* (trans. Norman Nagel; St. Louis: Concordia, 1986), 108.

In the more than six decades since Sasse penned those words, eschatology has become a major theme in both academic theology and popular spirituality, although the term is freighted with variegated definitions.[3]

Contemporary pastoral theologies are often hesitant to approach eschatology, opting instead for a focus on the therapeutic—that is, the healing of persons in distress with strategies for individual wholeness and social integration that sees death as a part of life to be accepted and managed.[4] At best, death is seen as an inevitable aspect of the human condition which calls for recognition and self-acceptance.

Martin Luther's reading of Psalm 90 provides a stringent yet necessary corrective for therapeutic pastoral theologies.[5] The reformer instead enabled the pastor to be the theologian of the cross who calls the thing what it is, and thus speaks God's words of wrath and grace, condemnation and consolation, law and gospel, to those who sit in the shadow of death. The commentary on Psalm 90 is a fitting eschatology for pastoral theology.

Luther began his lecture on Psalm 90 in late October 1534 and completed it on May 31, 1535. He declared that in Psalm 90 we have *Mosissimus Moses*, "Moses at his most Mosaic."[6] The lecture on Psalm 90 is a rhetorical defense of Moses aimed at confirming the authority of Moses' ministry of the law which Luther saw as under attack by John Agricola and his antinomian followers.

---

[3]For an overview, see Reinhard Slenczka, *Ziel und Ende: Einweisung in die christliche Endzeiterwartung: "Der Herr ist nahe!"* (Neuendettelsau: Freidmund-Verlag, 2008), 67–115; also see Steven D. Paulson, "The Place of Eschatology in Modern Theology," *Lutheran Quarterly* (Winter 1998): 327–53.

[4]Under the conditions of modernity, Oswald Bayer observes a "secularization of Christian eschatology." See Oswald Bayer, "Rupture of Times: Luther's Relevance for Today," *LQ* 13 (Spring 1999): 35. The therapeutic approach to death may be seen as an aspect of this secularized eschatology.

[5]Note the description of this psalm by Walter Jens: "A puzzling text, contradictory and dark, hopeful and somber, merciless and gentle. A song of dying and a word of life—a psalm marked equally by fear and trust, of terrible death and tender friendliness, lament and praise, wrathful judgment and hymnic eulogy." Walter Jens, "Psalm 90, On Transience," *LQ* 9 (Summer 1995): 177.

[6]On this see John Maxfield, *Luther's Lectures on Genesis and the Formation of Evangelical Identity* (Kirksville, Mo.: Truman State University Press, 2008), 19.

Luther focused on the theological reality of death as God's judgment, and asserted that Moses is "a stern minister of death, the
wrath of God and sin" (*LW* 13:77). In his treatment of Psalm 90
from 1514/1515, Luther employed letter/spirit terminology and
spoke of man's falling away from God's word. In this lecture of two
decades later, however, Luther used law/gospel language and spoke
more directly about sin in relationship to God's wrath and death.
As Werner Elert observed, "The basic total picture of man's existence is developed by Luther exhaustively but also with unparal-
leled gloom" in this later work.[7]

Sin blinds humanity to the actual potency of death. For Luther,
the fall into sin is so great that man "does not even know his own
sorry state, although he feels it and languishes under it. He neither
understands its origins nor does he see its final outcome" (*LW* 13:76).
Sin is not merely an act of moral disobedience, but a condition of
unbelief that puts humanity in opposition to God. Elert captured
Luther's understanding:

> If sin were only disobedience, that is deviation from the norm, the
> damage could be repaired forthwith by obedience, and the prob-
> lem of destiny would be solved by 'composure.' In reality, however,
> sin in the strict sense, is 'enmity against God,' that is, active opposi-
> tion to the will of God, which, to an equal degree, is active against
> sin. God replies to sin with a judgment that can only terminate in
> our death.[8]

Sin breaks the communion between God and man, between
the Creator who alone gives life and the creature who lives only as
he receives life from God. So Helmut Thielicke noted, "The terrifying
quality of man's death consists thus not merely in his loss of physical life, but in his forfeit of the living fellowship with God. To use
our earlier terminology, death is not merely a quantitative boundary,
but the imposition of qualitative limits; it is a fateful event in the

---

[7]Werner Elert, *The Structure of Lutheranism* (trans. Walter Hansen; St. Louis:
Concordia, 1962), 18.

[8]Elert, *Structure of Lutheranism*, 27.

personal relationship between God and man."[9] Death itself is the ultimate expression of God's wrath.

It is at this point that Luther observed the tendency toward the attempt to dissolve this linkage: "And so it happens that in their desire to soften the punishment of sin the wise men of the world become involved in greater sin" (*LW* 13:76). Luther saw this as a sentimentalizing of death. Theologians "of recent times," Luther said, were "following the example of pagan thinkers":

> [T]hey say in their funeral sermons that one should not grieve over death as if it were an evil; for death, so they assert, is a kind of haven, in which we are securely sheltered from the troubles and misfortunes to which the life of all men is subject. But this is the worst blindness and a further disaster—also a result of original sin—when we thus minimize sin and death, together with all other sorrows of the human race; when we thus oppose the universal judgment of mankind, yes, experience itself; and when we flatter ourselves with the most superficial and meaningless thoughts (*LW* 13:76–77).

Luther chided the Epicureans, accusing them of attempting "to find a way to mitigate an inescapable evil" (*LW* 13:96), which is death. In contrast to the Scottish skeptic David Hume's Stoic-like fortitude in saying, "I have done everything of consequence which I ever meant to do. . . . I, therefore, have all reason to die contented,"[10] Luther asserted that human beings cannot overcome death by composure or imagination. The fact that we die is the result of God's indescribable wrath over sin.

Luther saw Psalm 90 as an expression of God's twofold work in the face of death: judgment and mercy. Moses terrifies in order to bring consolation; he performs a double office of killing and making

---

[9] Helmut Thielicke, *Death and Life* (trans. Edward H. Schroeder; Philadelphia: Fortress, 1970), 153.

[10] Quoted in Dale Allison, *Night Comes: Death, Imagination, and the Last Things* (Grand Rapids: Eerdmans, 2016), 14. Here also see Thielicke, *Death and Life*, 159: "Death is not to be conquered by the illusion of security that comes from ignorance, nor by downgrading God and elevating myself above him in fearless and wanton contempt for death."

alive. "He does this," Luther said, "to humble the proud and to console those who have been humbled" (*LW* 13:79). Luther's eschatology
is one of both law and gospel. God's alien work of delivering death
brings to an end every proud but empty attempt to circumvent
death. His proper or natural work of forgiving sins creates life with
God for the sake of Christ:

> God indeed also claims for himself the work of slaying man, as
> we have heard above (v. 13). In Scripture God expressly says: "I kill
> and I make alive" (Deut. 32:39). But Isaiah distinguishes between
> these works of God and says that some are his "alien" works and
> others his "natural" works (Isa 28:21) (*LW* 13:135).

Further, when commenting on the title, "A Prayer of Moses,"
note how Luther said that Psalm 90 speaks to two kinds of sinners:
*smug* and *terrified and trembling*:

> Thus Moses suggests in the very title the remedy against the horri-
> ble doctrine of death and combines both—the remedy against, and
> the doctrine of, death—that those who as a result of this doctrine
> have been terrified and that others might not become hardened and
> smug. These two factors must be joined, so that smug sinners and ter-
> rified and trembling sinners are cheered and encouraged, since they
> are told to follow the example of Moses, therefore, to believe and to
> pray. The voice of the Law terrifies because it dins into the ears of
> smug sinners the theme: "In the midst of earthly life, snares of death
> surround us." But the voice of the Gospel cheers the terrified sinner
> with its song: "In the midst of certain death, life in Christ is ours"
> (*LW* 13:83).

God therefore kills both kinds of sinners with the express purpose of
making them alive again.

Here we might also note the connection between Luther's lecture on Psalm 90 with his 1524 hymn, "In the Very Midst of Life."[11]
In this hymn, the reformer painted a dark picture of life saturated
with sin, tormented by the powers of hell, and haunted by death. Yet
in the middle of it all, there is a refuge of grace and mercy in the blood
of Christ. Death oppresses to be sure, but Christ is the atonement for

---

[11]*Lutheran Service Book* (St. Louis: Concordia, 2006), 755.

our sins and his resurrection from the dead guarantees our victory
over the grave. Luther rightly saw that in the middle of life we are
confronted with death; the reverse is also true for Luther, as in the pit
of death there is life on account of Christ.

Elert connected Luther's interpretation of Psalm 90 with the
deconstruction of autonomy:

> From the inside we are autonomous—therefore also responsible.
> But when, as Luther demanded, we "look at our life with the eyes of
> God," life and at the same time autonomy shrink to the "mathemati-
> cal point." Before God, autonomy cannot achieve comprehensive ful-
> fillment. It remains merely a demand of our ego. But this demand
> embraces both our responsibility and our guilt before God. Thus
> what Luther pointed out in his commentary on Psalm 90 becomes
> entirely clear: the outer side of our life is death.[12]

For Luther, death is not simply part of the great and ever-
reoccurring circle of life. The death of the human being, in contrast
to that of animals, "is a genuine disaster. Man's death is in itself truly
an infinite and eternal wrath" (*LW* 13:94); thus, "Man's death is
truly an event sadder and more serious than the slaughter of a cow"
(*LW* 13:95). Death is not accidental, it is linked to the will of God
who himself is not only judge but also executioner: the third verse
of Psalm 90 explicitly states that God causes man to die. Drawing on
1 Samuel 2:16 and Romans 8:36, Luther asserted that "God indeed
uses the devil to afflict and kill us. But the devil cannot do this if God
does not want sin to be punished in this way. We are, therefore, 'as
sheep to be slaughtered' (Rom 8:36). We are subject to death because
of God's wrath over sin" (*LW* 13:97). There is, as Reinhard Slenczka
puts it, an inseparable connection between sin and death.[13]

The knowledge of God's wrath is a prerequisite for the fear of
God: "Man cannot be moved to fear God unless he has first been

---

[12]Elert, *Structure of Lutheranism*, 26. Also see the description of how death
moves out "from its chronological confinement in the last day and becomes
something that leaves its mark upon his (man's) entire life" in Thielicke, *Death
and Life*, 157.

[13]See Slenczka's treatment of this connection in *Ziel und Ende*, 120–21.

shown God's wrath" (*LW* 13:85). But reason, Luther argued, is incapable of recognizing God's wrath for what it is. Luther did not attempt to erase or evacuate the wrath of God as so often happens in modern theology. God's wrath is not so easily dispensed with. Where the wrath of God is denied or suppressed, it simply resurfaces as consciences are terrified by the anonymity of God's work in creation and human history. Hence we recall Luther's language about Adam and Eve being cut to the quick with terror at the rustling of a leaf: "No species of living beings is tormented by the fear of death the way man is" (*LW* 13:112). The reformer was unrelenting in his description of the human condition: "Thus the fear of death is the one misery that makes us more miserable than all other creatures. Although these, too, are subject to change and death, they are not changed because of God's wrath as are we, who spend our lives in the constant terror of death" (*LW* 13:116).

Moses aims, Luther asserted, to have us look at our perishing lives as God does. "And so Moses has us transport ourselves outside time and has us look at our life as God sees it" (*LW* 13:100). It is only *coram deo* that we come to recognize our true condition as perishing creatures rightly under the just condemnation of our Creator.[14] Like the fading flower, man's existence is limited; but unlike the flower, man dies under a divine death sentence. There is no escape even though human beings seek relief through idolatry. "Hence those theologians are right who maintain that the hellish punishment will be so terrible that the godless will wish to flee from God's presence but will be unable to do so, as Paul also tells us in 1 Thess. 5:3" (*LW* 13:93). Human reason cannot fathom God's wrath or his grace. God discloses the truth of our condition and the depths of his mercy for condemned sinners.

The disclosure of humanity's fate as death-bound creatures on account of sin is not the only or final word of Moses, that superlative minister of the law as Luther identified him. Moses teaches us also of

---

[14]Hans-Joachim Kraus observed that "human existence stands under the light of Yahweh's presence." From this reality, "The time is gone as if flown away (Ps 90:10). Why? Because human life in its real nature is subject to God's anger, to his 'No.'" Hans-Joachim Kraus, *Theology of the Psalms* (Continental Commentary; trans. Keith Crim; Minneapolis: Fortress, 1992), 168.

a merciful death, that is, we die that we might live. "He means to tell us that people die in order that they might be humbled and not abide in death" (*LW* 13:99). As Christ is the end of the law for faith, so too is he the end of death.[15] By his death he has destroyed death and established life with God through the forgiveness of sins. Only those who know the terror of God's wrath will come to rejoice in his mercy.

Death is magnified under the lens of the law precisely so that we might see it for what it truly is: our enemy.[16] But it is this "last enemy" that Christ himself has defeated by his sacrificial death. Luther saw Moses testifying to this work of Christ in Psalm 90. In Christ, we see that it is God who both kills and makes alive. This was particularly vivid for Luther in the prayer of verses 12–17 where Moses implores God for wisdom and mercy. He asks for wisdom to "number our days" in verse 12, and then confesses the mercy revealed in God's works which satisfy us with the forgiveness of sins. This divine mercy then establishes the work of our hands according to verse 17.

---

[15]So Dennis Ngien: "The force of the annihilating knowledge of divine wrath comes to an end as the negative voice of the law is negated by the voice of the gospel. What is ended is not the contents of the law but the condemnation under the law." Dennis Ngien, *Fruit for the Soul: Luther on the Lament Psalms* (Minneapolis: Fortress, 2015), 188.

[16]So Werner Elert: "For the Christian, physical death relates only partly to the question of God's providence, which is posed to him by his entire life. But this question also places us inescapably into the antithesis of Law and Gospel. The Law attests the judgment of God. It reveals that our entire life is 'judged' in a twofold sense: It is subject to the verdict of God's judgment, and it pursues an irreversible course toward death. Under the Law, death has teleological significance for all of our earthly life. The earthly way is a way to death. Whatever it may be that constitutes life itself, it cannot prevent death, and it is simultaneously a disintegration of life because it consumes the time of life which is delimited in advance by death. Under the Law the earthly way is the way of death and nothing else. The apostle's statement that the Law of God is inscribed into the hearts of the heathen is confirmed by nothing so much as the wisdom of the Greeks, which declares that the happiest man is he who was never born. Since he does not live, he also need not die. To live means to have to die." Werner Elert, *Last Things* (ed. Rudolph F. Norden; trans. Martin Bertram; St. Louis: Concordia, 1974), 15.

So we see Moses praying in this psalm for things essential in this life. He prays first of all for remission of sins and eternal life. Yet we are not to be idle in this life but must, to our dying day, establish the soul through the Word of God and, under peaceful conditions, provide also for the needs of the body; hence Moses prays that piety might be taught and peace preserved. When we have all this, our hope for eternal life is certain. Then we also have the pure ministry of the Word in the church. And we are, finally, able also to lead a quiet or peaceable life. Then we have everything and can live out our life in peace of body and soul (*LW* 13:141).

The forgiveness of sins does establish the works of our hands. Works cleansed by the blood of Christ now endure not as monuments which assure immortality, but as works which serve the neighbor. Delivered from the curse of the law, Christians now live in the law since they are not withdrawn from creation but located by their various callings in the world. "After we have been justified, grant that the doctrines might remain pure, so that the hypocrites do not set aside Moses' law when the law must prevail and so that the Gospel be not corrupted and this God and the Holy Spirit who dwells within us be grieved" (*LW* 13:139).

But our confidence remains in Christ alone: "Therefore there should be no uncertainty in doctrine, and souls should not be in doubt regarding God's will toward them" (*LW* 13:139). Luther saw Psalm 90 as providing Christians with certainty in the face of death precisely because now through faith we are in Christ. "God is the kind of dwelling place that cannot perish" (*LW* 13:85), Luther wrote in his comments on verse 1. Here observe Luther's connection with Colossians 3:3 where the apostle Paul writes that believers are hidden with Christ in God. Justification by faith alone, therefore, is the basis for eschatology.[17]

---

[17]This was helpfully expressed by Elert: "For Christ's person and work are taken seriously only if one binds them to the historical Christ. It is not the hope of the coming Christ which makes for certainty regarding the historical Christ, but vice versa. Something similar applies when the seriousness of the forensic doctrine of justification is made to yield to the formula of the 'eschatological' character of justification. Eschatology is concerned with hope. Justification, however, deals with faith and is not the object of hope, as the

Luther's exposition of Psalm 90 establishes a foundation and framework for pastoral care in the face of death. Rather than denying death or attempting to downplay it, Luther enables the pastor to face death for what it is. It means that the pastor is able to name death as the enemy, not suppressing its reality as the alien work of God's wrath which is overcome only by the proper work of his mercy enacted in the death and resurrection of Christ Jesus.

Werner Elert once wrote, "Death does not intrude the field of ethics as a stranger who really belongs in biology, but he is at home here."[18] We are more comfortable to keep death in the realm of biology, for then there can be completely naturalistic explanations of it. Death, after all, is just part of life and a natural one at that. Just as summer finally must give way to fall and fall to winter, so youth gives way to age and the aged must go the way of death. One generation passes from the stage to give room to the next. We can be rather stoic about death for it is no more than the final turn in the cycle of life's circle. Then the suggestion of the postmodern philosopher, Jacques Derrida, makes sense: You can give yourself the gift of death.[19] Death is yours for the taking. Thus enter euthanasia and the nobility of assisted suicide. If life will be taken from me, at least I can determine the time and the place. I don't have to go whimpering and whining into that dark night. I can choose the means, the locale, and the time of the final exit.

But death is not content to remain locked up in the clinic. Death knows itself to be more than an inevitable biological episode. Death is more than biology. "The sting of death is sin, and the power of sin is the law" (1 Cor 15:56). Death, sin, and the law—that is the trio. It is sin that gives death its sting. And it is the law—which comes in, as Paul says, "to increase the trespass" (Rom 5:20)—that is the potency of sin which Luther saw magnified in Psalm 90.

---

resurrection, for instance, is. Here too only the faith that 'we are justified' is able to sustain hope, and not vice versa." Elert, *Last Things*, 11.

[18]Werner Elert, *The Christian Ethos* (trans. Carl J. Schindler; Philadelphia: Fortress Press, 1957), 161.

[19]See Jacques Derrida, *The Gift of Death* (trans. David Wills; Chicago: University of Chicago Press, 1995), 108–9.

Death nails life down. It is irrevocable. You cannot do a retake. You cannot play it over again. There are no second chances. Death renders a verdict. The problem is not simply that we are mortal but that we die sinners. Sweet eulogies uttered at pagan memorial services are fake absolutions, pathetic attempts to declare the deceased righteous and good on account of his vocational achievements, his personal traits, his hobbies or whatever. Death still wins the victory.

Over and against this, we have another word. It is the prophetic word brought to fulfillment: "Death is swallowed up in victory. O death, where is your victory? O death, where is your sting?" (1 Cor 15:54–55). This is a word that shows death for what it is. It is sin that gives death its lethal poison and it is the law that gives sin its potency. From those tyrants we cannot free ourselves by retreating to nature, by fantasizing about a soul that migrates from one body to the next. Platitudes that invite us to ponder death not as judgment and destruction but as transformation and change fail. Death will not stay put with biology. It jumps over the fence and breaks out of the zoo every time! Death makes it certain that flesh and blood will not inherit the kingdom of God.

"The sting of death is sin, and the power of sin is the law. But thanks be to God who gives us the victory though our Lord Jesus Christ" (1 Cor 15:56–57). Alive or in the grave, there is victory in this Lord. At his coming the dead will be raised. The perishable nature will be clothed with that which will not rot or decay; the mortal nature puts on immortality. We wait for that day anticipating it every time we confess the Nicene Creed, saying, "and I look for the resurrection of the dead and the life of the world to come."

We know the truth about death. Indeed it is a terrible enemy whose sting is sin and whose power is the law. But Easter announces the victory. The one who was made sin for us gives us forgiveness in his blood. The one who died in our place gives us his indestructible life. The end of life's story is not the obituary; the final destination is not the cemetery. The end of the story is Christ Jesus crucified and risen from the dead. The end of the story is your resurrection. In light of this truth, we are set free to face the questions of mercy and care at life's end with the full confidence that the Lord who gives us life and who will one day recall this life to himself always has more to give. We will neither take our own lives or those of others, nor will we hold on to them selfishly when the Lord, who has already called us from death to life in Holy Baptism, calls us to die for that final time.

"When the true God disappears," said Luther, "the fairy tales arrive."[20] Our age is inundated with fairy tales regarding death. One fantasy is that death with dignity is something that can be sought after and achieved. But in the Holy Scriptures, death is the "last enemy," the result of sin. Luther said, "Originally death was not part of [man's] nature. He dies because he provoked God's wrath. Death is, in his case, the inevitable and deserved consequence of his sin and disobedience" (*LW* 13:94). Luther stated the biblical truth in his exposition of Psalm 90: Where there is sin, death reigns; and it is God himself who executes the death sentence! There is no dignity in death according to Psalm 90.

Contrast this with the way that death is often pictured today. It is seen as part and parcel of the grand scheme of things. Our culture perpetuates the myth that death is natural, nothing more than an inevitable and unavoidable turn in the cycle of life. As spring follows winter, as the brightness of the dawn comes after the darkness of night, so death comes after life. In the ever-turning and never-ending repetition of existence, life leads to death and death back to life.

Or else death is seen as arbitrary and accidental. Then it is thought that death can be prevented or stalled. Advances in medical technology prolong life and, at least temporarily, lessen the effects of aging and disease. Improved diet and regular exercise are thought to delay death. Efforts in education are marshaled to increase public safety making death less likely on the highways and in the work-place. Some even dream of a future where science will have found a way to renew and repair the body perpetually. Yet if death finally cannot be avoided, we will at least engineer the time and the place. We will take our own life before it can be ripped from us. It is called euthanasia or suicide.

Yet for all its attempts to naturalize death, to deny its linkage to our sin and God's wrath, and to beckon death to conform its arrival

---

[20]As cited by Adolph Köberle, *The Quest for Holiness: A Biblical, Historical, and Systematic Investigation* (trans. John C. Mattes; Minneapolis: Augsburg, 1938), 41.

to our timing, our age still retains some recognition that death is about a judgment. It is evidence of Oswald Bayer's assertion that the universe is structured so to demand justification.[21] We are always trying to justify ourselves. At the end, we want our lives to be accounted right, to be declared of worth and value. Listen to the eulogies delivered at the funeral rites for unbelievers. They attempt to justify—that is, they render a judgment, that the life of the deceased was worth something because he was a devoted husband who was faithful to his wife, a loving father who sacrificed for his children, a successful businessman or a skilled mechanic, an active member of the Rotary Club or Republican Party, and the list goes on. Is it not strange that those who would deny the existence of God feel themselves compelled to justify life in the face of death? If it is true that death is just part of life, why do people go to such great lengths to defend themselves against it?

Christians alone are finally able to see death for what it is: God's own termination of sin. God's law speaks and carries out a death sentence. It is not simply that human beings are mortal and are therefore deprived of life. Then the cure would be immortality. Rather, human beings are sinners who must die. The answer is not to be found in engineering a way around death or through death to "the other side," but by hearing a word of absolution that announces and bestows the forgiveness of sins. Where there is forgiveness of sins, death is robbed of its terror. Death swallowed up by the death of Jesus on the cross now becomes the portal to life everlasting. Luther put it like this in his great Easter hymn, "Christ Jesus Lay in Death's Strong Bands":

> No son of man could conquer death,
> Such ruin sin had wrought us.
> No innocence was found on earth,
> And therefore death had brought us
> Into bondage from of old
> And ever grew more strong and bold
> And held us as its captive. Alleluia!

---

[21]See Oswald Bayer, *Living by Faith: Justification and Sanctification* (trans. Geoffrey W. Bromiley; Grand Rapids: Eerdmans, 2003), 1–7.

Christ Jesus, God's own Son, came down,
    His people to deliver;
Destroying sin, He took the crown
    From death's pale brow forever:
Stripped of pow'r, no more it reigns;
    An empty form alone remains;
Its sting is lost forever. Alleluia!

It was a strange and dreadful strife
    When life and death contended;
The victory remained with life,
    The reign of death was ended.
Holy Scripture plainly saith
    That death is swallowed up by death,
Its sting is lost forever. Alleluia![22]

By Jesus' death, the last enemy is disarmed; for where the forgiveness of sins reigns, death is deprived of its sting. There is only life and salvation. So we confess in the Small Catechism that it is Jesus who has purchased and won us from sins, death, and the power of the devil "that I may be His own and live under Him in His kingdom and serve Him in everlasting righteousness, innocence, and blessedness, just as He is risen from the dead, lives and reigns to all eternity" (SC II, 2).

Jesus, who was made sin for us, died with the dignity of a condemned criminal bearing our shame. Handed over to wicked men, Jesus was stripped, beaten, and pinned to a cross as one judged guilty. Yet in this single death, sin is atoned for by the blood of God's Son. Death is defeated not by a raw act of God's power, but by the passion of God's Son—the suffering that submits to death and in doing so destroys it, for where sin is removed the last enemy has lost its grip on sinners. By becoming the victim, Jesus has won the victory. Luther put it nicely in an Easter sermon from 1529:

Christians from their own standpoint are a Judas, a Caiaphas, a Pilate and find themselves condemned. But there is another Person who took my sins on himself. On Good Friday they are all laid around his

---

[22]*LSB*, 458:2–4.

neck. But on Easter I look at him, and then he has none. . . . Thus sin is completely taken away in the resurrection. Everyone should learn this today, that all of us should abandon thoughts about ourselves and should not pass judgment on ourselves according to our feelings. For this is contrary to Christ and the Gospel, which says that Christ has taken away the sin from our hearts and consciences and laid them on himself. For this reason the apostles praise the resurrection unceasingly.[23]

Jesus' resurrection from the grave is more than a confirmation of the fact that there is life after death. It is not part of an inevitable cycle: life to death, and then back to life again. Jesus is raised from the dead without the sins he took to the cross; they are left buried forever. Put to death for our trespasses and raised again for our justification, Jesus' resurrection announces and declares that sins are forgiven.

When Jesus came to his disciples who had locked themselves up in fear on Easter evening (see John 20:19–23), he brought to them the glad news of his resurrection with his word of peace and the sight of his pierced hands and punctured side. His word of peace is in effect an absolution. Coupled with the marks of his passion, Jesus' words bestowed on his disciples the result of his death for sin: peace with God. When the Lord spoke his peace to the disciples a second time, breathing on them his Spirit, he sent them to forgive sins: "If you forgive the sins of anyone, they are forgiven" (John 20:23). Only Jesus' forgiveness, won at Calvary in his dying, holds power over death. Where there is no forgiveness of sins, death remains lord. But where Jesus forgives sin, death is toppled from the throne. Death no longer can hold sinners in its iron grip. It is ultimately this good news that Luther's reading of Psalm 90 enables pastors to proclaim to those who sit in the shadow of death.

---

[23] *The 1529 Holy Week and Easter Sermons of Dr. Martin Luther* (trans. Irving L. Sandberg; St. Louis: Concordia, 1999), 127.

# Martin Luther and the Ottoman Jihad

*Adam S. Francisco*

With all the events and media attention given to the Protestant Reformation in 2017, most people have become at least somewhat exposed to the basic story of Martin Luther's protest over the sale of indulgences, his ecclesiastical and secular trial for heresy and subversion, and the subsequent condemnation by both Pope and Emperor five centuries ago. His story also includes a host of other controversies and conflicts—from the peasant uprisings of the 1520s to the radical teachings of the Anabaptists, and of course the various issues surrounding Saxony's Jewish population. Towards the end of life, after he had spent his career engaging his foes in Europe, he wrote that it was now time to "prepare ourselves against Muḥammad" (WA 53:572). By the name "Muhammad," Luther plainly meant Muslims; and in his day and age he meant the predominantly Turkish Muslims of the Ottoman Empire.

## The Ottoman Empire

The Ottomans were the theological and political offspring of Muhammad (c. AD 570–632) who had passed on marching orders to his successors "to fight the world until it confessed there is no God but Allah" up "until the day of judgment."[1] The various caliphs—that

---

[1]Muhammad ibn Umar al-Waqidi, *Kitab al-Maghazi* (ed. Marsden Jones; 3 vols.; London: Oxford University Press, 1966), 3:113; Abu Dawud al-Sijistani, *Sunan Abu Dawud* (trans. Ahmad Hasan; 2 vols.; Lahore: Ashraf Press, 1984),

is, the vice-regents of Allah and successors and custodians of the traditions of Muhammad—pursued this struggle or *jihad* (as the Muslim
tradition describes it) after Muhammad's death. From the Arabian
Peninsula, the Rashidun caliphs (632–661) conquered Syria and
Mesopotamia. The Umayyads (661–750) extended the borders much
farther—to China in the east, and Spain in the west where they would
finally be stopped by Charles Martel in 732. The subsequent centuries saw the development of Islamic civilization under the Abbasids,
until the Mongols arrived in Baghdad in the middle of the thirteenth
century. While they eventually settled down and embraced Islam, the
Mongols never enjoyed the political legitimacy and so never bore
the title of caliphs. In Egypt, outside the domain of the Mongols, a
shadow caliphate was established instead. But when the Ottomans
conquered Egypt and Arabia in the year that Luther was nailing
the Ninety-Five theses to the Castle Church door in Wittenberg,
they became the uncontested and legitimate caliphs of Islam (and
remained so until 1924).[2] In doing so, the Ottomans reasserted the
duty of expanding the reach of Islam, and what Bernard Lewis has
called the "great jihad *par excellence*" was underway.[3]

It began with the greatest of the Ottoman sultans—Süleyman
the Magnificent (1520–1566)—who would bring the borders of this
Islamic empire and Islam deep into Hungary by the end of his first
decade in office. The greatest event, signaling that he intended to
take the rest of Europe, was the siege on Vienna in 1529. Although
the Turks eventually lifted the siege, their very appearance sent
Europe into a panic. "The Turk and his religion is at our very doorstep"
(WA 30, II:207) wrote Luther, and should Germany be conquered by
them "there is a great danger . . . we would fall from the Christian
faith to the Turkish faith, to the devil, into hell" (WA 30, II:184).

---

2:702. Cf. Mohammad Hashim Kamali, *Principles of Islamic Jurisprudence*
(Cambridge: Islamic Texts Society, 2003), 207.

[2]Caroline Finkel, *Osman's Dream: The Story of the Ottoman Empire 1300–1923*
(New York: Basic Books, 2005), 110–11.

[3]Bernard Lewis, *Islam and the West* (Oxford: Oxford University Press, 1994),
10. On the *jihad* ideology of the Ottomans, see Linda T. Darling, "Contested
Territory: Ottoman Holy War in Comparative Context," *Studia Islamic* 91
(2000): 133–63.

These were apocalyptic times. What was once "the most far-reaching problem of medieval Christendom"[4] was now firmly entrenched on European soil.

The Ottoman jihad on Europe was a jihad like no other. The Turks were not (and still may not be) the most stridently orthodox Muslims. They viewed themselves as the new rulers of a religiously-diverse Byzantium, but were still compelled and inspired by the Islamic tradition of expansion "fi sabil Allah," or "in the cause of Allah." They viewed Europe as the domain of jihad. This is the classical political worldview proffered in Islamic law. On the one hand, there is "dar al-Islam"—that is, the realm ruled by Islamic law and governments, which, in the sixteenth century, had Istanbul as its center. On the other hand, lands and populations beyond it have traditionally been called "dar al-harb"—that is, the house or abode of war. The Turks in particular called it "dar al-jihad."

## Luther and the War

This is the world that was bearing down on Europe in the early sixteenth century, and it became an issue at the very beginning of the Reformation. For example, just as he was entering the public limelight in 1518, Luther received a letter sent on behalf of his Elector concerning Pope Leo X's plans to crusade against the Turks.[5] He responded by rejecting war conceived of as a holy war, but took the opportunity to critique his own culture: "In vain we wage carnal wars abroad, while at home we are conquered by spiritual battles." At least the Turks were not "sunk in the depths of avarice, ambition, and luxury" like the papacy. Until this was cleaned up, any and all attempts to stop the Turks would be futile. Christians needed first to repent and mollify God with "tears, pure prayers, holy life and pure faith" (WBr 1:282).

Luther was convinced God was using the Turks to discipline a corrupt and unrepentant Christendom. "Many . . . dream of nothing

---

[4]Richard W. Southern, *Western Views of Islam in the Middle Ages* (2d printing; Cambridge, Mass.: Harvard University Press, 1978), 3.

[5]See Kenneth M. Setton, "Pope Leo X and the Turkish Peril," *Proceedings of the American Philosophical Society* 113 (1969): 367–424.

else than war against the Turk," he wrote. "They want to fight, not against iniquities, but against the lash of iniquity and thus they would oppose God who says that through that lash he himself punishes us for our iniquities because we do not punish ourselves for them" (*LW* 31:91).[6] For Luther, then, at this point, Europe's problems were internal. "Christendom is being destroyed not by the Turks," he wrote, "but by those who are supposed to defend it" (*LW* 44:70).[7] But, he explained,

> This article does not mean that we are not to fight against the Turk, as that holy manufacturer of heresies, the pope, charges. It means, rather that we should first mend our ways and cause God to be gracious to us. . . . God does not demand crusades, indulgences, and wars. He wants us to live good lives. But the pope and his followers run from goodness faster than from anything else, yet he wants to devour the Turks (*LW* 32:89–91).[8]

Luther was no pacifist, but he did reject ill-conceived military ventures and emphasized repentance before retaliation.

Moreover, up until early 1521 the Turks were a distant threat and posed no real challenge to the security of the German empire. A military response was not really required. Circumstances soon changed, however, when later that year the Ottomans advanced past Belgrade and shortly thereafter up the Danube River into the plains of Hungary. By 1526, they defeated King Louis II at the battle of Mohács, bringing an end to the medieval Kingdom of Hungary.

This forced Luther to reconsider his earlier aloofness. So in 1528, working with his colleague Philip Melanchthon, he strongly advocated for war against the Ottomans, exhorting pastors to "explain to [the laity] what a rightful service it is before God to fight against the Turks when the authorities so command" (*LW* 40:305–6).[9] The following year he published a work dedicated to the effort, entitled *On War Against the Turk*, where he argued that it was the Emperor's

---

[6] WA 1:535.
[7] WA 6:242.
[8] WA 7:443.
[9] WA 26:228–29.

obligation to lead the fight. The war should in no way be considered a holy war, however, for Charles V was "not the head of Christendom or defender of the faith"; and the fact that the Turks were non-Christians played no role in Luther's decision to call for war (*LW* 46:169).[10] It was a secular and defensive war, and anyone obliged by their vocation should make the necessary preparations for it.

About a year later Luther drafted another work, *Muster Sermon against the Turks*, addressing the war. He repeated his call to make war, and urged everyone to participate and resist the Turks at all cost. "I wish," he wrote, "that all Germans were of such a mind that they would allow no small town or village to be plundered or led away [into captivity] by the Turks, but when it comes time to struggle and fight, that those who would defend themselves would do so, young and old, men and women, man-servant and maidservant, until they are killed, burning their own house and home and destroying everything" (WA 30, II:183).

Luther remained committed to a defensive war against the Turks until his death in 1546. He was even willing to "struggle even unto the death against the Turks" himself (WBr 5:167). But he believed all would be for naught if military conflict was not accompanied by spiritual warfare; so throughout this and other works, he appealed to Christians to repent of their sins and pray without ceasing for victory against the Ottomans.[11]

## The Apocalyptic Significance of War

Between the publication of *On War against the Turk* and *Muster Sermon*, Luther began to see the Turks and their expansion into central Europe as a fulfillment of eschatological prophesy, interpreting the rise and extension of Ottoman borders especially in view of Daniel 7. In his preface to the book in the Luther Bible, he went so far as to confidently assert:

---

[10]WA 30, II:115.
[11]See, for example, "Appeal for Prayer Against the Turks" (*LW* 43:213–41); *Vermahnung zum Gebet wider den Türcken* (WA 51:585–625).

[C]ertainly we have nothing to wait for now except the Last Day. . . .
The world is running faster and faster, hastening towards its end, so
that I often have the strong impression that the Last Days may break
before we have turned the holy Scriptures into German. For this is
sure: there are no more temporal events to wait for according to the
Scriptures. It has all happened, all has been fulfilled—the Roman
Empire is finished, the Turks have come to the peak of their power,
the power of the Popes is about to crash—and the world is crack-
ing into pieces as though it would tumble down . . . for if the world
were to linger on, as it has been, then surely all the world would go
Muhammadan or Epicurean, and there would be no more Christians
left (WA DB 11, II:381).

What that meant for the meantime was that Christians needed to
stand firm and resist any temptations to sin that the Turks might
provoke.

One of the biggest temptations, in Luther's mind, was to give in
to the Turks or—even worse—to embrace Islam under the dominion of the Turks. He had heard reports that some Christians desired
"the coming of the Turk and his government because they would
rather be under him than under the emperor" (*LW* 46:193).[12] He
also learned that "Christians who are captured or otherwise enter
into Turkey fall away and become altogether Turkish, for one very
seldom remains [a Christian]" there (*LW* 46:175).[13] So he decided
to learn and explain to his readers as much as he was able about the
Muslim religion.

## Luther on the Qur'an

Luther's earliest attempt to describe Islamic doctrine is located in
*On War Against the Turks*. Admitting he only had access to parts
of the Qur'an quoted in anti-Islamic polemics, he kept his comments to a brief summary. He explained that Islam circumvented
the whole Christian religion. It replaced the Bible with the Qur'an,
Christ with Muhammad, and grace and faith with works. Moreover,

[12]WA 30, II:137.
[13]WA 30, II:121.

it destabilized civil society and its imperialism perverted the nature of government. Finally, just as civil society was undermined by Muslim expansionism, so too were its most essential institutions of marriage and family. All of this, he wrote, took "out of the world *veram religionem, veram politiam, veram oeconomiam*, that is true spiritual life, true temporal government, and true home life" (*LW* 46:182).[14] These three estates were basic to the order of creation. Islam destroyed them and thereby was not just an enemy of Christendom but to all civil societies.

Over time, Luther gained access to a Latin translation of the Qur'an, which prompted even more critical assessments of Islam. Towards the end of his life he described Islam as the "invention of Muhammad" (WA 30, II:127–28). While it claimed to be the religion of the Old Testament prophets, it rejected their most basic message. From the very beginning, Luther explained, the prophets taught and God's people (*perpetua ecclesia*, the perpetual church) believed that all of humankind was fallen and stood condemned before God's law. They also proclaimed from the beginning the "gospel . . . that the eternal Father willed that the Son of God become a sacrifice for sins" (WA 53:572). The Qur'an rejected both these teachings. Coupled with its rejection of the Trinity and deity of Jesus, this led to Luther's final conclusion about Muslims and Islam:

> They do not want to listen to his word, which he has revealed concerning himself from the beginning of the world until now through the holy patriarchs and the prophets and finally through Christ himself and his apostles. They do not recognize him in this way, but they blaspheme and rage against him. They imagine a god, who has neither a Son nor a Holy Spirit in his divinity, and thus they claim that God is nothing more than a mere dream and they worship it. Indeed, they claim lies and blasphemies as knowledge of God because they presume, without divine revelation, that is, without the Holy Spirit, to know God and to come to him without a mediator (which must be God's own Son). They are therefore fundamentally without God. There is truly no other God than the one who is the Father of our Lord Jesus Christ (WA 51:151).

---

[14]WA 30, II:127–28.

For Luther, then, Islam was an innovation designed to bend and replace the truth with religious lies.

## Luther's Defense Against Islam

In addition to mere criticism, Luther also addressed Islam apologetically. This began after the siege on Vienna as he became increasingly convinced that a number of Christians would find themselves living under Islam in the Ottoman Empire in the future. So "to forestall the stumbling block of Muhammadanism," that is, conversion to Islam, "our people must be warned, lest, moved by the outward appearance of their religion and the façade of their behavior, or taking offense at the lowliness of our faith or the deformity of our behavior, they deny their Christ and follow after Muhammad" (*LW* 59:261).[15] To that end, Luther's *Muster Sermon/Heerpredigt* was written for "Germans already captive in Turkey or who might still become captive" (WA 30, II:185). In it he described Turkish religious culture, explaining how its piety, orderliness, and austerity might be attractive for the Christian, particularly one moved to external religious trappings. "Several Christians have fallen away and willingly and freely accept the Turk's or Muhammad's faith because of the great appearances that they have in their faith" (WA 30, II:185). But do not be led astray, he urged, and "learn the Creed now, while you still have room and place, the Ten Commandments, your Our Father, and learn them well" (WA 30, II:186).

The second part of his *Muster Sermon* is filled with practical and theological advice for Christians so that they might "remain firmly in their faith against every scandal and *anfechtungen*" experienced in a Muslim context. It also contains a strong exhortation for Christians held captive or even enslaved to the Turks to "patiently and willingly accept such misery and service" (WA 30, II:192). Luther believed that such crosses were ordained for Christians by God as part of the fallen order of creation. After all, he added, Jacob was forced to work for Laban, and Joseph for Pharaoh. Israel was forced into captivity in Egypt, and then again under the Babylonians; and Christ, the apostles,

---

[15]WA 30, II:206–7.

and martyrs were subjects of the Jews and pagan Romans. "Why would you have it better than your Lord Christ himself with all his saints in the Old and New Testament?" It might also be, he added, that God meant to present Christians living in subjugation under Islam with opportunities to "make the faith of the Turks a disgrace and perhaps convert any when they see that the Christians greatly surpass the Turks in humility, patience, industry, fidelity, and similar virtues" (WA 30, II:194–95).

To further aid Christians in understanding what life would be like under the Turks and how to think about and respond to Islam, Luther published a few additional works on the issue. In 1530 he published the work of an escaped slave of the Turks entitled *Booklet on the Rites and Customs of the Turks*. In the preface Luther added, he made clear he was publishing it with the hope of shedding light on "the stumbling block of Muhammadanism. . . . If we do not learn this, the danger is that many of our people . . . will become [Muslims]" (*LW* 59:261).[16]

A little over a decade later, as the Turks were reasserting their dominance in Hungary again, he published his most extensive treatment of Islam—the *Verlegung des Alcoran*.[17] It was essentially a translation of one of the most comprehensive and influential medieval polemics against the Qur'an—the Dominican missionary Riccoldo da Monte di Croce's *Against the Law of the Saracens*.[18] Luther, however, made it his own by removing and paraphrasing parts and adding his own material throughout. Its purpose was expressly apologetic:

> I have written here what I have so that if this booklet should, whether by the press or through the preachers, come before those who are struggling against the Turks or who are already subject to the Turks or who might become their subjects hereafter, they will be able to defend themselves against the faith of Muhammad, even if they were unable to defend themselves against his sword (*LW* 60:261–62).[19]

---

[16]WA 30, II:207.

[17]Johannes Ehmann, ed., *Ricoldus de Montecrucis*, Confutatio Alcorani *(1300); Martin Luther* Verlgung des Alcoran *(1542)* (Altenberge: Oros Verlag, 1999).

[18]See Rita George-Tvrtkovic, *A Christian Pilgrim in Medieval Iraq: Riccoldo da Montecroces's Encounter with Islam* (Turnhout: Brepols, 2012).

[19]WA 53:392.

The work begins by attempting to demonstrate that the Qur'an could not be the word of God for the following reasons:

> Neither the Old nor New Testament bear witness to it, it does not [agree] in speech or doctrine with any other [authority], it contradicts itself, it is not confirmed by miraculous signs, it is contrary to reason, there are manifest lies within it, it promotes murder, it is disorderly, it is shameful, [and] it is [finally historically] untrustworthy (WA 53:378).

Over the course of ten chapters, each of these allegations is supported by constant reference to the Qur'an and other Islamic sources. Where the arguments become really interesting is at the end, when it transitions from polemics to apologetics. There, Luther (following Riccoldo) uses passages with what he assumes is quasi-Christian content to show that Muhammad unwittingly acknowledged the triune nature of God and the deity of Christ. Luther believed these passages might even be used by Christians to engage Muslims in theological discourse with the possibility that those who were "led astray [by Islam] might return back to God" (WA 53:378).

## The Qur'an Published in Germany

The greatest contribution Luther made to raising awareness of Islam for Christians, however, was his involvement in the 1543 controversy over the publication of the Qur'an. Ever since he first began writing on the Turks he expressed his desire to obtain a complete version of the text. It took over a decade, but he finally obtained a manuscript version in 1542. Shortly afterwards he heard that Johannes Oporinus, a publisher in Basel, having received the manuscript from Theodor Bibliander, had been thrown in jail for attempting to publish such a heretical book.[20] This prompted a flood of letters from various scholars, none of which seemed to move the city officials. But when

---

[20]See Harry Clark, "The Publication of the Koran in Latin: A Reformation Dilemma," *Sixteenth Century Journal* 15 (1984): 3–12. For the literature from the affair, see Karl Hagenbach, "Luther und der Koran vor dem Rathe zu Basel," *Beitrage zur Vaterländischen Geschichte* 9 (1870): 291–326.

Luther sent his endorsement, Oporinus was subsequently released from custody. The Qur'an and a host of other literature on Islam was published in a large, three-part volume that has been described by one scholar as the first encyclopedia of Islam.[21]

One of the six editions published in 1543 includes a preface that Luther wrote where he encouraged his readers, and especially teachers, to persist in studying the Qur'an. He was convinced, as he told the city officials at Basel, that its publication and dissemination would help against "the apostles of the Devil and teachings of the shameful Muhammad . . . that the publication of this blasphemous seduction might arm and protect the least of us against such poisonous teaching and not only us Christians but also that some Turks might themselves be converted" (WBr 10:162). Christians needed to study "the writings of their enemies—so that they may more accurately refute, strike, and overturn those writings, so that they may be able to correct some of them, or at least to fortify our own people with stronger arguments" (*LW* 60:294).[22]

## Conclusion

These are the various dimensions of Luther's response to and concerns with the Ottoman jihad. From a defensive war to the apocalyptic role they played in the end times, to studying and possibly engaging with Muslims in Ottoman territory, Islam loomed large in Luther's mind. This all makes sense as the rise and expansion of the Ottoman Empire played a major role in shaping the events of the 1520s–1540s.[23] Whatever can be said about his approach, one thing that is clear is that it was anything but simple. This is all the more remarkable given the demands on his time and attention over the last two decades of his life.

Looking back, five hundred years later, Luther's concerns with the Ottoman Empire ultimately proved unfounded. It is totally

---

[21]Pierre Manuel, "Une Encylopédie de l'Islam: Le Recueil de Bibliander 1543 et 1550," *En Terre de l'Islam* 21 (1946): 31–37.

[22]WA 53:572.

[23]Bernard Lohse, *Martin Luther: An Introduction to His Life and His Work* (trans. Robert Schulz; Edinburgh: T&T Clark, 1987), 4.

understandable that he spent so much time considering appropriate responses to their aggressive wars of expansion: everyone, but the French perhaps, was concerned. Had a Martian arrived in Europe at the time, wrote Marshall Hodgson, he would have been justified in concluding the world was indeed going Muslim and the Ottoman Empire was destined to overrun Europe.[24]

Following the Reformation, however, the Ottoman jihads eventually came to an end. Incompetent leadership from Istanbul, a competitive Europe, and—if Max Weber's thesis on the Protestant work ethic was onto something—the broader aspects of Protestant identity which the Turks actually unwittingly helped protect by distracting pope and emperor, began to take hold in political and economic life. It helped move Europe into modernity, ultimately leaving the Ottomans in their wake. The geopolitical challenge of Islam has, nevertheless, returned. Our response to it will need to be just as robust as Luther's.

---

[24]Marshall G. S. Hodgson, "The Role of Islam in World History" in *Rethinking World History: Essays on Europe, Islam, and World History* (ed. Edmund Burke III; Cambridge: Cambridge University Press, 1993), 97.

# How Pastors Can Help Laity in Defending the Faith

*Rod Rosenbladt*

*This essay is a revised version of an oral presentation given at the 2016 Declare and Defend seminar on evangelism and apologetics at Redeemer Lutheran Church in Huntington Beach, California. The content amounts to a concatenation of various addresses I have given to confessional Lutheran pastors who received no training in Christian apologetics but wish they had. My intent was to highlight ever-so-briefly the nature and need of apologetics, and to encourage pastors by telling them that their calling to help their laity defend the faith is nowhere near an impossible one. I now intend that these words would honor all the pastoral care, writings, work with DOXOLOGY, and especially the professorial service of Rev. Dr. Harold Senkbeil.—RR*

## I. The Basics of Apologetics

The Greek word *apologia* refers to "a reasoned defense," usually in the context of a court trial. The classic example is Socrates on trial for corrupting the youth of his day. He and others were called upon to offer arguments that the charge against him was false. In a Christian context, Peter writes, "Always be prepared to offer an *apologia* (a reasoned defense) for the hope that is within you, yet do it with gentleness and respect" (1 Pet 3:15). Grammatically, this is an imperative, a command to all Christians. We are to be prepared to answer the question, "*Why* do you believe that the gospel is true?"

The ancient meaning is almost diametrically opposed to our English word "apologize." Christians are *not* being commanded in this verse to apologize for the fact that they are Christians. So we must put our English meaning completely out of our minds when we hear that word in Scripture. Instead, we must understand it according to the ancient context (someone on trial). We are to take it as a command to be prepared with *arguments*—in this case, in favor of the *truth* of the gospel.

In the earliest years of Christianity (beginning in the Book of Acts), Christians chiefly made a case for the truthfulness of the gospel according to two lines of argument: (1) on the basis of fulfilled prophecy (particularly Messianic prophecies in the Old Testament) when the audience was Jewish; and (2) on the basis of miracles—Jesus' public miracles done at will, but chiefly his bodily resurrection from the dead.[1] Why miracles? Because Jesus himself pointed to these. For example: "The works that I do in my Father's name bear witness about me" (John 10:25); "Believe me that I am in the Father and the Father is in me, or else believe on account of the works themselves" (John 14:11); and "Just as Jonah was in the belly of the great fish for three days and three nights, even so shall the Son of Man be three days and three nights in the heart of the earth" (Matt 12:40).

In our American context, the usual defense of Christianity is in terms of what philosophers call "subjective immediacy," roughly the equivalent of the line from the old A. H. Ackley hymn: "You ask me how I know he lives? He lives within my heart!" The problem (in addition to how foreign such statements are to the text of the New Testament) is that this is a completely *subjective* response. Such responses are *impossible* for the non-Christian to evaluate for truth-value. What we call "Christ in our hearts" the non-Christian can legitimately interpret as nothing more than heartburn! And why should he *not* think that?

What is called for is an *objective* case for the truth of the gospel. But can that be made? Is it even *possible* to do such a thing? I contend that the field of apologetics is designed to do just that, and does it sufficiently well. (I am not, however, making the apologetic case itself in this essay. For that, I refer you to the resources listed herein.)

---

[1]See F. F. Bruce, *The Defense of the Gospel in the New Testament* (rev. ed.; Grand Rapids: Eerdmans, 1977), 16–17.

## II. Apologetic Urgency Today

There was a time in this country when multitudes had respect for the Christian claim and for the text of the Bible. Even non-Christians could (and often did) revere both. But such times are past. One need not point to the violent expansion of Islam to get the impression that something is deeply missing—even deeply askew—in today's Western world. On the positive side of this shift, no longer do most Westerners have the convictions we had prior to the two world wars—for example, that all men are basically good, or that history is somehow headed inevitably upward.[2] But on the negative side, what we have these days in the West is the situation described decades ago by media genius Marshall McLuhan: a society that is global, that is secular, and that is pluralistic.

Note, however, that we are in a situation not all that different from the one faced by the earliest Christians living during the time of the Roman Empire. Think, for example, of the Christians living in Corinth during those times. Corinth was roughly the equivalent of our Las Vegas![3] Yet, with all of the congregational problems in Corinth, St. Paul still had a singular message to them: "I decided to know nothing among you but Jesus Christ and him crucified" (1 Cor 2:2). Paul helped to clean up—to answer—the ethical and doctrinal problems within those congregations. But then he returned to his theme of the gospel—that Christ died for our sins and was raised on the third day, both in accordance with the Scriptures (1 Cor 15:3–4)—*and* Paul provided evidence in the form of eyewitnesses who could confirm that these events had actually taken place (1 Cor 15:5–8).[4]

---

[2]See John Warwick Montgomery, *The Shaping of America: A True Description of the American Character, Both Good and Bad, and the Possibilities of Recovering a National Vision before the People Perish* (Minneapolis: Bethany Fellowship, 1976; repr., Irvine, Calif.: NRP Books, 2015), 69–87.

[3]Though see the discussion of morality in Corinth in James A. Davis, "1–2 Corinthians" in *The Baker Illustrated Bible Commentary* (ed. Gary M. Burge and Andrew E. Hill; Grand Rapids: Baker, 2012), 1274.

[4]On the importance of eyewitness testimony for historical claims, see Richard Bauckham, *Jesus and the Eyewitnesses: The Gospels as Eyewitness Testimony* (Grand Rapids: Eerdmans, 2006), 5–11.

If ever there was a time when both a clear preaching of the gospel, and a defense of it as genuinely *true* was called for, it was back then in Corinth. Yet the same urgency exists for Western nations today! With all the forces aligned to see historic Christianity as no more than trivial, as somehow equivalent to belief in the Tooth Fairy, what are we to do? Christian representation is virtually absent in our culture's "think tanks"—in our news media, in our magazines, in the worldview of our significant institutions—by which I mean the ones that attempt to control how we think and what we think. And I am *not* simply talking about politics. Rather, I am talking about the categories which—for good or ill—provide the structure for how we all see our lives, our culture, our world. Is genuine Christianity something that can legitimately provide a view of the world, of self, of meaning that is adequate for such a time as ours? Is it not only equal to but *better than* today's secularism as an interpretive grid? Don't answer too quickly, because the next question is predictable: *On what basis* is it superior to all other views? Why should I think it is true at all? Is there anything about the Christian claim that would justify giving mental time and effort to seriously considering it? If so, what exactly *is* that?

The urgency of a well-thought-out Christian response at this point is critical—both for Christians and for the world at large. That answer has *got* to be more than "emotional" or on the basis of "inner satisfaction." Neither is adequate to the task. If we respond, "Because the Christian gospel is *true*," we are (as I just said) immediately going to be asked for the basis of such a statement. That is precisely what apologetics provides for us: a reasoned, objective response for a culture that assumes we have nothing serious or intelligent to say. In the case of today's secular Westerners, it might be the first time they have ever heard such a claim—even if they go to church! This was partly why C. S. Lewis was asked to give a series of radio addresses in England during World War II. Many who listened to these "Broadcast Talks" (which became the first third of *Mere Christianity*) had never heard arguments as to why they should believe Christianity is true, even if they attended church regularly.

First and foremost is proclamation. Any adequate presentation of the Christian claim must include the depth of the fall into sin, and its effects on us all. It will also set forth Jesus' claims regarding himself (claims to be nothing less than God-in-human-flesh) and, especially, regarding his saving work (claims to die for the sin of the world, to rescue real rebels from the just condemnation of God). It will lay out the central Christian teaching of justification by grace *alone*, through faith *alone*, on the basis of Christ's cross and death *alone*. And these themes will occupy center stage in everything a serious parish does, from preaching and teaching, to works of mercy, to various other activities.

But in times of great skepticism such as ours, a parish must, in addition, regularly have available a reasoned defense of the truth of the gospel. This is for members—especially for youth who will go off to secular colleges, but also for adults who are confronted with arguments against the faith. Yet this is also for visitors and adult confirmands—any who suspect they will have to check their brains at the church door before believing the good news. For non-members, a parish could, for example, have evening meetings *designed* for people who "believe nothing at all"—a venue that is "safe" and is for the purpose of answering questions, but also for offering arguments for the truth of the gospel. The parish could also pass out a free, short, printed bibliography of quality apologetics sources to such people, and have it available in the sanctuary for members as well.

Now while I am contending that this apologetic need in our day is urgent and critical, I am at the same time also claiming that, though we might think that preparing to respond to secular inquiry is the mental equivalent of climbing K2, in reality *it is not!* Lutheran theology in particular is well primed for this task, as I will now attempt to explain.

## III. Lutheranism's Unique Focus for Apologetics

For the better part of the twentieth century, confessional Lutherans published almost *nothing* in the field of Christian apologetics. And this should come as no surprise, because Lutheran seminaries' curricula had no courses in the field—required *or* elective. A Christian denomination that chooses not to offer training in apologetics will not develop in its young scholars the impression that the cognitive defense of the truth of the gospel is somehow important.[5] In the

---

[5] I am aware, however, that individual seminary professors have stressed the importance of apologetics in certain of their courses. Harold Senkbeil, for

classical theological curriculum, "apologetics" was one of the three components of systematic theology (the other two being dogmatics and ethics).[6] So it is not obvious why conservative denominations (including Lutheran ones) would *ever* jettison such a basic ingredient of systematic theology. But it appears we have.

Such a state of affairs *is* completely understandable in the case of Protestant liberalism, given that liberals long ago embraced the basic unity of all religions. Protestant liberals believed that, at its core, the message of all the religions of the world is the *same*. (That shared message was usually said to be *moral* in nature—perhaps what we call the Golden Rule—an effectively Christ-less message that renders an *apologia* obsolete.) But conservative denominations never accepted

---

example, made it a point to tell his students that they must talk about historical evidences when referencing biblical narratives during catechesis.

[6]The place of apologetics among the various theological disciplines has been debated for some time. Some have proposed it as a branch of pastoral theology. This position assumes that the "apologia" of the faith will be either proclaimed (homiletics) or taught (catechesis) and thus is performed under the guise of the pastorate. If apologetics is the defense of the Christian claim systematically organized, then it presupposes a development of a "system" using the exegetical, historical, and systematic disciplines. In this case, apologetics takes its place under the greater umbrella of systematic theology. Either scenario seems reasonable: that is, that apologetics either is a part of the discipline of systematic theology or as the intellectualistic side of practical theology (catechesis and preaching). For more see B. B. Warfield, "Apologetics" in *The New Schaff-Herzog Encyclopedia of Religious Knowledge: Embracing Biblical, Historical, Doctrinal, and Practical Theology, and Biblical, Theological, and Ecclesiastical Biography from the Earliest Times to the Present Day* (ed. Samuel Macauley Jackson et al.; 13 vols. Grand Rapids: Baker, 1951–1954), 1:232–38; based on the *Realencyklopädie für protestantische Theologie und Kirche* (ed. Albert Hauck; 24 vols.; 3d ed.; Leipzig: J. C. Hinrichs, 1896–1913). Also see the description of apologetics as it is classically included within the various nascent systematic and dogmatic works of the seventeenth-century Lutheran dogmaticians in Robert D. Preus, *The Theology of Post-Reformation Lutheranism*, vol. 2, *God and His Creation* (St. Louis: Concordia, 1970–1972), 34–39. Lastly, for an analysis of the history of Lutheran theology that usually places apologetics within systematic and dogmatic works, see John Warwick Montgomery, *Faith Founded on Fact: Essays in Evidential Apologetics* (Nashville: Thomas Nelson, 1978; repr., Irvine, Calif.: NRP Books, 2015), 129–53.

this imagined core sameness of all religions. Biblically oriented Christians always thought that this claim on the part of Protestant liberals was intellectual rubbish—and could be *shown* to be intellectual rubbish by even light research.

For many conservative Christians, however, offering an objective historical defense of the faith to skeptics, liberals, and secularists is *verboten*. Why? Usual anti-apologetic responses (which we cannot pursue here in detail) have been twofold. First, the more intellectual representation of the anti-apologetic position: so-called presuppositional apologetics. This method, which is very common in solidly Reformed Christian circles, asks the non-Christian to begin by *assuming* the truth of the Christian claim. They tell the non-Christian that his acquaintance with the external world will, as a result of having made this assumption, be *more* coherent, *more* understandable, than is the case in any other position than the Christian one. So the emphasis is on pointing out internal inconsistencies in all non-Christian positions, and the *lack* of inconsistencies in the Christian position. But the (unfortunate) weakness in the method is that at no point does the Christian actually *defend the truth* of the gospel.[7] This is because presuppositionalists claim that evidence in behalf of Scripture can only be rightly interpreted if one assumes the truth of Scripture *in the first place*, which of course the non-Christian does not do.[8] So why bother?

Second, the less intellectual representative opposed to apologetics: Protestant pietism. For most of us, this latter position is the more familiar of the two anti-apologetic stances. The basic idea in pietism is that all cognitive arguments in favor of the truth of

---

[7]On the philosophical shortcomings of this view, see Jeffrey C. Mallinson, "Epistemology of the Cross: A Lutheran Response to Philosophical Theisms" in *Theologia et Apologia: Essays in Reformation Theology and its Defense* (ed. Adam S. Francisco, Korey D. Mass, and Stephen P. Mueller; Eugene, Ore.: Wipf & Stock, 2007), 23–44. See also the critique of the Reformed presuppositionalist Cornelius Van Til in Montgomery, *Faith Founded on Fact*, 107–28.

[8]See John M. Frame, *Apologetics: A Justification of Christian Belief* (ed. Joseph E. Torres; 2d ed.; Phillipsburg, N.Y.: P&R Publishing, 2015), 10–15. For a comparison of presuppositional and evidential apologetic methods, see Gary R. Habermas, "Evidential Apologetic Methodology: The Montgomery-Bahnsen Debate" in *Tough-Minded Christianity* (Nashville: B&H, 2008), 426–51.

Christianity are "less than spiritual" and thus should be *avoided* by every Christian.[9] Instead of offering arguments, those who are "truly spiritual" should simply repeat the gospel message once more and pray for the non-Christian's conversion. Again—but for different reasons—the Christian is altogether discouraged from attempting to argue in favor of the truth! Many Christians have been told by Protestant pietists that arguing *that* the gospel is true, and *why* it is true, amounts to trying to undermine the work of the Holy Spirit.[10] Sadly, this includes many Lutherans, too, despite the fact that defending the faith through argument is neither at odds with our Confessions[11] nor the theology of Martin Luther.[12]

---

[9]For example, historian W. R. Ward noted that Nicolaus Zinzendorf eschewed intellectual doubts on the grounds that finding answers through rational argument and apologetics "made faith harder by creating the impression that belief was a mathematical problem." Ward went on to quote Zinzendorf on the necessary separation between philosophy and theology: "Let people clarify their minds with philosophy as long as they like, but tell them that as soon as they wish to become theologians they must become children and idiots." W. R. Ward, *The Protestant Evangelical Awakening* (Cambridge: Cambridge University Press, 1992), 123. See also the comments on Friedrich Schleiermacher's "inner apologetic" that "cannot be verified outside of faith" in Avery Dulles, *A History of Apologetics* (Washington, DC: Corpus Instrumentorum, 1971; repr., Eugene, Ore.: Wipf & Stock, 1999), 161.

[10]One of the biggest straw man arguments against utilizing apologetics is that apologists try to *argue* people into the kingdom—that is, apologists think that by simply demonstrating the reasonableness of Christianity people can and will come to faith in Jesus. I am unaware of any serious apologist who maintains this view, even among evangelical Christians; but even if some do, suffice it to say that they are wrong and have misunderstood the apologetic task.

[11]See John Warwick Montgomery, "Christian Apologetics in Light of the Lutheran Confessions," *Concordia Theological Quarterly* 2 (July 1978): 258–75.

[12]On the relation between faith and reason in Luther's thought, see B. A. Gerrish, *Grace and Reason: A Study in the Theology of Luther* (Oxford: Oxford University Press, 1962; repr., Eugene, Ore.: Wipf & Stock, 2005); David Andersen, *Martin Luther—The Problem of Faith and Reason: A Reexamination in Light of the Epistemological and Christological Issues* (Bonn: Verlag für Theologie und Religionswissenschaft, 2009); and Mark A. Pierson, "Putting Reason in its Proper Place: Luther versus Aquinas on Reason's Role in Salvation" in *Theology is Eminently Practical* (ed. Jacob Corzine and Bryan Wolfmueller; Fort Wayne, Ind.: Lutheran Legacy Press, 2012), 157–73. For

What does classical Lutheranism have to offer in the enterprise of apologetics? Much! And it is so familiar to many of us that we don't even notice! The undeniable emphasis in confessional Lutheran theology is that it begins with the person of Christ. As Luther said, true Christianity "does not start at the top, as all other religions do; it starts at the bottom" (*LW* 26:30)—namely, with this historical flesh-and-blood man who is also fully divine, fully God, and whose vicarious, substitutionary death paid for the sins of the whole world. The Christian claim is that three days after he died, Jesus then rose bodily, literally, from the dead. St. Paul not only writes that this was "for our justification" (Rom 4:25), he also defends the resurrection as fact and rests the truth of the entire faith on it, saying that if Christ has not been raised then we Christians are "of all people most to be pitied" (1 Cor 15:19).[13] But there is another aspect not often mentioned—even on Easter mornings. The resurrection of Christ was God the Father's factual vindication of the truth of all of the claims of his incarnate Son (Rom 1:4), such that Jesus' teachings about his death as a death that saves sinners *can* be trusted![14]

This Christ-centered nature of our theology puts Lutherans at an advantage in doing apologetics in a way that other denominations' theologies do not. (It is not accidental that Lutherans are sometimes accused of being "Unitarians of the Second Person of the Trinity.") For example, Lutherans are *not* known for deep studies in the classical arguments for the existence of God. Our students are expected to be familiar with them, but they are not really central for us. As strong as the philosophical arguments for theism may be, bare theism saves

---

examples of Luther defending the gospel by appealing to the witness of history, see Adam S. Francisco, *Martin Luther and Islam: A Study in Sixteenth-Century Polemics and Apologetics* (Leiden: Brill, 2007). For an argument that Luther and many of the sixteenth- and seventeenth-century Lutheran fathers offered an objective defense of Christian truth, see John Warwick Montgomery, "The Apologetic Thrust of Lutheran Theology" in *Theologia et Apologia*, 5–21.

[13]For a defense of the resurrection that is vigorous, thorough, and yet accessible, see Gary R. Habermas and Michael R. Licona, *The Case for the Resurrection of Jesus* (Grand Rapids: Kregel, 2004).

[14]See N. T. Wright, *The Resurrection of the Son of God* (Minneapolis: Fortress, 2003), 23–25; and Gary R. Habermas, *The Risen Jesus and Future Hope* (Lanham, Md.: Rowman and Littlefield, 2003), 110–12.

no one! Lutherans, rather, work from the center of the Christian timeline—the incarnate God-man Christ—"backward" to God the Father almighty, maker of heaven and earth, and "forward" to the Holy Spirit who calls, enlightens, and sanctifies the whole Christian church until the End. It is the case for Christ as the true Savior of the world that both keeps the conversation focused on the gospel and grounds the Christian claim in the world of objective facts.

The best twentieth-century Lutheran representative of this apologetic orientation is Dr. John Warwick Montgomery. Virtually *all* of his books and articles demonstrate this Christ-centered approach to the questions most often asked by unbelievers about the truth of the Christian claim. (And it is his training of me that undergirds anything in this little essay that is "good, right and salutary." It is I who am responsible for any aspect of it that is less than these!)

## IV. Apologetics and Adult Education

What about a possible connection between Christian apologetics and Christian adult education? My thesis here is that not only *is* there a connection between adult instruction and our apologetic calling, but that it is more important than most of us Lutheran pastors think it is.

Many Lutheran laity know that one of the key callings of a pastor, in all of his preaching, is to proclaim God's law and to proclaim the biblical gospel, with the emphasis on the latter. He is to proclaim the person and work of Christ—to proclaim what we call the "Chief Article" of justification by faith alone—particularly the *for you* aspect of it! And the laity are correct: this *is* the central aspect of a confessional Lutheran pastor's call to do word and sacrament ministry at his congregation. The vocation of pastor primarily has to do with the forgiveness of sins.

Yet there is also the closely related aspect of the Lutheran pastor's call that has to do with Christian catechesis, teaching not only the youth but also the adults. Part of that calling is to prepare his laity for *objections* to the faith that they will certainly encounter from family, friends, the workplace, the media—everywhere! And, on the positive side, the pastor is to aid the laity in their ability to offer *objective evidence* in behalf of the truth of the gospel. Put simply, we are doing our people a disservice if they are left with the impression that coming to church is like entering a stained glass wonderland.

For some, this will sound like a tall order. Where do you start? Does each Christian have to know how to answer every possible objection a skeptic might present? For those asking these questions, I have some good news. Coming up to speed in apologetics is nowhere near impossible. It does *not* require becoming a living, breathing encyclopedia of information, and in an unrealistically short amount of time. Helping laypeople here is much less daunting. For example, if a pastor reads only a handful of apologetic works (see below), he will be well prepared to do an introductory course—or a series of courses—on key apologetic issues. This will also provide the opportunity for pastors to introduce laypeople to books which may answer their own particular questions. The goal is not to get laity to memorize a series of facts, but to make them familiar with the evidential case for Christianity and to help inoculate them against any shoddy thinking they will encounter.

In addition, the pastor seeks to equip his parishioners to offer a defense for the hope that is in them when they, according to their vocations, speak the gospel to others. In adult education, then, a course could also be done on short apologetic books with which the laity should become acquainted—again, *not* to memorize, but to consider giving to particular non-Christians with whom laity are conversing. One book will apply to a certain unbeliever's questions, another book to other non-Christians who are asking different questions. The layperson just needs to know the case well enough to hand out the book with some knowledge of what is in it.

To aid in this, 1517[15] will be marketing *outlines* of many, many of these important (and often *short!*) books. These are not, of course, substitutes for actually reading the books themselves; rather, they are "maps" to the content of each. For example, would it be worth your time and energy to have in outline form the top 5–10 most important apologetics works of C. S. Lewis, or Dr. Montgomery, or

---

[15]1517 serves churches and the world by supplying theological resources that strengthen congregations, providing a safe place for those broken by the church, and modeling ways of engaging the culture in a manner that is thoughtful, courageous, and Christ-centered. For more information, visit www.1517.org.

others—especially if these outlines were not just accurate but cheap? These "maps" are meant to assist both pastors in teaching these books and laity in digesting their contents.

I always cut a lot of slack to Lutheran pastors in their apologetic calling because, for the better part of a century, *none* of them had seminary courses in apologetics available to them. No wonder the whole enterprise sounds strange and foreign to them! It would to me, too, had I never had a professor even mention the importance of arguments in behalf of the truth of the gospel. I therefore also encourage laypeople to be light in blaming their confessional Lutheran pastor for his lack of familiarity with the apologetic aspect of his calling. It is likely that nothing in his professional training offered it. In this aspect of his schooling, he (and all his classmates) were *cheated* by their own church! (If you are inclined to assign blame for this, know that you will have to search a long, long way back in time to find those who eliminated the whole apologetic enterprise from confessional Lutheran seminary training. Very simply, your pastor's professors got no such training either.) If you are a layperson who wants to get your pastor to help the congregation in this regard, please go easy on him.

## V. The Place of Printed Sources

My students are sort of surprised or taken aback when I tell them that, often times, the major aspect of the laity doing apologetics with friends, family, or acquaintances is simply lending to them great apologetics books or essays. We imagine that we have to become acquainted with *every argument*, have *all* of them on the tips of our tongues. But that is simply false. We do not!

When I was in seminary, such writings were almost unknown—other than Dr. Wilbur Smith's *Therefore Stand* and the magnificent books of C. S. Lewis. A young Dr. Edward John Carnell was just beginning to be published, as was Dr. Bernard Ramm. And Dr. Montgomery was still an undergraduate at Cornell, majoring in classics and philosophy. By and large, apologetics books were as rare as hen's teeth. C. S. Lewis stood out like a sore thumb! But his readers quickly began to number in the millions, and still do. There are a lot of reasons for this,[16] but one of the main ones is that he defended the *truth* of the Christian gospel with *arguments as to why it is true!*

How times have changed! Soon Inter-Varsity Press began to publish the books of Francis Schaeffer—books that served to change the intellectual axis of university students. And not only that, Inter-Varsity began to publish small monographs (which were physically the size of playing cards) by recognized evangelical scholars on apologetic subjects. Titles included "The Impossibility of Agnosticism," "Dangerous Christian Books I've Read," "Christianity for the Open-Minded," "Doubters Welcome," "The Evidence for the Resurrection," and so on. In Inter-Varsity's *HIS* magazine, students could read apologetics articles by Dr. Montgomery (for example, "History and Christianity" and "The Place of Reason") and the late Paul E. Little (such as "What Non-Christians Ask" and "Is Faith for the Ignorant?"). During the 1970s and 1980s, one of the most popular apologists was Josh McDowell, a non-academic whose little book, *More Than a Carpenter*, sold millions of copies. The book's success was due, in part, to the fact that it was short, made an objective case for the truth about Jesus, and was intended for a wide audience—meaning, not just believers. (It can still be bought in bulk to hand out to inquiring skeptics.) Today, we have a *plethora* of Christian apologetics books, articles, websites, audio sources, etc. But this has only come to be the case in the last 20 or 30 years.

Now for an important caveat or two. *First*, this emphasis on printed sources assumes that the average person is able to read—even able to read "complex sentences." This becomes more dubious with

---

[16]On the attractiveness of C. S. Lewis as an apologist, see Richard L. Purtill, *C. S. Lewis's Case for the Christian Faith* (New York: Harper & Row, 1981; repr., San Francisco: Ignatius Press, 2004); *C. S. Lewis, Light-Bearer in the Shadowlands: The Evangelistic Vision of C. S. Lewis* (ed. Angus J. L. Menuge; Wheaton, Ill.: Crossway Books, 1997); J. I. Packer, "Still Surprised by Lewis: Why This Nonevangelical Oxford Don Has Become Our Patron Saint," *Christianity Today* 42 (Sept. 7, 1998): 54–60; Louis A. Markos, "Myth Matters: Why C. S. Lewis's Books Remain Models for Christian Apologists in the 21st Century," *Christianity Today* 45 (Apr. 23, 2001): 32–39; and Michael Ward, "How Lewis Lit the Way to Better Apologetics: Why the Path to Reasonable Faith Begins with Story and Imagination," *Christianity Today* 57 (Nov. 2013): 36–41.

every passing year. Books are only useful for those who are willing and able to open and peruse them! I'll leave the matter at that.

*Second,* we must recognize that most people have been taught that, in the realm of religion, *nothing* could possibly be classified as genuine knowledge. And even if it somehow *could* qualify, they "know" that *every* source is written from some bias, vitiating *all* text-based claims anyway. To make matters even worse, today's Westerner holds that the best one can expect to find is some religion that provides inward or personal satisfaction. Why? Because, as everybody knows, *subjectivity* rules in matters religious! It is a very rare person who even imagines that the religious truth question could ever be solved in an *objective* manner.[17] Poor university students are taught that *all* claimed metanarratives are necessarily false. What would ever cause a student to accept such a strange *a priori* position? The answer is twofold: postmodernism (à la Jacques Derrida, Jean-François Lyotard, many others), and the presumed authority of his or her professors (at least in the humanities).

*Third,* we are all—no matter our denomination—going to have to severely limit utilizing books from our denominational publishing houses. Almost all of it is written only for "insiders"—meaning, most of it should *never* be given to a non-Christian. Ninety percent of what most denominations (including mine!) publish should purposely be kept away from non-Christians. Virtually none of it is directed to non-Christian readers who are searching for answers, or it is written in language that they will not be able to understand. That means that Christians (Lutherans included) must find *better* material than what comes from their own publishing houses: books designed and written for doubters; books that set forth genuine arguments; books that attempt to answer the most common objections to Christianity.

---

[17] I am reminded of the informal exchange between Michael Horton (the J. Gresham Machen Professor of Theology and Apologetics at Westminster Seminary in California) and the late Richard Rorty (an atheistic philosophy professor who denied the distinction between subjective perceptions and objective facts). When Horton presented a forceful, evidential approach to the truth claims of Christianity, Rorty replied in shock, "There are Christians who can actually do this?!"

Or think of this subject in another way. John R. W. Stott long ago published an excellent little book titled, *Basic Christianity*. In the opening, he offered a possible prayer for the reader to pray. It went like this:

> God, if you exist (and I don't know you do), and you can hear this prayer (and I don't know if you can), I want to tell you that I am an honest seeker after the truth. Show me if Jesus is your Son and the Savior of the world. And if you bring conviction to my mind, I will trust him as my Savior and follow him as my Lord.[18]

Does this sound anything like a book your seminary professors could have ever written? I doubt it does. I know our confessional Lutheran professors would *never* put such a prayer in the preface of their books. And not for the reason you are likely thinking—that is, on theological grounds. Rather, the reason is simple: our professors are not inclined to write books for non-Christian doubters! But Fr. Stott was part of the university world in England, he spoke and wrote for Inter-Varsity there, and he knew well what it was to present the gospel to hundreds of students who *did not believe it*.

Now for pastors who are asking, "Where do I start?" and "How do I get brought up to speed?" let me suggest some worthwhile reading *before* you attempt to engage unbelievers or help your laity to do the same. In my tenure as a professor of apologetics for more than three decades, a handful of books became standard texts that I would assign to my undergraduate students, year after year. Collectively, these books cover the basics of apologetics.[19] In my view, they provide a solid foundation that both enables Christians to handle the most common objections to the faith and prepares readers for

---

[18]John R. W. Stott, *Basic Christianity: Fiftieth Anniversary Edition* (Nottingham: Inter-Varsity, 2008), 26.

[19]That is, they cover the basic arguments and lines of defense. For a well-rounded primer on the discipline and practice of apologetics, see Alister E. McGrath, *Mere Apologetics: How to Help Seekers and Skeptics Find Faith* (Grand Rapids: Baker, 2012). For suggestions on how to navigate conversations with unbelievers, see Greg Koukl, *Tactics: A Game Plan for Discussing your Christian Convictions* (Grand Rapids: Zondervan, 2009).

further study. Every aspiring apologist will want to become familiar
with the following works:

- *Mere Christianity* by C. S. Lewis[20]
- *History, Law and Christianity* by John Warwick
  Montgomery[21]
- *Reasonable Faith: Christian Truth and Apologetics* by
  William Lane Craig[22]
- *The Universe Next Door: A Basic Worldview Catalogue* by
  James W. Sire[23]

There is always more to learn, always some nuanced version of an
old (and already refuted) argument against the truth of the gospel;
but these sources should help keep any pastor or layperson in good
stead.[24]

---

[20](New York: MacMillan, 1952); available in numerous reprint editions. The
first third has been published separately as *The Case for Christianity*.

[21](Downers Grove, Ill.: InterVarsity Press, 1971; repr., Irvine, Calif.: NRP
Books, 2015). For a similar defense of the historical reliability of the Gospels
that also offers an apologetic for Lutheran theology, see Craig A. Parton,
*The Defense Never Rests: A Lawyer's Quest for the Gospel* (2d ed.; St. Louis:
Concordia, 2015).

[22](3rd ed.; Wheaton, Ill.: Crossway, 2008). For a simpler text, see William
Lane Craig, *On Guard: Defending your Faith with Reason and Precision*
(Colorado Springs: David C. Cook, 2010).

[23](5th ed.; Downers Grove, Ill.: InterVarsity Press, 2009). For books that also
defend the Christian worldview but give more attention to standard apologetic
issues, see Norman L. Geisler and Frank Turek, *I Don't Have Enough Faith to
Be an Atheist* (Wheaton, Ill.: Crossway, 2004) and Nancy Pearcey, *Total Truth:
Liberating Christianity from its Cultural Captivity* (study guide ed.; Wheaton,
Ill.: Crossway, 2008).

[24]These books can be supplemented with numerous others. For simple books
that address specific objections see Alex McFarland, *The 10 Most Common
Objections to Christianity* (Ventura, Calif.: Regal Books, 2007); Timothy Keller,
*The Reason for God: Belief in an Age of Skepticism* (New York: Riverhead Books,
2008); Mark Mittelberg, *The Questions Christians Hope No One Will Ask* (Carol
Stream, Ill.: Tyndale, 2010); and the concise handbooks from Paul Copan:
*That's Just Your Interpretation: Responding to Skeptics who Challenge your Faith*

## VI. The Place of Audio/Video Sources

Next, and very quickly, I want to say a bit about audio and video sources that pastors can use in their congregations or make available for members to listen to or watch on their own. One of the best apologetics items you can add to your church library is Dr. Montgomery's audio series, "Sensible Christianity." He delivered these introductory-level lectures at parishes throughout America, having designed them to be understandable to laypersons and not just educated clergy. Pastors can walk their congregation through some or all of this 16-part series for weeks on end. If it is well received, I recommend moving on to Dr. Montgomery's other 16-part audio set, "A History of Christian Apologetics: The Defense of the Gospel through the Centuries." This study covers how the greatest apologists met the attacks leveled against the faith in their own age—from St. Paul to C. S. Lewis—and their relevance for our defense of the truth of the gospel today.[25]

---

(Grand Rapids: Baker, 2001); *How Do You Know You're Not Wrong? Responding to Objections that Leave Christians Speechless* (Grand Rapids: Baker, 2005); *When God Goes to Starbucks: A Guide to Everyday Apologetics* (Grand Rapids: Baker, 2008); *True for You, But Not for Me: Overcoming Objections to Christian Faith* (rev. ed.; Minneapolis: Bethany, 2009). Somewhat more involved are these books from the "Case for . . . Series" by Lee Strobel: *The Case for Christ* (updated and expanded ed.; Grand Rapids: Zondervan, 2016); *The Case for Faith* (Grand Rapids: Zondervan, 2000); *The Case for the Real Jesus* (Grand Rapids: Zondervan, 2009). Collections of apologetic essays by well-known and promising scholars are found in the following books edited by Paul Copan and William Lane Craig: *Passionate Conviction: Contemporary Discourses on Christian Apologetics* (Nashville: B&H, 2007); *Contending with Christianity's Critics: Answering New Atheists & Other Objectors* (Nashville: B&H, 2009); and *Come Let us Reason: New Essays in Christian Apologetics* (Nashville: B&H, 2012). See also the essays from Lutheran apologists in *Making the Case for Christianity: Responding to Modern Objections* (St. Louis: Concordia, 2014). Pastors are encouraged at least to view the table of contents in such books to see if the topics therein might address questions raised by their own laity.

[25]Both these sets are available for download at www.1517.org as are shorter series from Dr. Montgomery on the same topics, including "Defending the Biblical Gospel" and "The Truth of Christianity: More Than A Feeling."

For video sources, I am likewise only recommending here two introductory-level items that cover a handful of topics and are intended to be viewed over multiple sessions. First there is the DVD series of three films by Lee Strobel: "The Case for Christ / The Case for Faith / The Case for a Creator." Each video is based on Strobel's book by the same name, but these are not merely infomercials; rather, like the books, Strobel brings his own background as an investigative journalist to the questions at hand and, perhaps more importantly, includes the judgments of respected scholars on the evidence for the Christian claim.[26] Second, an outfit called "TrueU" has produced a series of DVDs geared especially for teenagers and college students (though their solid content makes them valuable for adults as well). Through a slew of 30-minute lessons a case is made for the truth of Christianity under three main headings: "Does God Exist?"; "Is the Bible Reliable?"; and "Who Is Jesus?" These videos also feature key experts on pressing issues. Since this pre-packaged curriculum has an accompanying discussion guide, it may be especially useful for busy pastors.[27]

In our day, there exists countless digital resources on the subject of Christian apologetics; yet I admit that I am not competent to recommend much more than I already have in the way of specifics. I am aware that the webpage "Apologetics315" attempts to be a sort of "catch-all" for apologetics and has a rather extensive MP3 audio page.[28] Individuals such as Greg Koukl, J. Warner Wallace, John Ankerberg, Frank Turek, and Ravi Zacharias have numerous audio and video resources available through their websites, podcasts, or YouTube channels.[29] There are debates galore online, with the likes

---

[26]I recommend showing the videos in the following order: 1) "The Case for Christ"; 2) "The Case for a Creator"; 3) "The Case for Faith."

[27]I recommend that this series be shown the following order: 1) "Is the Bible Reliable?"; 2) "Who Is Jesus?"; 3) "Does God Exist?"

[28]See https://apologetics315.com/2008/03/the-ultimate-apologetics-mp3-audio-page/.

[29]Koukl: "Stand to Reason" (www.str.org); Wallace: "Cold-Case Christianity" (www.coldcasechristianity.com); Ankerberg: "The John Ankerberg Show" (www.jashow.org); Turek: "Cross Examined" (www.crossexamined.org); Zacharias: "Ravi Zacharias International Ministries" (www.rzim.org). For short videos on various topics that can perhaps be used as jumping-off points in an apologetics

of William Lane Craig, Michael Licona, and James White taking on skeptics of all stripes. And our own *Issues, Etc.* covers a fair amount of apologetics-related topics as well.

The drawback, however, of many of these latter resources—and even for most apologetics material in general—can be threefold. First, they are often designed to handle individual or specific questions and do not always build a comprehensive case for the historical reliability of the Gospels and the identity of the Jesus found therein. Second, and similarly, they can spend ungodly amounts of time on theism, creation/evolution, cultural or moral issues, and all sorts of things without *ever* getting to the scandal of the cross and the significance of the empty tomb. Finally, since evangelicals and others have been doing the heavy lifting in apologetics instead of Lutherans, pastors may have to correct whatever flawed theology finds its way into an otherwise decent defense of the faith. That said, such shortcomings should *not* lead us to throw the baby out with the bathwater and simply choose not to do apologetics *whatsoever*!

Let that suffice for comments on audio/video sources. As I implied, I am sure there are plenty of other Christians who can search and navigate the world of webpages, podcasts, and videos far better than me.

## VII. Conclusion

Years ago a pastor friend in northern California told me that his area was filled with hostility toward Christianity—toward the claim that God was in Christ reconciling the world unto himself (2 Cor 5:19). He said, "I live in the land of Druids and Wiccans, Rod." This remark illustrates the fact that after two centuries of Enlightenment rationalism and skepticism—during which even many theologians and pastors didn't believe much—the door is wide open in our day for people to believe anything and everything. And they do! You might not have Druids and Wiccans in your midst; it might be Muslims,

---

study, pastors may wish to peruse the YouTube channels of "RZIM Canada" (for the series, "Short Answers to Big Questions") and "One Minute Apologist" (which features numerous scholars).

Buddhists, Mormons, psychics, spiritists, universalists, or those who are comfortably "non-religious." But whether it's to the run-of-the-mill atheist or a member of some strange suicide death cult, we are still called to be prepared to offer an *apologia* for the hope that is within us.

In my estimation, the apologetic task that lies before pastors today is both harder and easier than it was a generation or two ago. It is harder, on the one hand, not primarily because the marketplace of ideas has become saturated with religious options, but rather because most people are inconsistent postmodernists about it all. How so? They are quick to say that everything is relative and that one belief system is as good as another (so long as it "works" for you), but they are even *quicker* to condemn Christians who make the exclusive claim that Jesus is the only Savior this sinful world has ever known. To this, the prudent apologist can respond in a way that is consistent with the words of St. Paul in 2 Corinthians 10:4–5: "For the weapons of our warfare are not of the flesh but have divine power to destroy strongholds. We destroy arguments and every lofty opinion raised against the knowledge of God, and take every thought captive to obey Christ." This divine power that destroys strongholds and arguments amounts to what we call "the law." Logic, rational arguments, common sense, and whatever else exposes the flaws and contradictions in someone's opposition to the gospel is meant to convict them in their suppression of the truth. But of course, sinful man will fight tooth and nail *even to remain illogical* so long as it means he doesn't have to bend the knee to Christ.

On the other hand, the task is easier today because the conversation is currently open. Some people are actually willing to listen to a clear proclamation of the gospel *and* a reasoned defense as to why this religious option in particular is superior to all others. Again, only an *objective* case for the truthfulness of the Christian claim can set it apart from the cacophony of subjective voices peddling their own claims. To return to 1 Peter 3:15, the hope that is within us is none other than the gospel itself—that Jesus died for our sins, at a real time and real place in history, and rose from the dead, *also* at a real time and real place in history. This means that, as much as possible, doing apologetics will remain *centered on Christ* even while appealing to evidence and employing arguments. In short, apologetics is meant to serve in the communication of the gospel.[30] Let us therefore not keep silent or lose focus while this window of opportunity remains.

In closing, I realize that all I have said to you is highly hortatory—not exactly the same as preaching Christ and the forgiveness of sins into your ears. Forsooth! Still, I hope you pastors find some encouragement in this little essay. Learning the basics of apologetics is nowhere near as difficult as many assume. A careful reading of just a few of the best books on the subject will help prepare you to teach your laity how to withstand objections and defend their faith. And a fair percentage of them will be interested, too, with some even pleading for more. Why? Because in conversations every week they face apologetic issues and know all too well that they need some assistance. That is, in part, why you have been called and ordained to serve them. May God therefore grant you wisdom, resolve, and courage as you endeavor, in the words of Luther, to "use all your cleverness and effort" and act as "lion hearts" in your defense of the gospel (*LW* 26:29–30; WABr 10:162).

---

[30]See further, Alfonso O. Espinosa, "Apologetics as Pastoral Theology" in *Theologia et Apologia*, 317–31.

# Christ (and His Virtues) in Action

## Sanctification as a Platform for Virtue Ethics

*Lucas V. Woodford*

## Introduction

Harold Senkbeil's first book, *Sanctification: Christ in Action*, provided a much–needed examination of a neglected teaching in Lutheran circles. His eloquent confession on this topic remains as encouraging today as when it was first published. In short, Senkbeil demonstrates that the sanctified life is the receptive life, a life totally and completely dependent upon receiving Jesus Christ again and again.

> [W]hen speaking about power for the sanctified life, we dare never stop speaking about Christ. St. Paul put it this way: "For I resolved to know nothing while I was with you except Jesus Christ and him crucified" (1 Corinthians 2:2). The person and work of the crucified Lord is the sum total of our message. He is all in all—"our righteousness, our sanctification, and our redemption" (1 Corinthians 1:30). No wonder, then, that Luther could write, "Having been justified by grace, we then do good works, yes, Christ himself does all in us."[1]

---

[1] Harold L. Senkbeil, *Sanctification: Christ in Action* (St. Louis: Concordia, 1989), 121.

The present essay seeks to celebrate and build upon this confession by using it as a launching pad into the contemporary conversation on Lutheran virtue ethics. There is much in common between sanctification and virtue ethics. In fact, rightly understood, one can say the sanctified life is the virtuous life. But how that life comes to be is the question. Is it something we achieve with much effort and discipline, or is it something given to us and received over and over again? How we answer has profound implications for how we understand Christian identity and character, as well as how we live day-to-day as followers of Jesus.

In the generation or so that has passed since Senkbeil's publication, our culture has changed remarkably. We now live in a digital age of perpetual "likes" and "followers" that feed our egos. Sexual temptations of all kinds are no more than a click away; modesty and self-respect are seen as antiquated if not repressive ideals. Homosexual behavior has become normalized, and even the very notion that people are born a specific gender is under attack. In the words of Albert Mohler's blunt assessment,

> We are facing a complete transformation of the way human beings relate to one another in the most intimate contexts of life. We are facing nothing less than a comprehensive redefinition of life, love, liberty, and the very meaning of right and wrong.[2]

Thus, both to address accurately the above question concerning the origin of the virtuous Christian life, and to speak truth into our confused culture as it undergoes a moral revolution, we first need to be clear on our definitions of virtue and ethics.

*Virtue.* The wider Christian tradition holds that a "moral virtue is a settled disposition of a person to act in excellent and praiseworthy ways, cultivated over time through habit."[3] Similarly, the classical perspective (going back to Aristotle) asserts that virtues are habitual,

---

[2]R. Albert Mohler, *We Cannot Be Silent: Speaking Truth to a Culture Redefining Sex, Marriage, and the Very Meaning of Right and Wrong* (Nashville: Nelson, 2015), 1.

[3]Karl Clifton-Soderstrom, *The Cardinal and the Deadly: Reimagining the Seven Virtues and Seven Vices* (Eugene, Ore.: Cascade, 2015), 4.

affective dispositions that govern behavior. As such, practicing virtues—such as the cardinal virtues of prudence, justice, fortitude, and temperance—will "enable man to attain the furthest potentialities of his nature."[4] In other words, they will actualize within us a new state of being.

The debate here, however, is whether the mere practice of those virtues can change our being, or whether our being is first changed, after which it becomes capable of practicing those virtues. (A case will be made for the latter position—that is, for the receptive Christian life—which is consistent with the Lutheran doctrine of sanctification.)

The term "potentialities" (quoted above) is abstract; in fact, language for both sanctification and virtue ethics often remains conceptual. It is necessary, therefore, to unveil those abstractions to get to the core of daily Christian living and the spiritual reality that goes with it. Noted Lutheran ethicist Gilbert Meilaender is helpful in this regard, bringing the abstract into practical focus:

> The moral virtues—those excellences which help us attain the furthest potentialities of our nature—are, then, not simply dispositions to act in certain ways. They are more like skills which suit us for life generally—and still more like traits of character which not only suit us for life but shape our vision of life, helping to determine not only who we are but what world we see.[5]

By unpacking those "potentialities," Meilaender presents a clearer picture with his definition: virtues are skills, habits, dispositions, and traits that exemplify the morally excellent life.

*Ethics.* Quite simply, ethics deals with morality as it pertains to human behavior. There are three general subject areas here: 1) metaethics, which deals with the origin and meaning of ethical principles; 2) normative ethics, which seeks to discern standards that regulate

---

[4]Josef Pieper, *The Four Cardinal Virtues: Prudence, Justice, Fortitude, Temperance* (trans. Richard and Clara Winston, Laurence E. Lynch, and Daniel F. Coogan; New York: Harcourt, Brace & World, Inc., 1965), xii.

[5]Gilbert C. Meilaender, *The Theory and Practice of Virtue* (Notre Dame, Ind.: University of Notre Dame Press, 1984), 11.

right and wrong conduct; and 3) applied ethics, which addresses specific and often controversial moral issues. Both virtue ethics, which focuses on developing good habits of character, and Christian moral practice, where believers attempt to live their lives in conformity with the word and will of God, can be said to fall under the category of normative ethics. Thus, from one Lutheran perspective, ethics is the "critical and constructive reflection on Christian moral practice," which makes it "both descriptive and normative."[6] That is to say, it is both an intellectual theological activity and a practical moral activity.

Virtue ethics is invariably more complex; however, the point has been to draw out its emphasis on the role of character and virtue in our moral being. This brings us to the larger point. These definitions indicate a decidedly anthropocentric (man-centered) perspective: that is, the emphasis stands primarily upon human desire, action, behavior, and will, along with a humanly created identity. According to the doctrine of sanctification, however, there is certainly more going on in Christians' behavior than purely human effort and willpower. As Joel Biermann observes, "Broadly speaking, ethics can rightly be understood as a reflection on the subject of sanctification, or discipleship . . . shaped by the scriptural account of Christ heard within the church."[7]

Here is where Senkbeil remains so helpful. He unequivocally identifies Christ, his word, and his Spirit as the agents of moral transformation. In light of the massive moral revolution flooding our culture and church, Lutherans do well to continue delivering Christ as the source of all morality and life. In fact, the immorality of our time must be met with the sanctifying washing of what can be called "baptismal virtue ethics," which delivers the identity, character, virtues, and ethics of Jesus himself to believers, right along with his forgiveness, righteousness, holiness, and innocence. Both pastor

---

[6] Robert Benne, "Lutheran Ethics: Perennial Themes and Contemporary Challenges" in *The Promise of Lutheran Ethics* (ed. Karen L. Bloomquist and John R. Stumme; Minneapolis: Fortress, 1998), 11.

[7] Joel D. Biermann, *The Case for Character: Towards a Lutheran Virtue Ethics* (Minneapolis: Fortress, 2014), 11.

and parishioner will benefit from believing the sanctified life is the virtuous ethical life.

## Sanctification Revisited: Life in the Early Twenty-First Century

There remains a lack of agreement today about sanctification throughout the broader Christian church, as well as within Lutheranism.[8] Arguments go back and forth about the correct emphasis of sanctification. Is it an activity that primarily deals with our moral behavior and its practical implications—that is, virtue ethics and progressive sanctification? Or is it an activity that deals chiefly with the ritual reception of Christ's holiness and virtues—that is, an ethics of holiness, "Christ in action" in us?

Pastor Senkbeil offered a clarion call that applies as much today as when he first wrote it: "[W]e need a new Lutheran initiative in demonstrating the dynamic truth *and practicality* of our scriptural doctrine for every Christian's life."[9] In other words, Lutheran theology—particularly the doctrine of sanctification—confesses a spiritual reality that has practical application for the life of every Christian. Given the moral revolution facing the church today, not to mention the digital age that constantly teaches us to look *to* ourselves and *at* ourselves, as we post our segmented, fragmented, and exaggerated lives on Facebook, YouTube, Twitter, Instagram, and the like, we dare not shrink back from addressing the sanctified life. In fact, the tsunami of sexual expressiveness and gender dysphoria presently washing over our culture is wiping out the biblical institution of marriage and the divinely created distinctions of male and

---

[8]The whole of Senkbeil's work, *Sanctification*, contrasts the Lutheran position over and against the American Evangelical perspective. For a formal evaluation about the broader differences see *Christian Spirituality: Five Views of Sanctification* (ed. Donald L. Alexander; Downers Grove, Ill.: InterVarsity, 1988). For a brief overview of some Lutheran differences, see Lucas V. Woodford, "Holy God, Holy Things, Holy People: Pastoral Care in Proximity to God's Holiness." *Seelsorger: A Journal for the Contemporary Cure of Souls* 1 (July 2015): 105–35.

[9]Senkbeil, *Sanctification*, 18; emphasis original.

female human identity. Simultaneously, utter havoc is being wreaked upon the hearts and minds of both children and adults through digital pornography which is available and accessible with little to no restrictions.

All the sins associated with this moral revolution are more than just a matter of immoral acts. They include the corresponding spiritual contamination of those acts, as well as the completely new identity and foreign moral character being established by whole segments of people who often define themselves by such acts. (Simply consider what has become known as LGBTQA). Back at the turn of the millennia, James Davidson Hunter told us "character is dead." Sadly, he predicted that any attempts to "revive" it, at least in the traditional sense, "will yield little"[10] because society has willfully divested itself of its morality. "When the self is stripped of moral anchoring, there is nothing which the will is bound to submit, nothing innate to keep it in check."[11] Today we are observing what is perhaps the pinnacle of this cultural madness and mayhem.

Of course, many in the church are also adversely affected as a result. Christians, too, are often caught in the sexual temptations of alternate "lifestyles." They have been influenced by the cultural lies of newly created terms to justify their sexual identity and the normalization of their behavior. The non-biblical notions of "sexual orientation" and "gender identity" serve to validate what society as a whole formerly considered to be an immoral way of life. Now, as ever, the church needs to be clear on the cleansing, purging, and purifying work of Christ in sanctification. Now, as ever, the church must bring hope to the defiled, truth to the confused, and relief to tortured souls. They, along with every last sinner on the face of the planet, need the healing and sanctifying power of the gospel—not just for the forgiveness of sins, but also for the reception of a holy identity and a holy lifestyle that comes through Jesus Christ.

Accordingly, the argument advanced here comes from the Lutheran perspective that sanctification and the Christian virtuous life are both a matter of the receptive life—both refer to life lived out of

---

[10]James Davison Hunter, *The Death of Character: Moral Education in an Age Without Good or Evil* (New York: Baker, 2000), xiii.

[11]Hunter, *Death of Character*, xiv.

the ritual and habitual reception of the gifts of grace from our Triune God. Receiving the righteousness and holiness of Jesus are especially significant. Though perhaps abstract terms, these create a definite reality which shapes moral behavior and gives a distinct holy identity. As will be demonstrated, this is true because the receptive life includes the reception of the virtues of Christ himself, which are what give shape to moral behavior and content to Christian identity. In other words, Christ gives his virtuous works, behaviors, desires, and passions to believers to be their very own, in which to live and move and have their being. As Paul says, "I have been crucified with Christ. It is no longer I who live, but Christ who lives in me. And the life I now live in the flesh I live by faith in the Son of God, who loved me and gave himself for me" (Gal 2:20). The same is true for the identity of believers. Jesus' identity becomes our identity. Again, as Paul says: "[F]or in Christ Jesus you are all sons of God, through faith. For as many of you as were baptized into Christ have put on Christ" (Gal 3:26–27).

## The Receptive Life

Believers receive all from Christ. Begun in Holy Baptism, and situated amid the habitual life of repentance and prayer (the daily dying and rising with Christ), the Christian life is the receptive life that is lived out of Christ.[12] In his first book Pastor Senkbeil aptly calls this "Christ in action" among us. In his second book, *Dying to Live: The Power of Forgiveness*, he expounds on this even more saying: "[T]he work of every Christian in the world is actually the work Jesus Christ is doing in and through that Christian."[13] Christ is quite literally all in all.

---

[12]One who is very influential upon Senkbeil's thought is Australian Lutheran John W. Kleinig, who offers this about receptive spirituality: "Christian spirituality is, quite simply, following Jesus. It is the ordinary life of faith in which we receive Baptism, attend the Divine Service, participate in the Holy Supper, read the Scriptures, pray for ourselves and others, resist temptation, and work with Jesus in our given location here on earth." Kleinig, *Grace Upon Grace: Spirituality for Today* (St. Louis: Concordia, 2008), 23.

[13]Harold L. Senkbeil, *Dying to Live: The Power of Forgiveness* (St. Louis: Concordia, 1994), 161.

Sanctification, then, is not merely the believer's practical living and good works *for Jesus*, but rather Jesus' life-giving work *for us* through his cross and resurrection. There Christ is at work *in us* by his word and Spirit, given *to us* in Holy Baptism, for a good conscience and the forgiveness of sins. By it, God sanctifies and makes sinners holy[14] and the resulting fruit of the Spirit (Gal. 5:22–23) produced *in us* is for the good of our neighbor and the glory of God. Therefore, sinners are not to look inward for strength and life, but rather outward to Christ and his Word.

The true Christian lifestyle consists of sinners daily living out their baptism by dying and rising with Jesus through contrition and repentance. In baptism our "being" is made new. Contrary to the classic approach to virtues and identity, which emphasizes self-development, we are a "new creation" in Christ (2 Cor 5:17). Thus, our identity and life flow from him and not from our own works, behaviors, passions, or desires. That is why Senkbeil is so adamant that "the Christian life is a daily return to our baptism—a life lived under the cross, in partnership with Jesus."[15] Likewise, the Christian is given a holy identity, not by our own efforts, conduct, or achievements, but by Christ who baptismally covers us with his righteousness, holiness and even his very self (Gal 3:27). Simply put, sanctification is the life of Christ for us, and the life that Christ lives through us.[16]

---

[14]The little word "holy" is often overlooked and underemphasized. To be made holy is nothing of our doing; it is entirely the work of God. Yet part of the confusion, as Senkbeil notes, is that many think they can attain holiness through acts of the law. But the holy living as spoken of here refers to life lived in the holiness borrowed from Jesus Christ. For fine treatments on holiness, see the following works by Kleinig: "Luther on the Christian's Participation in God's Holiness," *Lutheran Theological Journal* 19 (1985): 21–29; "Sharing in God's Holiness," *Lutheran Theological Review* 7 (1995): 105–18; *Leviticus* (Concordia Commentary; Concordia: St. Louis, 2003); "Worship and the Way of Holiness," *Logia* 16, no. 1 (Epiphany 2007): 5–8; *Grace Upon Grace: Spirituality for Today* (Concordia: St. Louis, 2008). See also Woodford, "Holy God, Holy Things, Holy People."

[15]Senkbeil, *Sanctification*, 140.

[16]"By baptism into Christ we have a whole new life ahead of us. Our old life has disappeared—baptized, dead, and buried into the death of the Crucified

This certainly does not reduce the place of virtues in the life of Christians. Rather, it clarifies exactly what occurs in virtue ethics from a distinctly Lutheran perspective. The goal is to identify the power and source of the virtuous life, to proclaim it, and to enact it. The Lutheran view of sanctification will therefore be harnessed as a framework and approach to virtue ethics.

As sanctification is Christ in action in us, Christian ethics is the virtues of Christ in action in us. Significant implications for Christian identity and lifestyle result from this understanding. For instance, Christian ethics can reveal how the baptismal identity of an individual becomes a crucial active agent in the struggle against temptation and sin—particularly sexual sins and alternate lifestyles. This becomes vitally important for pastors of the early twenty-first century to utilize amid our culture's infatuation with gender identity and sexual expressiveness.

What is more, in a culture obsessed with normalizing moral transgressions and its debased byproducts, the Lutheran doctrine of sanctification confesses the full, defiling effects of sin. Not only do the moral infractions (that is, the bad deeds) of sin need to be treated and remedied, so does all of the corresponding spiritual contamination. Our theology recognizes that the sins we commit, as well as the sins committed against us, require the holiness of God and the cleansing blood of Jesus Christ to sanctify and heal us from all unrighteousness (1 John 1:7).

Ultimately, this approach seeks to provide the church with an ethics of holiness that hinges upon the receptive life of faith in Christ, with a distinct focus on the regenerative power of the gospel. This will be unpacked as baptismal virtue ethics. Although space does not permit for an expansive and detailed treatment of this proposal, a beginning practical framework will prove useful for pastoral care and catechesis.

---

One. A new man emerges from that watery grave. Joined with our risen Lord, we rise to live a new life in Him." Senkbeil, *Dying to Live*, 62.

## Towards a Baptismal Virtue Ethics: The Virtues of Christ in Action

The classic tradition of virtue ethics notes that people must practice habits that lead them to acquire various virtues. In so doing, each person actualizes his or her potential and creates a new being within. This approach emphasizes human willpower and effort as the mode of acquisition. However, Christian virtue ethics asserts God as an active participant in the process. While there are various Christian approaches to virtue ethics,[17] it must suffice here to note that the different perspectives assert different degrees of God's activity within the life of the believer. Most tend to assert that God is active, but that it is ultimately up to the individual to strive for and acquire the various virtues and corresponding moral character.

The perspective taken here, however, recognizes the utterly depraved nature of the human soul, which cannot draw goodness or virtue from within the self (Gen 8:21). We are completely dependent upon Christ and his gifts of grace, and are likewise dependent on him for virtues, character, and identity. Christ actualizes the virtues within us, not by magic or some secret, but through the washing and renewal of Holy Baptism (Titus 3:5–8). Thus, as the sanctified life flows out of baptism, so does the virtuous life. Luther brings this out in his Large Catechism:

---

[17]Some prominent differing perspectives to consider are: 1) the abundant works of Stanley Hauerwas, especially *A Community of Character: Toward a Constructive Christian Social Ethic* (Notre Dame, Ind.: University of Notre Dame Press, 1981) and *Sanctify Them in the Truth: Holiness Exemplified* (Nashville: Abingdon, 1998); 2) the Roman Catholic perspective given by Pope John Paul II's *Veritas Splendor* and Pope Benedict XVI's *Deus Carita Est*. However, a more accessible and helpful aid to understand these teachings is offered by Romanus Cessario's *The Moral Virtues and Theological Ethics* (2d ed.; Notre Dame, Ind.: University of Notre Dame Press, 2009); and 3) the insightful Lutheran perspective of Meilaender, *The Theory and Practice of Virtue*. For a differing Lutheran perspective, see Biermann, *A Case for Character*. In my estimation, since Biermann's final conclusion ultimately focuses on law as the impetus for the virtuous life, this is problematic and conflicts with a Lutheran understanding of sanctification that is rooted in the gospel.

Every Christian has enough in Baptism to learn and to do all his life. For he has always enough to do by believing firmly what Baptism promises and brings: victory over death and the devil, forgiveness of sin, God's grace, the entire Christ, and the Holy Spirit with His gifts.

Thus a Christian life is nothing else than a daily baptism, begun once and continuing ever after. For we must keep at it without ceasing, always purging whatever pertains to the old Adam, so that whatever belongs to the new creature may come forth. What is the old creature? It is what is born in us from Adam, irascible, spiteful, envious, unchaste, greedy, lazy, proud—yes—and unbelieving; it is beset with all vices and by nature has nothing good in it. Now, when we enter Christ's kingdom, this corruption must daily decrease so that the longer we live the more gentle, patient, and meek we become, and the more we break away from greed, hatred, envy, and pride. This is the right use of baptism among Christians (LC IV, 41, 66–68).

Since sanctification is Christ in action within us, the corollary proposition is that Christian ethics is simply the virtues of Christ in action within us. This section explains how Christ's virtues are at work in the life of the baptized, a phenomenon referred to here as baptismal virtue ethics.

Baptismal virtue ethics begins with the faith given in baptism, which apprehends the whole of Christ and all his gifts. Christ never gives himself out in parts or pieces. One either gets all of him, with all of his gifts, or nothing at all. An example of this is when Paul tells the Corinthians, "It is because of [God] that you are in Christ Jesus, who has become for us wisdom from God—that is, our righteousness, holiness and redemption." Mixed in with these is the cardinal virtue of wisdom: Christ "has become for us wisdom from God" (1 Cor 1:30). As such, we can conclude that the virtues of Christ are most certainly included in the baptismal gifts of Christ. Christ is all in all, and he gives to receptive souls all of his good gifts of life and salvation.

It becomes readily apparent that the gospel, rather than the law, operates as the power and force behind baptismal virtue ethics. The law can certainly describe that life, demand that life, and guide one in that life, but it cannot *give* that life. That power comes from the gospel alone.

Similarly, the law can certainly instruct in Christian character, virtue, and habits. But it cannot deliver these things. Jesus Christ delivers them all to us in his own person. Yet, he did not come to abolish the law, but to fulfill the law (Matt 5:17). He did so with perfect obedience to his heavenly Father, never once sinning, and yet he was put to death for our sins to suffer the wrath of God in our place. By faith in Christ, we receive the righteousness of one who fulfilled the law, just as if we fulfilled the law ourselves. Therefore, to say Jesus gives us the fulfilled law along with his righteousness is not out of line. As Paul says, "Christ is the culmination of the law so that there may be righteousness for everyone who believes" (Rom 10:4). Again, Christ is all in all: he supplies everything we need, giving us his own virtuous acts, deeds, desires, and passions.

Accordingly, we are no longer under the law or slaves to the law, but in Christ we are under grace (Rom 6:14). The Christian, then, believes he has access to moral character, virtue, and a holy, righteous identity through Jesus Christ. This is more than a mere mental thought or intellectual exercise designed to encourage someone to act like Jesus. This is an exercise of faith, an exercise that believes what Jesus has given us and clearly acts upon it. Paul helps us again: "For as many of you as were baptized into Christ have put on Christ" (Gal 3:27). Plain and simple, baptized believers have put on the virtues of Jesus such that "we are his workmanship, created in Christ Jesus for good works, which God prepared beforehand, that we should walk in them" (Eph 2:10). Faith calls us to believe the gospel and trust that Jesus not only gives us his forgiveness, righteousness, and holiness to secure our standing before our heavenly Father and gain eternity in heaven, but that he also gives us his character, his identity, and his virtues to take as our very own and lead us in our earthly life, in this particular culture and at this precise time.

Consider, for example, someone who desires courage and self-control (the classic virtues of fortitude and temperance). Bearing up under the pressures of this decaying culture with a resolute and faithful witness to Christ is not easy. But Christ gives us the virtues we need to endure and withstand scorn of the unbelieving world (Luke 12:12; 21:15). Just as Jesus was mocked, beaten, and bloodied, and his suffering was paraded out in front of everyone, so too do baptized believers put on the very virtues he displayed while he suffered—not magically, not secretly, but the same way he gives all of his good gifts: by faith. And faith calls us to receive his courage and self-control, and then put it into action in our lives. The point is to look to Christ for strength, to see what Christ has placed upon us, and then to act upon it by faith. Faith is a living and active thing after all.

Another example: Perhaps someone is seeking justice. Here we must be sure to distinguish between the desire for justice, and the desire to be a just person. This becomes significant in a society filled with the continual loss of religious liberty, and the injustices that continue to occur to United States citizens who are Christians (such as to certain bakers, florists, and photographers). Even so, we look to the cross by faith and see Jesus enduring the just punishment we deserved. Yet, we also see his self-control, his courage, and his love, which have all been baptismally imparted to us. Therefore, with the hope that comes with Christ's resurrection and ascension, Christians walk by faith and put this justice, self-control, love, and hope into action, even if it means suffering and loss. We are united to that part of Christ as well. As the Scriptures say: "We always carry around in our body the death of Jesus, so that the life of Jesus may also be revealed in our body. For we who are alive are always being given over to death for Jesus' sake, so that his life may also be revealed in our mortal body" (2 Cor 4:10–11). The virtues of Christ do not guarantee a trouble-free life; rather, they guarantee a life united to Christ and his cross.

In sum, this essay presents a description of how the virtues of Christ are received, and what the virtues of Christ in action look like. Though brief, this introduction has demonstrated that the reception of the virtues of Christ are part of the regenerative effects of the gospel upon the Christian. This occurs by faith, which looks to Christ, but certainly also utilizes reason and logic. Of course, a more detailed explanation of this, along with the comparative aspects of other understandings of virtue ethics would need to be more carefully explained in a broader treatment. Nonetheless, the power behind this baptismal virtue ethics is always Christ, a point which has been illustrated here.

Yet the question remains: how does the believer maintain, cultivate, and sustain these virtues of Christ? If we are beggars and receive it all from him, what does the receptive life look like and sound like? What habits are seen and heard? How are these different than the virtues of

Christ lived out in the believer? The habits that make us receptive to the virtues of Christ are indeed different than enacting the virtues of Christ. Therefore, it will prove helpful to explore how the habits of prayer and repentance are vital elements of baptismal virtue ethics.

## Towards a Baptismal Virtue Ethics: The Holy Habits of Prayer and Repentance

The sanctified life is the receptive life. The depravity of our souls means we must borrow and receive everything from Jesus. "We are beggars" as Luther said, which is why this proposed baptismal virtue ethics follows his lead, recognizing it is not a practice of spiritual self-development, "but a process of reception from the Triune God."[18]

The receptive life means faith is exercised in specific ways as it receives the gifts of God through his appointed means of grace. Prayer and repentance are two such ways, for both function as doorways that open us up to receive more and more of Jesus and his sanctifying and regenerative power. We sin much—indeed, we are defiled and contaminated by sin daily. Consequently, we need more and more of Christ's righteousness, holiness, and virtues to bear up and deal with our sinful lives. But how do prayer and repentance aid in receiving more and more of Jesus? To help answer this, Luther's explanation of the baptized Christian life in his Large Catechism is again worth quoting at length:

> Therefore it may serve to remind us and impress upon us not to become negligent about praying. We all have needs enough but the trouble is that we do not feel or see them. God therefore wishes you to lament and express your needs and wants, not because he is unaware of them, but in order that you may kindle your heart to stronger and greater desires and spread your cloak wide to receive many things. Each of us should form the habit from his youth to pray daily (LC III, 27–28).

> What is repentance but an earnest attack on the old creature and an entering into a new life? If you live in repentance, therefore, you are

---

[18]Kleinig, *Grace Upon Grace*, 16.

walking in Baptism, which not only announces this new life but also produces, begins, and exercises it. In Baptism we are given the grace, Spirit, and strength to suppress the old creature so that the new may come forth and grow strong. Therefore Baptism remains forever. . . . Even though we fall from it and sin, nevertheless, we always have access to it so that we may again subdue the old man (LC IV, 75–76).

Repentance, therefore, is nothing else than a return to Baptism, to resume and practice what has earlier been begun but abandoned. . . . Therefore let everybody regard Baptism as the daily garment which he is to wear all the time. Every day he should be found in faith and amid its fruits, every day he should be suppressing the old man and growing in the new. If we wish to be Christians, we must practice the work that makes us Christians (LC IV, 79, 84–85).

Luther pointedly emphasized the habits we must keep if we are to continue receiving life from Jesus. Practicing the "work that makes us Christian" does not refer to specific good works or virtues, but to the habits of prayer and repentance.

Prayer is simply communication with our Triune God in words and thoughts. Simple as it seems, it is often difficult to do. Our sinful nature and the assaults of the devil make that certain. However, Jesus draws us into himself and gives us words to pray, most especially in the Lord's Prayer. He also demonstrated the important regular habit of prayer throughout his earthly ministry.

As we are baptized into Jesus, he gives us more than just a set prayer to follow. Jesus also "gives us His own status as God's Son and allows us to share in all the privileges of His unique relationship with His heavenly Father."[19] This is no small occurrence. Once again, Christ is all in all! Our union with Christ even permeates our prayers. As Kleinig notes:

By giving us His prayer, He includes us in His relationship with His Father and allows us to act as if we were Him, dressed up in Him (cf. Romans 13:14; Galatians 3:26–27). By giving us His prayer, Jesus puts us in His shoes and involves us in His royal mission, the holy

---

[19]Kleinig, *Grace Upon Grace*, 163.

vocation as the royal Son of God. We may therefore stand in His shoes and pray with Him for the hallowing of His Father's name and the coming of His Father's Kingdom.[20]

Prayer, then, keeps us receptive to the gifts of God. One example is giving thanks to God for what he has given to us. Such prayer keeps us all the more mindful of what we need, and therefore we return all the more to Christ to receive from his gifts what we lack (such as the cardinal virtue of wisdom). Paul describes this for us in numerous places, but one in particular brings everything together in three verses: "Therefore, as you received Christ Jesus the Lord, so walk in him, rooted and built up in him and established in the faith, just as you were taught, abounding in thanksgiving. . . . For in him the whole fullness of deity dwells bodily, and you have been filled with him, who is the head and rule of all authority" (Col 2:6, 9–10). Clearly, the habit of prayer is essential to baptismal virtue ethics.

Now we press on to the final component of this proposal, the role of repentance. To put this into practical, daily-life terms, we again turn to Luther. In his Small Catechism, he noted the vital connection between baptism and repentance when considering what baptism indicates for the Christian:

> It indicates that the old Adam in us should by daily contrition and repentance be drowned and die with all sins and evil desires, and that a new man should daily emerge and arise to live before God in righteousness and purity forever (SC IV, 4).

Putting it simply, to live out our baptism we must repent. When dangerous passions and "evil desires" disorder life, lead to sin, and defile us, baptism calls every sinner to repentance. Not just here and there. Not just once a week at church. But daily. And to be clear, in repentance Christians not only confess sin, but also turn away from that sin or evil desire in sorrow and contrition. Our sinful thoughts, behaviors, and vices stop. We confess them as wrong. We plead for mercy and forgiveness. In so doing, we spiritually crucify the sinful

---

[20]Kleinig, *Grace Upon Grace*, 163.

self and bury it with Christ (Rom 6:4), we spiritually drown the sinful self and mortify the flesh. The habit of daily repentance therefore brings with it an ethic of faith.

Most Christian virtue ethics give little or no treatment to repentance, but it is an essential part of baptismal virtue ethics. Dietrich Bonhoeffer reminded us that discipleship is costly. It cost Jesus his life, so it costs us our life as well.

> When Christ calls a man, He bids him come and die. It may be a death like that of the first disciples who had to leave home and work to follow him, or it may be a death like Luther's, who had to leave the monastery and go out into the world. But it is the same death every time—death in Jesus Christ, the death of the old man at his call. . . . In fact every command of Jesus is a call to die, with all our affections and lusts.[21]

Indeed, we must die to ourselves. Our desires, passions, and lusts, along with our sinful behaviors, unclean acts, and our immoral identity, must all be put away. In repentance, we constantly throw ourselves before Jesus, asking for forgiveness and receiving his holiness, receiving more and more of his virtues, by which we resist temptation and do good works that serve our neighbor.

Jesus himself began his ministry by saying, "The time is fulfilled, and the kingdom of God is at hand; repent and believe in the gospel" (Mark 1:15). In practical terms, this means a submission of the will, a reordering of the intellect, a changing of the passions, and a remaking of our character, which includes changes to our thinking, acting, and speaking, and replacing them all with the fruits of the Spirit (Gal 5:22–23)—all of which are virtues of Christ. But repentance does not produce the Christian's new being, just as prayer does not. The "new man" results from the work of Christ and his Spirit upon the sinner. Christ gives his own identity (Gal. 3:26–27) to the baptized sinner so that our identity becomes united with his, with our behaviors, thoughts, and desires all emanating from Christ and his virtues at work in us.

---

[21]Dietrich Bonhoeffer, *The Cost of Discipleship* (repr., New York: Touchstone, 1995), 89–90.

## Conclusion: A Baptismal Virtue Ethics for Pastor and People

The words of Paul go to the core of baptismal virtue ethics: "I have been crucified with Christ. It is no longer I who live, but Christ who lives in me. And the life I now live in the flesh I live by faith in the Son of God, who loved me and gave himself for me" (Gal 2:20). This is good news for the people of our time and culture! With the moral revolution going mad, baptized Christians have the hope of Christ in them. Christ in action defines the sanctified life. Thanks in part to Harold Senkbeil's encouragement for "a new Lutheran initiative in demonstrating the dynamic truth *and practicality* of our scriptural doctrine for every Christian's life,"[22] the Lutheran understanding of sanctification provides a grand platform to develop a baptismal virtue ethics. Though a small beginning, this provides a framework of thought for future development.

Advocating for moral character and the virtuous life remains a noble endeavor, but this must be done from the strength and power of the gospel. Focusing upon specific virtues or the behavior of the believer to attain them is misguided; rather, the focus must be on upon Christ, who lived a life of perfect virtue and who gives his virtues to believers through baptism. Through these, as in sanctification, he works within the daily lives of believers. Cultivating character and virtue therefore remains a baptismal endeavor of living out one's faith and identity in Christ. To make it simply a moral endeavor omits the fullness of the gospel's regenerating power and falls short of the mark.

This understanding becomes particularly helpful for pastors as they strive to care for souls in our time. Baptismal virtue ethics provides important habits of faith in prayer and repentance; it keeps sinners united to Christ through word and sacrament; and it provides a distinct identity, with distinct character, for daily living amid temptations in the various vocations of one's life.

---

[22]Senkbeil, *Sanctification*, 18; emphasis original.

# The Congregation as Family

## Form and Commission

### *Timothy Pauls*

## Two Families

The natural family and the church have abundant parallels and for good reason. Both are households instituted by God in Genesis 2. Each is blessed with a commission for the increase of life: husband and wife are to be fruitful and multiply (Gen 1:28), while the church is to make disciples of all nations (Matt 28:18–20). Children are born into each: by the will of the flesh and of man in the family, and by the will of God in the church (John 1:12–13). Both have a God-given structure: the natural family is to feature husband and wife, then children as God so blesses; and the church in any location is to have pastor (in the stead of Christ) and congregation (the bride of Christ in that place), composed of the children of God.[1]

---

[1] This essay builds upon its companion piece, "The Congregation as Family: A New Testament Survey," *Seelsorger: A Journal for the Contemporary Cure of Souls* 3 (2017): 5–23. In that essay, I argue that "family" is not merely a helpful metaphor and lens for examining congregational life but that the church *is* the family of God, with each congregation existing as the family of God in a certain location. Were it not for the fall into sin, the biological family of Adam and his descendants and would be identical to the church, but the fall has caused the division. Thus a Christian is part of two families: one born of the flesh and one born of the spirit; one by the will of man and one by the will

It is further no coincidence that households in Scripture involve fatherly instruction (Eph 6:4) and meals, while the church's worship is centered upon the Lord's gifts of word and sacrament. In fact, both institutions are given by God to point to Christ. The church does so explicitly, endeavoring always to proclaim "Christ and him crucified" (1 Cor 2:2), whereas the marital relationship of love and subordination in the natural family (established in Genesis 2:24) is interpreted by Paul as a mystery that refers to "Christ and the church" (Eph 5:32). This analogy is continued in the *Haustafel* of Ephesians 6:1–9, which says fathers are to provide instruction to their children in lieu of wrath, and masters and slaves are to act in goodwill toward one another.[2]

Though not utilizing domestic nomenclature, the Augsburg Confession presents a consonant view of the church as family: "It is the assembly of all believers among whom the gospel is purely preached and the holy sacraments are administered according to the gospel" (AC V, 1). That is where Christ and his bride are found together, where the Holy Spirit is at work in the means of grace to create and sustain the children of God. That is where the pastor stands in the stead and by the command of Christ, as surrogate husband and father to Christ's bride and her children.[3]

---

of God. This scriptural revelation should have a profound influence in shaping pastoral care and congregational life.

[2] For an extensive treatment of the *Haustafel*, see the commentary of Thomas M. Winger, *Ephesians* (Concordia Commentary; St. Louis: Concordia, 2015), especially pages 598–696.

[3] To illustrate the point, it is helpful to insert familial terminology into a summary of the Augsburg Confession: There is a God (AC I) from whom we are lost because of sin (AC II). That we might be brought into his family, the Son of God was born of Mary to reconcile us to the Father (AC III); and it is through the work of Christ, the bridegroom, that we are forgiven, justified, and restored as the children of God (AC IV). So that we might be his children, God has instituted the ministry of word and sacrament (AC V), through which the Holy Spirit works to make us alive so that we might do what living children do (AC VI). This gathering, this family, is the church (AC VII); and even if the word is preached and the sacraments administered by evil fathers, they still create and sustain life in the children of God (AC VIII).

What, in particular, are the means of grace which create and maintain children in the family of God? They are born in Holy Baptism (AC IX); thusly born again, they are fed with the Lord's Supper (AC X) and taught that they are

The parallels between the church and the natural family continue outside of Scripture in our present day: both are in decline and under attack in American society. Political scientist Mary Eberstadt argues convincingly that the mutual decrease is inevitable: "family and faith are the invisible double helix of society—two spirals that when linked to one another can effectively reproduce, but whose strength and momentum depend on one another."[4] As goes one household, so goes the other. Far from conceding the argument that creeping secularization is responsible for the church's demise, Eberstadt instead points to the weakening of the traditional family and vice versa. Her thesis ought not come as a surprise: rather than a double helix, the church and natural family were designed by God to be a single strand. This was the case ever so briefly in the Garden of Eden, when all of humanity (Adam and Eve) was both one family and the church. Faith and family divided with the fall into sin: Adam transferred all of his descendants from the church to those dead in sin (Rom 5:12), thus destroying the family of God. Additionally, Adam did no favors to the natural family as he promptly threw his wife under the bus (Gen 3:12), later begetting the first murderer.

Both households are under attack, and both are suffering the same assaults of a shared enemy. Indeed, one of the reasons that pastoral ministry is so demanding, if not exhausting, is that the pastor finds himself on the front line of two separate (though inseparable) battles.

---

forgiven children (AC XI) in an ongoing manner. They sometimes disobey and are tempted to reject their Father and mother, but they are restored by repentance: a wayward child does not re-earn sonship by his works (AC XII) anymore than he earned re-birth into that family in the first place. Instead, life is given and maintained by the sacraments, received by faith (AC XIII).

In the stead and by the command of Christ, and thus as surrogate father to the congregation, the pastor teaches and administers the sacraments to the family of God (AC XIV). These are to be preserved if the church is to be the church, yet ceremonies and traditions may vary from place to place (AC XV).

[4]Mary Eberstadt, *How the West Really Lost God* (West Conshohocken, Pa.: Templeton, 2013), 22. A somewhat expanded discussion of Eberstadt's thesis, as well as a greater exploration of the New Testament's description of the church as family, can be found in Pauls, "Congregation as Family."

## The Enemy

The enemy of both is expressive individualism, pervasive and parasitic. This amounts to a troublesome "chicken-and-egg" problem. On the one hand, disintegration of the family leads to this individualism: divorce teaches that even the most intimate relationships and promises can be broken, while cohabitation never makes promises in the first place. Those who suffer through a broken home, be they parents or children, easily learn to trust only themselves because exemplars prove untrustworthy. Children are left to develop their own morality and faith, often caught in the crossfire of warring parents with opposing values. All of this encourages individualism and a reliance only on self.

In turn, expressive individualism leads to broken families. Adultery destroys a marriage because one spouse betrays the other out of selfish desire. Parents neglect or abandon families and responsibilities for vain personal dreams. Children from divorced families can have difficulty sustaining relationships and marriages of their own. Sex is reduced from an act of love between husband and wife for intimacy and procreation to an exercise in personal pleasure with no regard for the partner. Even in the locus of sexual intimacy, individualism argues that it is good for the man to be alone (as evidenced by recent headlines heralding the development of sex robots). Disdain for the unborn and the elderly reshapes the family along Darwinian lines, rather than it being a place of service to those most in need. Marriage and family, always sustained by mutual sacrifice and love, are destroyed by selfish pursuits of self-centered dreams and self-gratifying sins.

The disintegration of the natural family leads to decline in the congregation. The reduction in family size correlates closely to decreasing church membership. Those who favor sexual indulgence apart from marriage have little use for a church that still takes seriously the Sixth Commandment. Those who have suffered through divorce often feel marginalized, either by others' comments or their own sense of guilt. Tossed back and forth in joint-custody arrangements, many children only attend church half-time at best and resist a church's teaching that parents are subject to God's wrath unless they repent. As the church declines in influence, secular philosophies sway family members toward individualism at the expense of each other. Thus, the double helix of faith and family cycles downward.

Pastoral care takes place at the nexus where both battles collide, as pastors care for natural families in crisis while shepherding congregations that are often in concurrent decline. Their labors are complicated in a third way, however, for expressive individualism seeks to infiltrate and supplant Christian doctrine. One valuable analysis is the landmark study of Christian Smith who extensively interviewed youth across America and documented the development of a belief system he calls "Moral Therapeutic Deism."[5] This religious form of individualism has five common beliefs:

- There is a God who created and watches over the world.
- God wants people to be good and nice.
- The goal of life is to be happy and feel good about oneself.
- God does not need to be involved in one's life unless he is needed to resolve a problem.
- Good people go to heaven when they die.[6]

This deistic god is "something like a combination Divine Butler and Cosmic Therapist."[7] He is on call in times of need; otherwise, it is left to the individual to be good, nice and happy according to his own designs. In the present discussion, two points from Smith are especially noteworthy. First, Smith observes that this is not a creation of youth, but that they have learned and developed it from the example of grownups. Indeed, individualism has increasingly dominated society since its blossoming in the 1960s, leaving few in the pew or pulpit who have not been subtly indoctrinated throughout

---

[5]These findings and their implications were originally published as the fifth chapter of Christian Smith, *Soul Searching: The Religious and Spiritual Lives of America's Teenagers* (Oxford: Oxford University Press, 2005), 118–71. They have since been summarized by the author in "On 'Moralistic Therapeutic Deism' as U.S. Teenagers' Actual, Tacit, *De Facto* Religious Faith," which can be accessed online through Princeton Theological Seminary: http://youthlectures .ptsem.edu/?action=tei&id=youth-2005-05.

[6]Smith, *Soul Searching*, 162–63.

[7]Smith, *Soul Searching*, 165.

their lives. Second, expressive individualism is not just attacking Christianity from the outside, but from within. Smith warns that this "misbegotten step-cousin" of Christianity is working its way into the minds and hearts of individual believers and thus into Christian churches and organizations. "Christianity is actively being colonized and displaced by a quite different religious faith."[8] Thus, while the natural family and the congregation struggle to bar the door under relentless assault, the battle is further complicated because the enemy is already inside.

## Does the Church Need to Change?

There's little disagreement about nature of the battle, but how best to fight it is a current controversy within the church. In essence, the disagreements can be boiled down to how one responds to this crucial question: does the church need to adopt a new paradigm to survive and to evangelize? There can be no way forward in the fight without the correct answer. Yet there exists another element of conflict for pastors as well. Numerous so-called experts lecture and reprimand those who seek to remain faithful shepherds by contending that such pastors are actually *detrimental* to the future of the church. Commonly, these criticisms are accompanied by the opinion that current seminary training in the Lutheran Church—Missouri Synod (LCMS) is outdated. To explore both the question and this harsh criticism, I will consider one of the most prevalent paradigms of today—the missional church. I will then examine related questions about the church's survival using the argument that the church is the family of God.

## The Missional Church

It is somewhat difficult to describe missional thought because it is intentionally vague in definition. It is united by task, not form. Specifically, the Christian church exists primarily to fulfill the Great Commission. In the words of Ed Stetzer and David Putman,

---

[8]Smith, *Soul Searching*, 171.

[The church] is not about us! It is about Jesus saying, "As the Father has sent Me, I am sending you" to "Go and make disciples of all different kinds of people" with a message of "repentance and forgiveness of sin" as a people who have "received the Holy Spirit." We are missionaries. Your church is intended to be God's missionary church. The only question is this: Are we being good missionaries?[9]

They go on to declare:

*The church is one of the few organizations in the world that does not exist for the benefit of its members.* The church exists because God, in his infinite wisdom and infinite mercy, chose the church as his instrument to make known his manifold wisdom in the world.[10]

Elsewhere, they cite Reggie McNeal who says that "if we are not focusing on missiology then we are being disobedient to the Great Commission."[11]

The Great Commission, therefore, is the material principle of missional church thought, the lens through which all doctrine and practice are viewed. A successful and faithful congregation is one that experiences numerical growth because its primary purpose is to make disciples.[12] Because the church makes disciples by going into the world, it is a bad thing when a congregation "settles" into a form that presumably results from members' preferences, develops

---

[9]Ed Stetzer and David Putman. *Breaking the Missional Code: Your Church Can Become a Missionary in Your Community.* (Nashville: B&H, 2006), 42.

[10]Stetzer and Putman, *Breaking the Missional Code*, 44; italics original.

[11]Quoted in Stetzer and Putman, *Breaking the Missional Code*, 2.

[12]Missional thought holds this emphasis in common with the Church Growth Movement (CGM) and with good reason: the former has evolved from the latter. Missional advocates praise CGM for its emphasis on statistics, measurements and business methods; however, they are critical of CGM for viewing the congregation as primarily "attractional." In other words, the philosophy of CGM was to build a large campus with a variety of services that would draw the neighborhood in, while missional philosophy views the church as adapting to the neighborhood's context and inserting itself into the neighborhood. One might put it this way: if a CGM congregation is styled as a mall of Christian teachings and services, a missional congregation is styled as a niche boutique.

its own culture, and expects the world to come by attraction. In contrast, a mission-focused congregation is constantly adapting itself to the cultural context around it.

Part of the reason that congregations are to adapt to the local culture is for the sake of appeal to the unbeliever. But there is another reason: missional thought holds that the Holy Spirit is at work in the world apart from the means of grace, preparing converts apart from the word. In a sense, the Holy Spirit has set the pace, and it is up to the lagging church to catch up with him and solve the mystery of how he is working uniquely in a particular place. Because the Spirit works so enigmatically, deciphering his agenda takes guesswork, and so pastors and laity are left to imaginative innovation and risk. Allen Roxburgh and M. Scott Boren write enthusiastically that the Holy Spirit is at work "in the world"[13] and "in the neighborhood,"[14] as well as "in the midst of our questions,"[15] "shaping a new imagination" in God's people.[16] They also maintain that we "imagine new ways of being Jesus' people" through the uncertainty of "trial and error."[17] Stetzer and Putman echo this sentiment:

> It is arrogant to assume that God is not already at work in most places. We need to ask, What is God doing? Where is he blessing? As we discover what he is doing, we must learn from others and join God in how he is already at work. Those who break the code join God in his activities.[18]

It is no surprise, then, that missional theology is not sacramental. If the material principle is the Great Commission, the formal principle appears to be the Holy Spirit, who has been readily divorced from the means of grace and who works apart from the word.

---

[13] Allen J. Roxburgh and M. Scott Boren, *Introducing the Missional Church: What It Is, Why It Matters, How to Become One* (Grand Rapids: Baker, 2009), 18.

[14] Roxburgh and Boren, *Introducing the Missional Church*, 20.

[15] Roxburgh and Boren, *Introducing the Missional Church*, 26.

[16] Roxburgh and Boren, *Introducing the Missional Church*, 21.

[17] Roxburgh and Boren, *Introducing the Missional Church*, 22.

[18] Stetzer and Putman, *Breaking the Missional Code*, 83.

Examined through the missional lens, Scripture takes on a different message. Through this prism, the first Christians in Acts provide a case study of the good and the bad. Positively, they spread the gospel widely because the church "recognized that its primary mission was to 'go and make disciples' of all nations."[19] Negatively, however, when they began to "settle" in Acts 8, the Holy Spirit employed persecution to move them to "a missional imagination of being the church in the world."[20] In fact, the error of Saul as persecutor was not his violent rejection and persecution of Jesus (Acts 9:4), but his need for "a radical transformation of his imagination—of the way he saw the world"![21]

Similarly, key passages of Scripture are reinterpreted based on missional thought. The point of John 20:19–23 is not that the risen Jesus came to institute the Office of the Keys, but that "the disciples were behind closed doors, and many churches still are today"[22] thus failing to engage the community. Matthew 28:18–20 becomes a warning against complacency: "After announcing his authority, though, [Jesus] did not say, 'Make sure all of your needs are met' or 'Make sure all of your preferences are satisfied.' What he said was, 'Go therefore and make disciples of all nations.'"[23] Everything is interpreted through the lens of outreach, and thus as law, since the focus is always on what Christians ought to be doing. As Skye Jethani wryly notes, in missional theology "an individual is either *on* the mission, the *object* of the mission, an *obstacle* to the mission, an *aid* to the mission, or a 'fat' Christian who *should* be on the mission."[24]

---

[19]Stetzer and Putman, *Breaking the Missional Code*, 120.

[20]Roxburgh and Boren, *Introducing the Missional Church*, 16. Stetzer and Putman chime in that "God used persecution to move the early church beyond its comfort zone." This accusation has no scriptural support, but it serves a double purpose: it discredits the church "model" of the earliest Christians (who were living *under direct supervision of the apostles*); and it facilitates the narrative that outreach is more important than the life of the congregation. Stetzer and Putman, *Breaking the Missional Code*, 122.

[21]Roxburgh and Boren, *Introducing the Missional Church*, 27.

[22]Stetzer and Putman, *Breaking the Missional Code*, 30.

[23]Stetzer and Putman, *Breaking the Missional Code*, 34.

[24]Skye Jethani, "Has Mission Become Our Idol? (Cont.)," CT Pastors, July 20, 2011, http://www.christianitytoday.com/le/2011/july-online-only/has -mission-become-our-idol-cont.html; italics original.

In practice, missional thought has several common themes. To begin, it holds that the church is formless. Advocates of missional theology normally affirm that certain doctrines and practices are necessary for a congregation to remain Christian, but beyond "the gospel" (which is typically undefined), they are hesitant to clarify what those doctrines and practices are. Forms of worship and church are deemed culture-specific that grow outdated as the world evolves. For example, some claim the practices of the church in Acts were only for first-century Eurasia; today, however, "we are called by the Spirit to imagine and shape forms of being church that address our time and place."[25] Traditional congregations are suspect because traditions are seen as barriers that only believers understand. In contrast, "Missional leaders [are to] bring the gospel into a context by asking, 'What cultural containers—church, worship style, small group ministry, evangelism methods and approaches, discipleship processes, etc.—will be most effective in this context?'"[26] Thus, the form of a congregation is to be determined by the culture around it.

Missional theology also emphasizes the work of "ordinary people" because it has a low view of the pastoral office. Roxburgh and Boren argue that "the Spirit is not the province of ordained leaders or superspiritual people; instead the Spirit is in what we call ordinary people of a local church."[27] Though such a statement is not without truth, it harbors the belief that all Christians are called as ministers and that it is wrong to reserve word and sacrament ministry for ordained pastors. Stetzer and Putman fret that pastors "tend to build monuments to themselves and monuments to their churches" rather than reach out, adopting a "refuge mentality" of "survival and preservation."[28] In fact, a barrier to the imagination and risk that are necessary to a missional church is an "inappropriate clericalism" that "communicates that these professionals (clergy) are the only ones who have control and knowledge over the mysteries of what God is up to in the church and in the world."[29]

---

[25]Roxburgh and Boren, *Introducing the Missional Church*, 33.

[26]Stetzer and Putman, *Breaking the Missional Code*, 55.

[27]Roxburgh and Boren, *Introducing the Missional Church*, 122.

[28]Stetzer and Putman, *Breaking the Missional Code*, 70, 193.

[29]Roxburgh and Boren, *Introducing the Missional Church*, 183.

With its separation of the Holy Spirit from the means of grace and the subsequent assertion that church and ministry are formless, missional theology bears the hallmarks of the theology of the *Schwärmerei*. Far from the transgression of "inappropriate clericalism," a pastor might very well quash an "imaginative" idea for outreach not because he claims a superior imagination, but because he can demonstrate that the idea is contrary to Scripture. In the place of such pastors, missional theology looks for leaders who shun the status quo:

> Leaders who break the code have a high level of courage in regard to making the tough decisions. They are almost rude about vision. They have the courage to protect the unity of the church. They hire and fire the right people. They are simply willing to make the tough calls to break through.[30]

More alarmingly, they "aren't afraid of deconstructing the existing church with all of its traditions, programs, methods, and preferences."[31] To do so does not protect the unity of the church as claimed, but instead casts it adrift from all the saints who have gone before. It risks a congregational amnesia in which continuity is not based upon consistent doctrine and practice, but upon the leader whose time is limited.

Practically speaking, since every neighborhood will have unique characteristics and the Spirit is expected to act innovatively, it stands to reason that every missional congregation will differ to adapt to the neighborhood. How might this appear? In some cases, it may be as simple as a street fair in the church parking lot or a community center; in others, the missional paradigm has spawned congregations that present themselves to the world as coffee shops, beer pubs, and health clubs.

Even among supporters of the missional church, there is concern about the emphasis on innovation, imagination, risk and statistical gains. Gordon MacDonald has labeled "missionalism" a disease,

---

[30]Stetzer and Putman, *Breaking the Missional Code*, 75.
[31]Stetzer and Putman, *Breaking the Missional Code*, 203.

with which "the worth of one's life is determined by the achievement of a grand objective" and "the passionate need to keep things growing and growing so that one proves his/her worth."[32] Similarly, Skye Jethani writes that leaders who are mission-minded tend to replace a "vision of a life with Christ" with "a vision for ministry,"[33] with their own efforts becoming the focus. This yields predictable results for those who stress outreach as the basis of the church, since the law never ceases to be a taskmaster. Pastors often burn out and leave the ministry or develop addictive behaviors. Indeed, the disease is contagious with lasting effects:

> When church leaders function from this understanding of the Christian life, they invariably transfer their burden and fears to those in the pews. If a pastor's sense of worth is linked to the impact of his or her ministry, guess what believers under that pastor's care are told is most important? And so a new generation of people who believe their value is linked to their accomplishments is birthed. *If the cycle continues long enough, an institutional memory is created in which the value of achievement for God is no longer questioned.*[34]

Such a congregation runs the risk of amnesia, focusing on its efforts and forgetting its identity as the family of God.

We now turn from our survey of missional thought to the important query posed above: how will congregations survive the assault of destructive individualism and the concern of declining numbers? Do they need to change by adopting a missional or other outreach-focused paradigm?

---

[32]Gordon MacDonald, "Dangers of Missionalism," CT Pastors, January 1, 2007, http://www.christianitytoday.com/le/2007/winter/16.38.html.

[33]Skye Jethani, "Has Mission Become Our Idol?," CT Pastors, July 18, 2001, http://www.christianitytoday.com/le/2011/july-online-only/has-mission-become-our-idol.html?start=2.

[34]Skye Jethani, "Has Mission Become Our Idol?"; italics added.

## Questions for Consideration

If marriage is given by God to tell the story of Christ and the church, then alternatives to marriage are going to tell a different story. For instance, if marriage vows illustrate the Lord's faithfulness, then divorce can exhibit the false teaching that God breaks his promises, and cohabitation may give the impression that God makes no promises in the first place.

In an age where marriage and family are under attack, the solution is not to change the natural family to fit the context of the surrounding culture but to strengthen it against the ongoing assault. The same concern must exist for the congregation. In an age where the family of God is under attack, the solution is to strengthen the church as family, not to change its form. The answer is surely *not* to change the paradigm in a way that weakens the congregation as family. Rather, an internal alarm should sound when we hear that the missional church is intentionally formless, because formlessness is exactly what the culture is imposing on the natural family. A formless paradigm is not what the Holy Spirit intends for the family of God; on the contrary, the de-formation of God's gifts (marriage, family, gender identity, etc.) is an unwitting concession to the expressive individualism of our time, one that facilitates the pursuit of personal preference over faithfulness to the word of God.

Eberstadt quips that secularization is "the phenomenon through which Protestants, generally speaking, go godless and Catholics, generally speaking, go Protestant."[35] It appears also to be the process through which Lutherans go missional, and it is difficult to see how one can "Lutheranize" missional theology. In fact, one is more likely to end up missionalizing Lutheran theology until it is Lutheran no more. The context of this discussion, however, is that the congregation is the literal family of God in a place. It therefore behooves us in all things to work to strengthen both congregational and natural families, not to redefine them. I thus pose the following questions for discussion:

---

[35]Eberstadt, *How the West Really Lost God*, 53.

## (1) Does the insistence on the preeminence of the Great Commission help maintain a congregation as family?

Imagine a natural family where a father tells his children, "You're all very important to me, but the rest of the kids in the neighborhood are more important."[36] This would devastate the family, yet it is precisely the consequence of outreach-first paradigms. If the needs of the unbeliever are primary, then those of the church family must not be. Consequently, worship and preaching will be designed for the comfort of potential visitors (who may never visit!) rather than for the nurture of family members (who are regularly present). What is more, the pastor must focus on visiting non-members more than members, perhaps even those who are sick or homebound.

The emphasis on the Great Commission is a recent innovation in the church's history. It is generally traced back to William Carey, a missionary to India and the author of *An Enquiry into the Obligations of Christians, to Use Means for the Conversion of the Heathens*.[37] Understanding the context for Carey's efforts is vital. Over and against his fellow clergy who asserted that *any* overseas mission efforts rejected the doctrine of election, Carey argued that "the commission" of Matthew 28:19–20 and Mark 16:15 was not restricted only to the apostles and the apostolic age.[38] The church was therefore to continue sending missionaries to all nations.

Carey wrote to encourage churches to conduct foreign missions, not to persuade them to change form to accommodate their local culture. Over time, his argument for "the commission" has been remodeled into the Great Commission—so great in fact that, for some, other doctrine is subservient to it and subject to compromise.

---

[36]This is, in fact, the description given me by a man who had left a missional congregation. Similar telltale statements from others in comparable situations include, "Coming to this [traditional] church is like *coming home*" and "My church doesn't feel like my church anymore . . . but I guess it's what you've got to do to reach people."

[37]Lucas V. Woodford, *Great Commission, Great Confusion, or Great Confession?* (Eugene, Ore.: Wipf & Stock, 2012), 55.

[38]William Carey, *An Enquiry into the Obligations of Christians, to Use Means for the Conversion of the Heathens* (Leicester: Ann Ireland, 1792; repr., London: Hodder and Stoughton, 1891), 8.

As Lucas Woodford notes, "It remains curious how a relatively recent and primarily evangelical development—one that did not have any specific New Testament, early, medieval or Reformation church tradition—came into regular practice by the majority of North American churches."[39] Now it appears that the disease of missionalism has taken hold, and the Great Commission as material principle has become the institutional memory of those churches.[40]

## (2) Is ongoing change a good thing for a family?

The repetitive nature and ordinary practices of family life are a help and comfort. Parents know what a change in routine will do to children, and husbands and wives often adopt habits regarding household chores, financial responsibilities, even certain meals on certain days. Families establish traditions and then maintain them, which helps cement family identity. In contrast, as Eberstadt notes, our highly individualized culture has left the family in a state of permanent reinvention, leading to instability and confusion.[41] So it is within the family of God: coupled with the gifts and commands given by God for good and for order, tradition is a valuable part of family identity, so long as the tradition points to or serves Christ.

A family that is grounded in routine and tradition is a stable family, and a stable family is comfortable inviting others to join them. In fact, this is the basis of evangelism. Within the family of God, the pastor feeds the Lord's children with the word; as they grow in faith, the children tell others what their Father is doing. They invite others to come to church and join the family for worship. This is the strength of vocational evangelism: as the children of God

---

[39]Woodford, *Great Commission*, 55.

[40]Though the missional church may seem too young to establish institutional memory, it is simply a later iteration of the Church Growth movement, which traces its doctrinal roots back to revivalism. See Klemet Preus, *The Fire and the Staff* (St. Louis: Concordia, 2004), 313–30.

[41]Eberstadt, *How the West Really Lost God*, 162. One should also note Eberstadt's speculation (on page 160) that this unfocused, changing view of family makes it all the more difficult for individuals to understand *the* family of Mary, Joseph, and Jesus, which in turn makes the gospel all the more bewildering.

go about their callings in the world, they share the gospel with those whom they encounter.[42] Thus evangelism grows out of family, rather than apart from—or at the expense of—the family's identity.

When a family is constantly changing, no one knows quite who they are anymore. The household loses its story and self-understanding, existing only for the here and now. There is an inherent instability that easily communicates indecision to others: church might feel like an event, but not a family. Instability is a dangerous thing for the long term and unhelpful to evangelism.[43]

### (3) Is it beneficial or wise for a family to measure success by statistical growth?

How does one measure the success of a family? Is a large family more successful than a small one? What about a family with better finances, more vacation stories, or healthier children? To the world, these may indeed be ways to gauge prosperity. Before God, however,

---

[42]"They are lived out naturally, in tandem, and not at the expense of the other. Here we can, as Eugene Bunkowske invites, 'gossip the Gospel' and 'make and multiply disciples by positively and naturally introducing our good friend Jesus to other people in our everyday life.' In this way, homes, workplaces, and neighborhoods become places of mission when, in the course of natural conversations and service to those around us, we have the opportunity to share the Good News of Jesus Christ, where, through the 'gathering' of the Holy Spirit, others are invited into the community of saints." Woodford, *Great Commission*, 39.

[43]As noted by Klemet Preus, tradition is a blessed thing between sister congregations: "Historically, congregations of The Lutheran Church—Missouri Synod have valued the common practice shared between them. We followed the same church year, wore the same vestments, used the same hymnal, employed the same Divine Service, confirmed the young people at roughly the same age, held the same Communion practice, expected the same education of pastors, expected the same from their pastors both during the service and elsewhere—basically tried to do things the same way. We were uniform in practice, not because the way we did things was always the best way, but because we recognized that uniformity is good. For the sake of one another and the unity they shared, individual pastors and congregations gave up their quest for uniqueness. Unity of practice reflected unity of doctrine in Christ." Preus, *Fire and the Staff*, 430–31.

all families are equally precious since each member is redeemed by the blood of Christ.

When the Lord instituted marriage in Genesis 2:24, his criterion for success was (and is) the union and lifelong commitment between one man and one woman who become one flesh. It is rather startling that God does not require children for a marriage to be a success, even though he inaugurated procreation with his blessing: "Be fruitful and multiply" (Gen 1:28). Sometimes he blesses a couple with abundant children and sometimes he does not. Regardless of size, he requires fidelity and love among those in the household.

When it comes to the family of God, the Lord likewise does not measure success by quantifiable numbers. Instead, he places a premium on fidelity, holiness, and love. Sometimes he blesses a congregation with an abundance of members, and sometimes he does not. What chiefly matters is that the word is preached and the sacraments are administered according to the Lord's institution, for that is where Christ and his bride interact. It is where the Holy Spirit is at work to give life, where children of God are born and sustained, and where the Father evangelizes his children and nurtures them to tell others the good news.

Missional advocates will often point to swift statistical gains as proof of the Spirit's work, but even apart from doctrinal considerations, the numbers rarely reflect longevity. In reality, a smaller congregation that remains in a place for a century might easily reach more people with the gospel than a missional effort that lasts only a few years. For example, Roxburgh and Boren cite "The Landing" as "a center of life in Eagle [Idaho] and an outstanding example of the conviction that God is up to something in the local contexts in which we live."[44] Seven years after this praise was printed, no trace of "The Landing" can be found. A few miles away in Emmett, however, the liturgical Our Redeemer Lutheran Church continues to proclaim the gospel as it has for 95 years. Similarly, Stetzer and Putman point to Mars Hill Church in Seattle—which averaged 12,000 in weekly attendance across 15 campuses during its heyday—as a shining example.[45] Yet the entire enterprise dissolved in spectacular

---

[44]Roxburgh and Boren, *Introducing the Missional Church*, 53.

[45]Stetzer and Putman, *Breaking the Missional Code*, 17.

fashion on January 1, 2015. Meanwhile, nearby Messiah Lutheran Church is approaching its 70th anniversary of faithfully proclaiming the word and administrating the sacraments. Against the insistence that we reach the lost *now*, the family of God also looks to remain for children yet unborn (Ps 78:6).

There will be times when, despite the greatest intentions and efforts, a marriage is barren and the family line discontinues in a place. There will be times when families cannot make ends meet or are torn apart by conflict, and thus must give up their homes and take up residence with relatives. This will also be the case with congregations. It is not a welcome thing, but in a world so hostile to church and family, it is inevitable. Nevertheless the Lord will have his people, and the gates of hell will not prevail against his church (Matt 16:18).

### *(4) Is a father's vocation to be measured by his ability to lead and implement change?*

In 2015, *Business News Daily* asked business owners to define "leadership." These were some of the answers given:

- "Leadership is having a vision, sharing that vision and inspiring others to support your vision while creating their own."
- "In my experience, leadership is about three things: To listen, to inspire and to empower."
- "Leadership is stepping out of your comfort zone and taking risk to create reward."[46]

Missional advocates adopt the same terminology and praise the same qualities in pastors. These are excellent and necessary qualities for an entrepreneur, but fatherhood is seldom praised for inspiring family members to embrace a new vision of family or empowering family

---

[46]Brittney Helmrich, "33 Ways to Define Leadership," *Business News Daily*, June 19, 2015, http://www.businessnewsdaily.com/3647-leadership-definition.html.

members or risking the family's wellbeing to create a greater reward, whatever that might even mean. Fathers are rightly praised for maintaining stability in an adversarial world, holding families together, nurturing their children in the discipline and instruction of the Lord, and protecting them from ungodly influences. Their calling has little to do with statistical measures of success established by the world.

In the congregation, the pastor serves as surrogate father in the stead and by the command of Christ. He therefore does not need a new vision because he is not called to envision anything new. He does not need to lead the congregation to a new place; even if they have strayed from the Lord's word, he is merely to lead them back home. He is not called to inspire or empower, but to feed and nurture with the means of grace. There is no reason to change the identity of the family to match the neighborhood better; there is already enough risk and discomfort in simply maintaining the family and in inviting members of the neighborhood into the family of God to be reborn.

### (5) Is "everyone a father" an advisable philosophy for family life?

With the breakdown of the natural family in our present day, it is all too easy to envision a household in which a husband abdicates the responsibilities of his calling as father. This normally happens in a passive form, where other family members are left to fill the void and perform the tasks that the father ought to be doing. It might be a little harder, however, to imagine the following scenario: a family meets and decides that each member will now be the father, that each is now to do whatever the father normally does in his role. Some of this seems entirely sensible when it comes to function: if the father normally mows the lawn, now several mowers are available. (It does, however, lead to the question, "Now, will *anybody* mow the lawn?") Other aspects, however, are far more controversial: is it given to a three-year-old girl to discipline her teenage brother for missing curfew? Is it given to the teenage boy to be a husband to his mother? Of course not. The vocation of father consists of far more than just the tasks he performs but is rooted in the unique calling he is given by God.

Hand in hand with a low view of the pastoral ministry is the missional idea that everyone is a minister, for it seems sensible and pragmatic to expand the workforce by spreading the pastor's tasks around. However, just as a father is called by God to love his wife and nurture his children, so too is a pastor called by God to guide the church by the proclamation of the Lord's word (2 Tim 4:1–5). This is not a matter of inappropriate clericalism or abuse of power, but rather how God has instituted the pastoral office for the sake of serving his people. To ignore this doctrine is to pose the question, "Does 'everyone a minister' in fact teach that no one is the father in the church family?"

As we have seen by considering the above questions, congregations are not in need of a missional church paradigm. To emphasize the Great Commission over the congregation as formed by God is akin to emphasizing "Be fruitful and multiply" over the institution of marriage. In each case, the commission is only proper when the form is first established and preserved. Outreach-preeminent paradigms are designed with noble intent: they seek to reach unbelievers. They often do so, however, at the expense of the congregation as family. If Eberstadt's thesis holds, then weakening the church family will do nothing good for the natural family either.

It is appropriate to address briefly one other concern expressed by critics: are pastors properly and adequately trained in LCMS seminaries, or is the current curriculum outdated? Clearly, no amount of training is adequate for the pastoral ministry: it is an art learned in daily life, built upon a solid foundation of theological instruction. However, the training that pastors currently receive at LCMS seminaries establishes the proper foundation for nurturing the family of God. Exegetical theology prepares the pastor to tell God's children what the Lord has to say to them, while systematic theology pieces the message together. Historical theology provides a sense of family history, so that the children of God might know their ancestors and be strengthened in a sense of identity. Practical theology is a necessary aspect as well: just as the father of a newborn must learn the practical tasks of swaddling, diaper changing, and installing car seats, the pastor must learn the nuts and bolts of caring for the children of God.

## The Family into Winter

God's gifts are always under assault in a sinful world. In a time when pernicious individualism runs rampant, it is no surprise that his institution of family is suffering. Whereas the fall into sin divided the one family into two, individualism seeks to render them both formless in the pursuit of personal fulfillment. But the church is not a formless thing that can be fitted into different templates depending on one's imagination, situation, or cultural context. Rather, the church has a definite form: it is the family of God; it is the children of Christ and his bride. It is vital to maintain the church as family and not impose paradigms that weaken its identity as such. The church will not be nurtured by an emphasis on the Great Commission over the gospel or by incessant change. Congregations will not be blessed by the constant comparison of pastor and people against statistical expectations, nor will the bride of Christ be helped if her pastors are overwhelmed by inappropriate populism among her children.

This is not to say that the coming years will be easy. Expressive individualism has the momentum, which means that things will get worse before—*if*—they get better. The current decline may herald that the Last Day is near. Until the Lord returns, however, the congregation is his bride and her children gathered around his word and sacraments. The pastor remains the surrogate father who stands in the stead and by the command of Christ. The people are fed by the Lord's grace, go about their vocations, and speak the gospel to those whom they encounter. This is not true because it is the favored paradigm of traditional Lutheran theology. It is true because the Lord declares it to be so in his word.

Like traditional natural families today, it is given to the church in her congregations to continue to be the family of God. It will not be an easy time. Hermann Sasse's encouragement to pastors seems as fitting today as it did in 1950:

> With deep concern we are all thinking about the future of the Lutheran Church in all parts of the world. To us it is not given, as it was to the fathers of the previous century, to experience a springtime of the church. But in the church it cannot always be spring. God also sends to his church the storms of autumn and the seeming death-sleep of

winter. What he has allotted to us is simply that we faithfully administer his means of grace. It is certainly easier to preach in times when masses of men flock into the church than in times when only a handful of the faithful hold fast to the word of God. But the latter is at least equally important as the former. Even in the life of the Preacher of all preachers both occurred.[47]

If the winter is upon us, it is still given to fathers to feed their children, though food may be harder to find when days grow cold. Likewise, it is still given to pastors to care for the family of God in and out of season, even if that season seems especially dark or bleak. But they do so with joy even in winter, for since Christ the Bridegroom has purchased his children with his own blood, he will certainly not forsake them now.

---

[47]Hermann Sasse, "The Results of the Lutheran Awakening of the Nineteenth Century" in Hermann Sasse, *Letters to Lutheran Pastors* (ed. and trans. Matthew C. Harrison; 3 vols.; St. Louis: Concordia, 2013–2015), I:329–30.

# Pastor as Servant vs. Pastor as Leader

*Seth Clemmer*

*"The pastor is not a leader, but a servant."* Such a statement is often met with great resistance in today's church, where the pastor is commonly referred to as the "leader of the congregation."[1] It seems self-evident that only a leader would conduct the divine service, possess authority to forgive and retain sins, teach Bible classes, set the tone for the congregation, and have a commanding influence in many of the decisions made by the parishioners. In fact, this view is so widely held that it sounds almost redundant to refer to the pastor as the leader, for what is he if not that? Yet it is difficult to justify the use of the English word "leader" when looking at the terms found in the Greek New Testament that pertain to pastors. On the contrary, designations such as "servant," "overseer," and "shepherd" are plain and prevalent. In cases when Greek terms for "leader" can be found in the text, the words refer to an office that has been given unique authority to serve the people in some capacity, whether political, as with military leaders, or religious, as with synagogue officials. Pastors have also been given such an office, solely to serve and to shepherd

---

[1]For example, Rick Warren asserts, "You must change the primary goal of the pastor from minister to leader." Rick Warren, "Structuring Your Church to Grow and Not Plateau," Pastors.com, https://pastors.com/structuring-church -grow-not-plateau/.

others, with the forgiveness of sins being the chief end. Thus, pastors are servants and not leaders.[2]

There is a further problem, however, that impairs modern Christians who either follow translations that employ the term "leader" for pastors or who simply presume the word makes up part of the pastor's job description. The secular ideology of Marxism has strongly affected (and thus grossly altered) the proper understanding of this term. Karl Marx's sociology was concerned with class struggle and the mobilization of the working class toward a revolution, which required a leader to bring about this political and economic change through movements. Thus, the subtle influence of Marxist ideology has recast the idea of "leader" beyond an office with given authority that was intended to serve others, and shifted it to the power of one or more individuals to control the people on behalf of the masses.[3] There are at least three related ways this approach can be seen in the church today: 1) the church is often considered a "movement" and not an institution; 2) as such, pastors are needed to be leaders who will (presumably) speak for the collective; and 3) the power they possess resides in themselves rather than having received it from another. This Marxian construction stands in direct opposition to the biblical teaching of "pastor as servant."[4]

---

[2]The persistence of "pastor as leader" is seen in the "servant-leader" idea; yet because "servant-leadership" sounds like such a positive thing, this self-contradictory notion is frequently promoted in the church as a necessary characteristic for Christians in positions of authority.

[3]This is not to suggest that the characterization of a leader as a person of intrinsic power rather than consigned authority is unique to Marx. Rather, Marx is identified as a key figure in how the understanding of the term has shifted due to the popularization of his ideological analysis of society consisting of struggles between classes and movements which necessitates forceful and controlling leaders.

[4]To be sure, those who advocate the concept "pastor as leader" likely do so innocently. The goal of this essay is not to criticize any who might refer to the pastor as a leader, nor is it to equate them with the supporters of Marxist dictatorships. Rather, the intent is to emphasize the fundamental distinction between the biblical understanding of a pastor and today's common perception of a leader, while stressing that referring to the pastor as leader is potentially harmful to the Lord's church.

Jesus told his disciples, "The kings of the Gentiles exercise lordship over them, and those in authority over them are called benefactors. But not so with you. Rather let the greatest among you become as the youngest, and the leader as one who serves" (Luke 22:26). Letting Scripture interpret Scripture, a brief word study on "leader" will show that pastors are servants under authority and not leaders in command. This will become all the more apparent upon recognizing how current ideology that lionizes leadership is a phenomenon that is historically traceable to Marx's insistence on innate men of power.

## The Use of "Leader" in the New Testament

The Greek text of the New Testament uses different terms that are simply rendered as "leader" in many English versions. While this is an accurate translation in some cases, in others it can be misleading. A cursory look at the following terms should help underscore the nuanced and often preferred meanings for the varied vocables.

### ἄρχων or ἀρχηγός

According to Gerhard Delling, the Septuagint's use of these words for "leader" refers to "one who exercises authoritative influence; the term is used for the national, local or tribal leader." Included are officials and overlords, as well as "a general" or "the political or military 'leader' of the whole people, or of a part of it."[5] It is essential to note that a "leader" in this sense stands in a specific office because of the authority given to him. In other words, he is not a leader because of some ability or power he possesses, but authority has been bestowed upon him from outside of himself. Delling explained: "The ἄρχων has a prominent position in which he exercises authority; he is thus in the first instance a 'high official.'"[6] Thus, what makes one a leader is his office, and his office is defined by the authority given it.

---

[5]Gerhard Delling, "ἄρχων," *TDNT* 1:487–88. The term ἀρχηγός refers exclusively to Jesus in the New Testament: Acts 3:15; 5:31; Heb 2:10; 12:2.

[6]Delling, "ἄρχων," 488.

In the New Testament, this label is employed when describing many different offices. It refers to worldly political rulers (Matt 9:18; Luke 12:58; Rom 13:3; 1 Cor 2:6–8), the devil—the prince of demons (Matt 12:24; Mark 3:22; Luke 11:15; John 12:31; 16:1), and the rulers of the Gentiles who lord their authority over others (Matt 20:25). It is also used within religious contexts, including: the "rulers" within the synagogue, such as Jairus (Luke 8:41); Nicodemus (John 3:1); other "rulers of the Pharisees" (Luke 14:1; John 7:48; Acts 4:5); and the "rulers of the people" who were leading the charge against Jesus before his crucifixion (Luke 23:35; 24:20). In every instance, the term denotes those who occupy an office from which they derive their authority. Yet it is never used in reference to the office of the pastor.[7]

## ὁδηγός

This term for leader, and the verb related to it (ὁδηγέω), is seldom found in the New Testament. It refers to anyone escorting others,[8] in the sense of "the blind leading the blind" (Matt 15:14) or when Judas leads the soldiers to Jesus (Acts 1:16). The authority of this type of leader is limited to his giving guidance during a specific and limited action. His leadership, therefore, ceases after escorting the person to the desired destination. This word also never refers to the pastoral office.

## ἡγέομαι

ἡγέομαι and its derivatives are found frequently throughout the New Testament, and are most commonly used in the sense of "consider or regard."[9] For example, Paul considers (ἥγημαι) all earthly gain as loss for the sake of the gospel (Phil 3:7), and Peter admonishes his readers to regard (ἡγεῖσθε) the Lord's patience as salvation (2 Pet 3:15). The participle form of this word is also used when referring to

---

[7]ἄρχων is only used specifically of Jesus in Revelation 1:5, as he is set above all other kings as the "ruler of kings."

[8]Wilhelm Michaelis, "ὁδός," TDNT 5:99.

[9]BDAG, 434. It refers to worldly leaders twice (Matt 2:6; Acts 7:10), with both instances carrying the sense of "office" and "one acting under authority."

people, meaning, "one who is considered," "one who is regarded," or "one who has regard for."

Of particular interest is when this word specifically refers to those in the pastoral office, which it does three times in Hebrews 13. The English Standard Version offers the following translations:

> Remember your leaders (τῶν ἡγουμένων ὑμῶν), those who spoke to you the word of God. Consider the outcome of their way of life, and imitate their faith (Heb 13:7).
>
> Obey your leaders (τοῖς ἡγουμένοις ὑμῶν) and submit to them, for they are keeping watch over your souls, as those who will have to give an account. Let them do this with joy and not with groaning, for that would be of no advantage to you (Heb 13:17).
>
> Greet all your leaders (τοὺς ἡγουμένους ὑμῶν) and all the saints (Heb 13:24).

Friedrich Büchsel posited why the author of Hebrews employs this term in these passages:

> The community is obviously divided into those who lead and those who are led. In 13:17 they are pastors responsible to God. God has entrusted the other members of the community to them, and therefore these owe them obedience. . . . Reverent subjection to human officers with divinely given pastoral authority is now integral to Christian piety.[10]

Büchsel assumed that the community must be led, and thus concluded that the participle of ἡγέομαι denotes "leaders." If one removes the assumption of the *necessity* of leading, however, then the word could be more freely translated as "one who is regarded" (if passive) or "one who has regard for" (if active). That is to say, this man "has regard for his people" as one who cares for them. Thus, in this sense, there are those who *regard* (that is, pastors) and those who *are regarded* (that is, the congregation). This shift emphasizes that the pastor's office as "one who regards" is distinct from the congregation

---

[10]Friedrich Büchsel, "ἡγέομαι," *TDNT* 2:907.

(those regarded) only because of the authority given to that particular office. The pastor has no power in himself to lead, but acts only as one given authority by the Lord to shepherd the church, to consider and regard his people.[11]

Since almost every other New Testament instance of ἡγέομαι refers to the act of "considering or regarding," importing "leader" into the meaning of the term in Hebrews 13 seems unwarranted if not unhelpful. "Those who regard you" or "those who consider you" would be a more accurate rendering, which may make for awkward English but at least avoids a misleading alternative.[12] This nuanced understanding, then, maintains a distinction between "leader" and "pastor" while not diminishing the authority possessed by those in the pastoral office. Hebrews 13 assumes this authority by noting that preaching and keeping watch over souls is precisely what pastors are called to do.[13]

---

[11]Büchsel did, however, make the following point: "The interest of Hb. in the ἡγέομαι is ethical and religious rather than ecclesiastical." Büchsel, "ἡγέομαι," *TDNT*, 2:907 n.6. In other words, Hebrews is not necessarily laying out a model of church hierarchy here, but is giving ethical guidance to the church and making a religious distinction within the congregation between the preacher and the people. Hence these people are called the "heads of the Christian congregation" in BDAG, 434.

[12]John Kleinig speaks of these pastors as "those who regard the congregation," as they are given to guard those in their care with Christ and his word: "Pastors are commissioned to perform guard duty for those in their care (Heb 13:17). If they damage or destroy the church, the holy temple of God, by building it up with anything else than Christ and his Word, they, though purged and saved, will suffer from the fire of God's wrath, and their work will be undone (1 Cor 3:12–17)." John W. Kleinig, *Leviticus* (Concordia Commentary; St. Louis: Concordia, 2003), 238.

[13]Similarly, in reference to the "leaders" of verse 17, the Apology of the Augsburg Confession agrees that such authority does not require obedience apart from the gospel but only "under the gospel." Thus, "Bishops must not create traditions contrary to the gospel nor interpret traditions in a manner contrary to the gospel" (Ap XXVIII, 20).

## ἐπίσκοπος

The pastor is often described as an overseer (ἐπίσκοπος), with the purpose or manner of the overseeing always being given along with that title. For example, Paul says, "an overseer, as God's steward, must be above reproach. He must not be arrogant or quick-tempered or a drunkard or violent or greedy for gain" (Titus 1:7). Similarly, Paul both praises and notes limitations for those in this office: "The saying is trustworthy: If anyone aspires to the office of overseer, he desires a noble task. Therefore an overseer must be above reproach, the husband of one wife, sober-minded, self-controlled, respectable, hospitable, able to teach" (1 Tim 3:2). Moreover, Paul states that the authority of the overseer is bound to the word itself (Titus 1:9).

In his address to the Ephesian elders, Paul identifies the task of shepherding as belonging to the office of overseer and pastor. "Pay careful attention to yourselves and to all the flock, in which the Holy Spirit has made you overseers, to care for (ποιμαίνειν) the church of God, which he obtained with his own blood" (Acts 20:28). The authority of the overseer is for no other purpose than to shepherd—to care for—the church. Jesus, as the one shepherd and overseer, has instituted and given boundaries to this office, and has bestowed authority upon his undershepherds and overseers who tend to his sheep (1 Pet 2:25).[14]

Peter likewise admonishes pastors to avoid abusing their authority and to serve in a godly manner: "Shepherd (ποιμάνατε) the flock of God that is among you, exercising oversight (ἐπισκοποῦντες), not under compulsion, but willingly, as God would have you; not for shameful gain, but eagerly; not domineering over those in your charge, but being examples to the flock" (1 Pet 5:2–3). Scripture is clear: stepping beyond this God-given authority and mistreating members of the congregation is strictly prohibited.

## The Marxian Concept of "Leader"

If a leader is one who serves under authority—authority that belongs to a particular office and which has been given by another—then

---

[14]See also John 21:15–17; Eph 4:11; Heb 13:20.

any act of taking power by force would seem to disqualify one from being called a "leader" in the proper sense. In contemporary usage, however, the term "leader" is regularly applied to virtually any head of state or elected official—including dictators, tyrants, and autocrats who have obtained power by usurpation. What is more, the moniker is even used for one whose position of power is self-proclaimed. This modern understanding of "leader," which clashes with the biblical understanding, is largely due to the influence of Karl Marx.

Marx built on G. W. F. Hegel's interpretation of history. Hegel insisted that history is a progressive struggle moving toward an ideal form of Spirit—that is, toward the purest form of human consciousness—which allows for freedom through self-determinism.[15] This evolutionary philosophy of history, where the strong survive and are strengthened in the process, is often expressed as Hegel's "dialectic." In the first phase, one movement dominates society but its inadequacies lead to independent and reflective thought. This divergence and freedom from established customs eventually brings about the collapse or negation of the original movement. The second phase, however, also shows itself to be insufficient. It ends up being too abstract and, as a movement, absolute freedom from preexisting norms is an impractical basis for society. The third phase, then, amounts to a sort of harmony between the two previous phases—a movement that is organic yet maintains individual freedom.[16] Although the three terms "thesis," "antithesis," and "synthesis" did not originate with Hegel himself, they are often used to describe his phases of mankind's progression toward self-awareness through rational reflection.

Yet whereas Hegel's philosophy of history focused on the metaphysical "unfolding of Spirit in time" through reason and knowledge,[17] Marx held a materialistic understanding. There is no God who institutes authority (according to the Fourth Commandment); there is

---

[15]On Hegel's use of the term "Spirit" (or "*Geist*"), see Glenn Alexander Magee, *The Hegel Dictionary* (New York: Continuum, 2010), 226–28.

[16]For a concise explanation of Hegel's interpretation of history, see Peter Singer, *Hegel: A Very Short Introduction* (New York: Oxford University Press, 1983), 100–102.

[17]G. F. W Hegel, *Introduction to the Philosophy of History* (trans. Leo Rauch; Indianapolis: Hackett, 1998), 75.

nothing transcendent from which authority comes. Marx's biggest influence on leadership stems from his view that "The history of all hitherto existing society is the history of class struggles"—that is, of movements that vie for power.[18] Basic human needs and economic factors are what determine the course of events; material life conditions social life. Historical progress, then, occurs when an economic structure undergoes revolution and a society moves closer to the ideal of thoroughgoing communism.[19] Marx thought such change required the exploited proletariat (one movement) to overthrow their hostile oppressors (another movement)[20] who own the means of material production.[21] This struggle, however, demanded two things from the working class: their own self-transforming action, and the use of violence.[22]

---

[18]Karl Marx and Friedrich Engels, *The Communist Manifesto* (ed. Gareth Stedman Jones; trans. Samuel Moore; repr., New York: Penguin, 2002), 219.

[19]On the transition from capitalism to communism, and the need for the state to be the revolutionary dictatorship of the proletariat, see Marx as quoted and interpreted in V. I. Lenin, *The State and Revolution* (trans. Robert Service; New York: Penguin, 1992), 77–82.

[20]"Our epoch, the epoch of the bourgeoisie, possesses, however, this distinctive feature; it has simplified the class antagonisms. Society as a whole is more and more splitting up into two great hostile camps, into two great classes directly facing each other: Bourgeoisie and Proletariat." Marx and Engels, *Communist Manifesto*, 15.

[21]Marx thought "mental goods" were a part of the equation as well: "The ideas of the ruling class are in every epoch the ruling ideas, i.e. the class which is the ruling material force of society, is at the same time its ruling intellectual force. The class which has the means of material production at its disposal, has control at the same time over the means of mental production, so that thereby, generally speaking, the ideas of those who lack the means of mental production are subject to it. The ruling ideas are nothing more than the ideal expression of the dominant material relationships, the dominant material relationships grasped as ideas." Karl Marx and Frederick Engels, *The German Ideology, Part One* (ed. C. J. Arthur; New York: International Publishers, 1947), 64.

[22]Jonathan Wolff, "Karl Marx," in *The Stanford Encyclopedia of Philosophy* (ed. Edward N. Zalta; Winter 2015 Edition), http://plato.stanford.edu/archives/win2015/entries/marx/.

Practically speaking, these factors required an individual, a
leader, who would seize power and use it to control the movement
for the greater good of the masses. As in evolution, progress toward
the ideal only comes through struggle and death. This is perhaps
unfortunate, yet such violence is justified because it is considered
part of the natural godless order and because it is necessary if one
class is to overthrow another.[23] Thus, in Marx's version of Hegel's dialectic, "the antithesis *destroys* the thesis and the synthesis *swallows*
what survives."[24] As Marx said, "Force is the midwife of every old
society which is pregnant with a new one."[25] His secular philosophy
of history, therefore, presupposes an individual who will emerge
as "leader" and use power for the sake of the collective.

What is more, the leader's voice is not to be understood as
that of a single person, but as representing the oppressed group as a
whole. He himself, then, is above critique since his words are thought
to embody the shared voice of the domineered class. This concept
is known as the *Führer Principle*. (*Der Führer* literally means "the
Leader.") Whatever the leader does is considered the will of the collective, is necessary, and is irreproachable even when irrational.[26] In
fact, to question the leader would be to question the will of the entire

---

[23]For example, in *The Civil War in France* the overthrow of the state by the
Paris Communal was thus explained by Marx: "The task was to amputate
the purely repressive organs of the old government power, to wrest its legitimate functions from an authority with pretensions to standing above society
itself and to hand them over to the responsible servants of society." Quoted
in Lenin, *State and Revolution*, 46. Note that this amputating, wresting, and
handing over required the use of force by "leaders" who were not given authority but claimed it for themselves.

[24]Jacques Barzun, *Darwin, Marx, Wagner: Critique of Heritage* (Boston:
Little, Brown and Co., 1941), 208; emphasis added.

[25]Karl Marx, *Capital: Volume 1: A Critique of Political Economy* (trans. Ben
Fowkes; Harmondsworth: Penguin, 1976; repr., New York: Penguin, 1992), 916.

[26]According to Kenneth Minogue, those who espouse ideologies allege
to stand above the conflicts within society, thus enabling them to offer transcendent and saving critique. Since the critique is transcendent, it is necessarily irrefutable; and since the alleged goal of the ideology is to bring relief
from oppression, to question the leader is to join oneself to the oppressors.
"Ideological theories . . . as the pronouncements of higher rationality, cannot
be abandoned without calling the superiority of that rationality into question."

collective, and thus is punishable with violence or exile. As historian Anthony Read noted, after Adolf Hitler promised to execute all who disobeyed the state,

> [The] Reichstag President [gave] an emotional endorsement. The entire German people, he declared, "man by man and woman by woman" was united in a single cry: "We always approve everything our Führer does."[27]

The *Führer Principle* was perhaps best expressed in the words of Rudolf Hess. Hess was Hitler's deputy leader in the Nazi party and held by many to be Hitler's most loyal follower. In a public speech, he declared: "Hitler is Germany and Germany is Hitler. Whatever he does is necessary. Whatever he does is successful. Clearly the Führer has divine blessing."[28] It is not difficult to see how this type of leader could easily earn the title "dictator"—whatever orders he dictated were infallible because they flowed, not from a single man, but from the spirit of the collective. Indeed, when discussing Dietrich Bonhoeffer's public radio address against the *Führer Principle*, Eric Metaxas claimed this "profoundly misguided concept of leadership [is what] enabled Hitler's rise to power and led to the horrors of the death camps."[29]

In sum, the Hegelian, Darwinian assumptions upon which Marx built his understanding of history caused him to recast the meaning of "leader." No longer is a leader one who occupies a particular office and receives authority to serve others; nor is he even one who merely abuses his power. Instead, Marx identified leaders as those who rise up within movements and take power into their own hands to bring about change. This necessarily entails violence and can result in the

---

Kenneth Minogue, *Alien Powers: The Pure Theory of Ideology* (Wilmington, Del.: ISI Books, 2008), 136.

[27] Anthony Read, *The Devil's Disciples: Hitler's Inner Circle* (New York: W. W. Norton and Co., 2003), 377.

[28] C. N. Trueman, "The Fuehrer Principle," The History Learning Site, http://www.historylearningsite.co.uk/nazi-germany/the-fuehrer-principle/.

[29] Eric Metaxas, *Bonhoeffer: Pastor, Martyr, Prophet, Spy* (Nashville: Thomas Nelson, 2010), 144.

*Führer Principle.* While "dictator" remains a negative term in modern vernacular, this misappropriation of the concept "leader" has led people to desire someone who will direct a movement by having a voice over the group and steer the collective toward an ideal. As people seek such a person to lead their movement, however, attributes belonging to the dictator frequently remain, such as power, vision, and the ability to control and punish. Thus, when a person reading Scripture sees the pastor referred to as "leader," our modern post-Marxian understanding often causes a misinterpretation. Contrary to the meaning found in the biblical text itself, the reader is subject to misunderstanding the term with its freighted concept of a leader who commandeers and controls a movement.

## The Church as Movement vs. the Church as Institution

The language of "movement" is a hallmark of how the Marxist categorizes things in the world, with one group struggling against the next. Thus, the language of "movement" invites the question, "Movement over and against what?" When the church speaks of herself as a movement, this gives the notion of a struggle of one party against another. Whom, however, is the church struggling against? The Scriptures are clear that "we do not wrestle against flesh and blood, but . . . against the cosmic powers over this present darkness, against the spiritual forces of evil in the heavenly places" (Eph 6:12). The Christian understands himself in a struggle against his own sinful nature and the devil, yet these enemies have already been defeated by the death of Jesus on the cross. In this way, the Christian is not in a physical struggle but only a spiritual one. Thus, no earthly movement against these enemies is needed. So again, whom would the church be struggling against if she were considered a "movement"?

Perhaps individuals within the church have accepted the concept of "movement" as opposed to being "stagnant." One might think, "If the church is not 'moving,' then she is not going into the entire world with the gospel and serving the neighbor." The Hegelian progression of history, however, is not contrasted with being stationary, but instead characterizes the church as a movement struggling toward a utopian ideal. When the church defines herself as a "movement," she is adopting the notion that a temporal fight for power and the domination over opposing groups is part of her mission. More harmfully, it assumes the church is incomplete as given by the Lord, and a movement mentality is needed to help the church realize her "ideal."

The church, however, is an institution built firmly upon the rock of Christ (Matt 16:18) and has no need for a leader in the Marxist sense as though she were a movement. She is not struggling against opposing worldly forces, but has been placed in the world to deliver the gifts instituted by Jesus—namely, comforting his sheep with the gospel and being a light to the nations. It is precisely the "un-movement-ness" and unchanging character of the gospel that brings comfort and salvation in the midst of an ever-changing world where death and chaos reign.

The pastor, therefore, is not leading a movement but is serving others through the authority given him by virtue of the office he holds in the church. As stated above, he is to shepherd the flock of God, not exercising lordship in a domineering way but caring for those entrusted into his care (Luke 22:25–26; Acts 20:28; 1 Pet 5:2–3). In fact, the man placed into the office of the ministry regularly faces the temptation to succumb to the *Führer Principle*. Warnings are given in Scripture that the pastoral office is a place where the devil can do significant damage to the church (2 Pet 2:1; 2 Tim 4:3). This is why pastors are given as servants in contrast to leaders (or *Führers*). However, today's clichéd use of "leader" creeps into the church and creates confusion regarding the office of the ministry. Shepherds are regularly deceived into becoming dynamic and strong leaders of the collective instead of servants coming in humility. Thus did Paul remind the Corinthians that he came to them not with human wisdom or eloquent speech, but "in weakness with great fear and trembling" so that their faith might rest on God's power alone (1 Cor 2:1–5).

## Power vs. Authority

In contrast to a position wielding power, the Lord instituted the office of pastor to be one of a servant, having no power in himself but acting only under the authority given from another. The Scriptures make a clear distinction between power and authority, which helps clarify the difference between a servant and a leader in terms of Marxian categories.[30] The concept of power (δύναμις) refers to the ability inherent to a person to carry out a function.[31] For example, in the parable of the talents, the talents are given to each "according to his ability (δύναμιν)" (Matt 25:15); and the Son of Man will return with "power (δυνάμεως)" over creation (Mark 13:26). On the other hand, authority (ἐξουσία) is given to someone from outside himself, such as the authority given to a governing official.[32] This is precisely what Jesus makes clear at the end of Matthew's Gospel: "All authority (ἐξουσία) in heaven and on earth has been given to me" (Matt 28:18). Likewise, Jesus tells Pontius Pilate, "You would have no authority (ἐξουσίαν) over me at all unless it had been given you from above" (John 19:11). The authority bestowed defines an office, not the inherent power of an individual holding that office. As such, the word denotes weakness and service, not control and power, because the authority has been given by someone greater and is used for the sake of others. In other words, the one given authority is necessarily a servant to the one who gave it and to those he attends by this authority.

The pastor, then, is nothing other than a man serving in an office according to given authority.[33] He has no power in and of himself, but has been set as a servant in weakness. Pastors vary with regard

---

[30]For example, Luke 4:36 says Jesus commands the unclean spirits "with authority and power," and Ephesians 1:21 says he has been exalted "far above all rule and authority and power and dominion."

[31]BDAG, 262–63.

[32]BDAG, 352–53. The distinction between power and authority is further clarified here by describing ἐξουσία as the one given the right or potential to exercise power. Authority gives power to certain individuals, but limits that power within a certain sphere.

[33]Harold Senkbeil speaks of pastors as officers and agents of Christ who forgive sins according to the authority of their office: "[Christ] works uniquely in the church through His ministers for the forgiveness of sins. The church calls pastors from her own midst, but it is Christ Himself who stands behind the office of the ministry. They are earthly agents for our Heavenly Lord. . . ." Harold L. Senkbeil, *Dying to Live: The Power of Forgiveness* (St. Louis: Concordia, 1994), 84.

to their abilities, persuasiveness, administrative skills, and ability to lead a meeting. None of these, however, have anything to do with the authority given the man; none of them make him a pastor. The people are not his to control as the powerful voice of the collective. Rather, he shepherds and serves those entrusted to his care according to the scriptural descriptions of the office.

The Lord Jesus specifically set "leaders as servants" (Luke 22:26; Matt 20:26). Paul, someone we might designate a "leader" of the church, never referred to himself as such. He instead often called himself "a servant of Jesus Christ" (Rom 1:1). James, Peter, Jude, and John each referred to himself in the same way—as a servant (Jas 1:1; 2 Pet 1:1; Jude 1:1; Rev 1:1). The term "servant" is extended further by Paul to all those given the attributes of the office in 2 Timothy 2:24: "And the Lord's servant must not be quarrelsome but kind to everyone, able to teach, patiently enduring evil." In reference to the ministry, Paul writes, "This is how one should regard us, as servants (ὑπηρέτας) of Christ and stewards of the mysteries of God" (1 Cor 4:1). Interestingly, Paul's use of ὑπηρέτας is often translated as "servants," but elsewhere in the New Testament it is translated as "officer" (that is, one who holds an office and is therefore under authority). Thus, the pastor is the Lord's officer, which makes him a servant rather than a leader.

The pastor is not only a servant *of Christ* but also a servant *for the church*. Paul indicates that "we proclaim not ourselves, but Jesus Christ as Lord, with ourselves as your servants for Jesus' sake" (2 Cor 4:5). Paul goes on to characterize these servants as weak jars of clay in contrast to the power of God (2 Cor 4:7). The office of pastor is one of weakness, a trait that stands in opposition to the power of the worldly leader. Being a servant, the pastor is to shepherd his flock in humility and kindness, as the weakness of his office ripples into all of his words and actions. He is not in control of a movement, in control of people, or leading anything; rather, he is serving.

## Potential Abuse When Servants Are Understood as Leaders

In the Smalcald Articles, Luther described the church as the place where "the little sheep hear the voice of their shepherd" (SA III, XII, 2). To accomplish this, the Lord speaks through the man he has placed into his office. This brings together the pure voice of the Shepherd—holy, blameless, right, without error—and the sinful mouth of a pastor—unholy, immoral, corruptible, power-thirsty. The little sheep hear from *one* mouth. Yet, the same mouth that speaks the Shepherd's voice of absolution can and does just as easily speak the pastor's sin-corrupted words. The sheep, then, are to recognize that not all words of that mouth are the Shepherd's voice.

While this may seem obvious, it introduces the potentiality of abuse of the Lord's office—namely, whereas the office of pastor is given to speak of the Lord's mercy, it can also be wielded to control toward man's preferences. One may wonder, "Does the voice I hear come from the ordained, sin-forgiving pastor, or does the voice come from the man in the office who *may and does* sin?" The counsel of the pastor to "stop sinning" is good; but when this instruction is attached to that which is not sinful, or when that counsel is given in such a way as to lead the sheep not to repentance but to servility, what is the sheep to do? The voice that distinguishes law and gospel to comfort souls can carry more weight than it perhaps should when, for example, it speaks concerning advice for the finance committee. If the pastoral ministry is to be "obeyed" and "submitted to" according to Hebrews 13:17, this can create a situation in which the pastor (a sinful man) has tremendous power within the congregation if he understands himself to be a "leader."

The church has been aware of this potential abuse of the office since her very institution. Paul recognized the wrong action/teaching of Peter (Gal 2:11–15), and Paul cautioned the church through his letters to Titus and Timothy that a man should not be ordained haphazardly (1 Tim 5:22), but carefully and with attention to certain qualifications. One may wonder, "Why bother with the qualifications? Surely the words spoken by any man who occupies the office are efficacious regardless of his inherent qualities!" It can be argued, however, that the requirements serve in part to guard the church against abuse from the ordained mouth.

More important than the qualifications from Paul, the Lord Jesus himself actually instituted the words given to the office in addition to the office itself. In other words, no one looks to the pastor as pastor for sports analysis, since the office was never established for this. People do, however, look to the pastor for advice, counsel, wisdom, and comfort with regard to spiritual, theological, and ecclesial matters. To be sure, an abusive pastor would be tempted to include everything in the church as "in the realm of the forgiveness of sins," but the Scriptures never give the pastor's office such open-ended authority.[34] When the pastor gives counsel "as pastor" in areas in which he has not been given authority, he potentially brings confusion to his sheep. Such mistaken pastoral counsel weakens the clarity and certainty of his authority when he speaks regarding those things he is specifically authorized to say.

Put simply, the voice of the pastor is given to be obeyed, but *only* for that which he has been given authority. His office has been instituted for the purpose of delivering the forgiveness of sins (John 20:23). Undeniably, the words of the law and gospel are many and various with regard to endless circumstances (2 Tim 4:3–4); but when the pastor's voice speaks with the authority of the office, his words are *always* toward the forgiveness of sins—even his retaining of sins. In the Large Catechism, Luther spoke similarly regarding the church: "Therefore everything in this Christian community is so ordered that everyone may daily obtain full forgiveness of sins." (LC II, 3).

---

[34]Such authority is predictable in any Marxist progression or movement. For example, Mussolini's motto was "Everything in the State, nothing outside the State, nothing against the State," allowing him to justify whatever the State did. Jonah Goldberg, *Liberal Fascism* (New York: Doubleday, 2007), 52. If the pastor can encapsulate everything in the church as "belonging to the realm of the gospel," then the congregation must seemingly obey his every whim.

## The Pastor as Servant—the Lord's Gift to the Church

A confusion exists today of who rightly qualifies as a "leader." Is it someone who acts on behalf of others according to God-given authority, or someone who controls a movement through his own power or force? When terms in Scripture are translated as "leader," it is not always the best option. In referring to pastors in particular, it may be better to opt for the rough rendering of "one who is regarded" or "one who has regard for" to avoid confusion. Since "overseer," "shepherd," and "servant" are clearly used of pastors, and since those in positions of political and religious authority occupy an office from which they receive that authority, the consistent understanding of the biblical text is that those in the pastoral office do not lead but rather serve.

Compounding any issues of translation is the fact that it remains challenging for moderns to avoid subconsciously interpreting "leader" according to Marxist influence. For Christians, this often results in a conflation of the pastoral office with the characteristics befitting the powerful motivator of a movement. In essence, a toxic quasi-office is created in which one attempts to serve God's sheep by speaking as their collective voice or by exerting control over them. When the pastor becomes a leader in this sense, it negatively impacts his actions, words, and demeanor. Rather than a loving shepherd who distributes the Lord's gifts, the visionary leader domineers with power and force. The "pastor as leader" assumption may be an innocent mistake, but the consequences can be dire. The church must therefore be diligent in correcting this false teaching.

# Johann Gerhard's *Sacrae Meditationes*

## On the Piety of Reformation Doctrine

*William C. Weinrich*

The Reformation is usually regarded as a revolution in doctrine and theology.[1] The theology of works and merit articulated by the schoolmen of the medieval universities was replaced by Martin Luther's insight that we are justified before God by grace alone (*sola gratia*), through faith alone (*sola fidei*) and for the sake of the innocent sufferings of Christ. That Reformation insight required a thorough theological reassessment of the biblical data, and the Lutheran reformers expended considerable energy reformulating the western theological heritage in light of the *sola gratia* doctrine. We are especially familiar with the significant works of this period. The *Liber Concordiae* (Book of Concord) is a compendium of definitions and expositions in light of questions arising from controversy with the Roman Catholics, with the Calvinists, and even among the Lutherans themselves. Further, the Reformation released a remarkable industry of biblical commentary and theological treatises, of which the *Loci Communes* of Philip Melanchthon and the *Loci Theologicae* of Martin Chemnitz are but two, albeit significant, examples.

---

[1] The care of souls, whether as a pastor or as a leader of the very successful *DOXOLOGY* program, has been the defining mark of Harold Senkbeil's vocation and practice. Indeed, within the circles of our church few have equaled the focused attention that the Reverend Senkbeil has given to that goal. It is an honor for me to offer the following reflections as a tribute to my long-time colleague and friend.

Yet we should remember that the Reformation was not merely an intellectual revolution. Luther was not in the first instance a university professor. He was a monk. And in this way he remained a monk: he desired to live in communion with God in freedom and without fear. To be sure, Luther came to understand that the life of the monastery—the life of the love of God—could be lived faithfully also in the vocations of the world. Nevertheless, the point is this: the Reformation freed man to live before God without fear; it freed man to love God wholly. To believe in God is to trust and to love him. As we know from Luther's Small Catechism, this is the meaning of the First Commandment.

It is recognized too little, however, that the Reformation resulted in a plenitude of devotional and spiritual works. The truth of the Reformation doctrine suggested a corresponding life of the spirit, and Reformation writers were not slow in producing books to assist evangelical congregations in the practice of the spiritual life according to the gospel. A classic example of this is the *Sacrae Meditationes* of Johann Gerhard. Gerhard was himself an accomplished theologian who produced one of the most learned and profound of all early Lutheran dogmatical works, his *Loci Theologici* (1610–1621). What characterizes his work is a thorough knowledge and use of patristic and medieval sources. His theology thus fruitfully incorporates the fullness of the catholic heritage. Indeed, the word now used for the study of the early fathers, *patrologia*, was first coined by Gerhard.

Gerhard was something of a prodigy. Born in 1582, as a young man he came under the influence of Johann Arndt, a Lutheran theologian whose *Sechs Bücher vom wahren Christentum* remains a classic of Lutheran devotional writing.[2] After studying theology at the universities of Wittenberg and Jena, Gerhard received a lectorship at Jena at the age of 23. In the following year, 1606, he wrote his *Sacrae Meditationes*.[3] In 1616 Gerhard was promoted to professor of theology at Jena, a post that he held until his death in 1637.

---

[2] For an English translation, see Johann Arndt, *True Christianity* (ed. and trans. Peter Erb; Mahwah, N.J.: Paulist Press, 1979).

[3] All citations in the present essay are from Johann Gerhard, *Sacred Meditations* (trans. C. W. Heisler; Philadelphia: Lutheran Publication Society, 1896; repr., Malone, Tex.: Repristination Press, 1998).

Luther was much influenced by late medieval piety and devotional writing. He was fond of John Tauler, a late fourteenth-century spiritual writer of Strassbourg, as well as of the anonymous spiritual treatise entitled, *Germanica Theologia*. Luther's indebtedness to St. Bernard of Clairvaux is well known. These late medieval devotional writers, in addition to the *Imitatio Christi* of Thomas á Kempis, form the background also of Johann Arndt's great devotional writing, *Wahres Christentum*, which Arndt was composing at the very time when Gerhard was writing his own *Sacrae Meditationes*. Indeed, Gerhard's *Sacrae Meditationes* stands firmly in the western spiritual tradition represented by St. Augustine, Gregory the Great, and St. Bernard. Consider these words of Gerhard's Ninth Meditation: "Without the love of God we have no desire for eternal life; and how then can we become sharers of that highest Good, if we do not love it, if we do not desire it, if we do not seek it?"[4] In this sentence Gerhard echoes the deep well-springs of Augustinian spirituality passed on through the medieval period by Gregory, Bernard, and Thomas á Kempis.

Yet, the language of love, of desire, and of seeking does not arise from Augustine. It is the language of the Bible. And this language of love is not that of *agape*, which is also the language of mercy and of unmerited favor. The language of the Bible concerning love for God is the language of *eros*, erotic love which is filled with desire for its object and seeks union with it. "Love Wisdom passionately (ἐράσθητι αὐτῆς) and she will preserve you; . . . embrace her (περιχαράκωσον αὐτήν) and she will exalt you" (LXX Prov 4:6, 8). The language of passion, of love, had proven difficult for early Christians. While the language of love was common in the Bible, they were faced with a Stoic philosophy which limited, if it did not exclude, passions from the moral life. According to the Stoics, the passions—such as fear, anger, and passionate love—were unruly like an angry sea and tossed the human person toward the rocks of unwanted and unstable ends. The wise man, therefore, seeks to free himself from such disordered impulses that hinder him from

[4]Gerhard, Meditation IX on "Loving God Alone" in *Sacred Meditations*, 52.

attaining good and noble goals. The mark of wisdom is tranquility and the absence of passion (ἀπάθεια).[5]

The church fathers could not, however, adopt this Stoic understanding of tranquility. The Scriptures demanded that they make spiritual sense of passionate love and the desire that lies within it. What mattered, they argued, was not the affections in themselves; they are neither good nor evil. What is important are the ends that the passions serve and those ends are determined by the object of love and desire. The truly spiritual man loves God; indeed, the love of God was implanted in man at the beginning as that which moved man to do the good. As Gregory of Nyssa could simply write: "We are led to God by desire as though drawn by a rope."[6] For Gregory, the infinity of God implied that throughout all eternity the love of God would move the blessed to a greater and greater love, without ever loving God perfectly. Eternal life was the movement of love. But the desire of love was not only the substance of eternal life; Christian life itself was a movement of love. In his famous exegesis of Romans 5:5, St. Augustine argued that the hope of faith is secure and certain because in the gift of the Holy Spirit love for God has been poured into our hearts. The activity of the Holy Spirit is to redirect our desire, our love, toward God and so direct our lives toward their true end and goal. In his *Homilies on First John*, Augustine described the "whole life of a good Christian" as a "holy longing" (*sanctum desiderium*), that is, a desire made holy through the divine Spirit who binds us with God in love. To desire is to seek after that which you do not possess fully. And so Augustine wrote: "What you long for you do not yet see, but by longing you are made capacious so that when what you are to see has come, you may be filled."[7] Our holy desire for God is the very "place" that is filled by God, the proper goal and

---

[5] An outstanding study of the Stoics (Seneca, Epictetus, Marcus Aurelius) and the moral life is C. Kavin Rowe, *One True Life: The Stoics and Early Christians as Rival Traditions* (New Haven: Yale University Press, 2016), 13–82.

[6] Gregory of Nyssa, *Homily on the Song of Songs* 1 (PG 48:89).

[7] St. Augustine, "Tractate 4.6.2," *Tractates on the Gospel of John 112–124. Tractates on the First Epistle of John* (trans. John W. Rettig; Fathers of the Church 92; Washington, DC: Catholic University of America Press, 1995), 179.

end of all pure love. Thus Augustine wrote in his *Confessions*[8] that his desire was not to know more about God, but to be more stable *in* God.[9] The goal of human life is not a matter of the intellect; it is a matter of the heart. Man was made to love God, and so the goal of human life, the purpose of human life, is to know God and to be known by him. In such a mutual knowledge lies a perfected delight in the vision of God. Man finds himself in that joy which is nothing other than to see the face of God. As the psalmist sings: "You have said, 'Seek my face.' My heart says to you, 'Your face, Lord, do I seek'" (Ps 27:8).

At the very beginning of his *Confessions*, Augustine wrote that man was made for God and man's soul is restless until it finds its rest in God.[10] In this world of change and instability man's soul experiences an aimless wandering which is the result of man's sin of pride. Man desires to praise God (for to that he was created), yet too proud to praise God, man is set upon a life of frustrated loves that are the witnesses of his sin.[11] Pride, unfulfilled love, restlessness: these are the elements of man's life apart from God.

When one turns to the *Sacrae Meditationes* of Gerhard, one quickly detects the influence of such Augustinian notions. The Ninth Meditation of Gerhard is entitled, "On Loving God Alone" (*de amando solo Deo*). As did Augustine, Gerhard wrote that our purpose as human beings is to "love Him who is the Highest Good, in whom is every good thing and without whom there is nothing that is truly good."[12] In words that seem to echo Augustine's *Confessions* directly, Gerhard stated: "No created thing can really satisfy our soul's desires, for no creature possesses all of perfect good in itself." And toward the end of

---

[8] All citations in the present essay are from Saint Augustine, *Confessions* (trans. Henry Chadwick; Oxford: Oxford University Press, 1991).

[9] Augustine, *Confessions*, VIII.1: "My desire was not to be more certain of you but to be more stable in you. But in my temporal life everything was in a state of uncertainty, and my heart needed to be purified from the old leaven" (Chadwick, 133).

[10] Augustine, *Confessions*, I.1: "You stir man to take pleasure in praising you, because you have made us for yourself, and our heart is restless until it rests in you" (Chadwick, 3).

[11] Augustine, *Confessions*, I.5–6 (Chadwick, 5–6).

[12] Gerhard, Meditation IX on "Loving God Alone" in *Sacred Meditations*, 49.

this meditation Gerhard wrote: "The love of God is life and rest to our souls."[13] The influence of Augustine is on the surface and easily recognized. Gerhard even adopted Augustine's exegesis of Romans 5:5, which he explicitly quoted: "He dwells in our souls by love, because the love for God is shed abroad in the hearts of the elect by the Holy Spirit." Echoing Augustine again, he continued: "There is no peace of mind without the love of God."[14] In these passages concerning our love for God, Gerhard employed the verb *amo*, the Latin term equivalent to the Greek ἐράω and signifying the passionate love of the heart.

Yet Gerhard was not only a disciple of St. Augustine; he was also a disciple of Martin Luther and a staunch defender of the doctrine of the Reformation. Thus, although in many ways Gerhard echoed Augustine, there is nonetheless a different sentiment, a different devotional quality or tone in Gerhard. One can see this straightaway in the First Meditation, "True Confession of Sin." For Augustine, the restlessness of the soul arises from a disordered desire. That is, the wayward soul desires what is disharmonious with the immortal soul whose rest lies in the immortal God. The wayward soul loves what is in fact dissimilar to itself and is, so to speak, out of place and in search of a home. For Gerhard, however, the restless soul is restless for another and very different reason. The soul is sinful and lies under the judgment of God. While Augustine thought of man as lost, Gerhard thought of man as judged. Thus, Gerhard began his First Meditation by addressing the holy God who is the just judge: "O holy God, You just Judge, my sins are ever before Your eyes and present to Your thought."[15] Man stands before God as sinner and so is restless like a convicted thief who cannot look the judge in the eye. This restlessness of the sinful soul is captured by these words of Gerhard that immediately follow those just quoted: "Every hour I think of death, for every hour death threatens me. Every day I think of the judgment of God, because for every day I must give an account at the Day of Judgment."[16] The restlessness of the soul is the anxiety of the convicted before the final judgment.

---

[13]Gerhard, Meditation IX on "Loving God Alone" in *Sacred Meditations*, 54.

[14]Gerhard, Meditation IX on "Loving God Alone" in *Sacred Meditations*, 54.

[15]Gerhard, Meditation I on "True Confession of Sin" in *Sacred Meditations*, 11.

[16]Gerhard, Meditation I on "True Confession of Sin" in *Sacred Meditations*, 11.

The emphasis of the First Meditation, however, is not on judgment and death. It is on "true confession of sins." The restless soul is restless because it is everywhere accused of sin and there is no place of respite from this accusation. Consider the all-encompassing scope of these accusers: "My adversary, the devil, accuses me"; "All the elements [air, water, fire, earth] rise in judgment against me";[17] "The holy angels . . . accuse me also"; "The very voice of God, the divine law, is also my accuser"; and finally, "God, the inflexible Judge, the almighty executor of His own eternal law, accuses me."[18] Our souls are restless because they are accused and found wanting *coram deo*, before the tribunal of God.

One cannot say that the analysis of man's restlessness is more universal or all-encompassing in Gerhard than in Augustine. But it is fair to say that in Gerhard man's predicament is more dire, more fearful. The Augustinian restlessness has a certain psychological element in it which makes the world strange with false allures. That is absent from Gerhard. For Gerhard man's restlessness possesses a sense of dread, for man faces an accusing world before a holy and just Judge. That sense of dread is absent from Augustine.

But what about the rest that every soul seeks and desires? Our souls find their rest when they rest in God. So wrote Augustine. It was as if the soul had found its way back home after being lost in the woods. And indeed, the Parable of the Prodigal Son provided the basic framework for Augustine's *Confessions*, which depicts the soul as in a far country being led back home by the still voice of God. In Gerhard things are very different. The rest of the soul lies in the safety of a refuge. "Where shall I flee?" asked Gerhard, quoting Psalm 139.[19] Gerhard's rhetorical question may be compared to the

---

[17]Typical is this: "The earth declares, 'I have supplied you with bread and wine for your nourishment. Yet you have abused all these things, and hast brought our common Creator into contempt; let all our blessings therefore be turned into instruments to torture you!'" Meditation I on "True Confession of Sin" in *Sacred Meditations*, 13.

[18]For the entire passage see Meditation I on "True Confession of Sin" in *Sacred Meditations*, 12–14. There can be no place of respite on the earth because the sinner has "offended the Lord of all creatures."

[19]Gerhard, Meditation I on "True Confession of Sin" in *Sacred Meditations*, 14.

rhetorical questions of Augustine at the beginning of his *Confessions*. Augustine asked, "How shall I call upon my God?" To call upon God is to beseech him to come into me, but God who fills the universe is already in me. According to Augustine's understanding, God is ever close to us; it is the heart of man that is far from God. Therefore, it is in the interior of the restless heart that God calls to us. Gerhard's rhetorical question, "Where shall I flee?" expresses very different spiritual sentiments and experiences. For Augustine, to seek God is to go deeper into one's own heart. For Gerhard, to seek God is to flee from oneself and find safety in another: "To You, O blessed Christ, my only Redeemer and Savior, do I flee for refuge. . . . In me there is nothing but sin that deserves Your condemnation; in You there is nothing but grace, which affords me a blessed hope of salvation."[20] The soul finds its rest when it has received the God of grace—and this God of grace is the Crucified One. Quoting Canticles 2:14, Gerhard wrote: "I hear a voice which bids me, hide in the clefts of the rock." And Gerhard interpreted this Old Testament text through 1 Corinthians 10:4: "You are the immovable Rock, and Your wounds are its clefts. In them I will hide myself against the accusations of the whole world."[21] At this point it was not Augustine but perhaps Bernard who influenced the thought of Gerhard.

The spirituality of the late medieval period was centered upon the sufferings of Christ. The frequency of the *ecce homo* paintings which depict the suffering Christ by way of his wounds is illustrative. This emphasis, however, also entered Christian hymnody as is evidenced by the famous hymn, *Salve caput cruentatum*. Attributed to Bernard but perhaps written in the fourteenth century, this hymn was well-known at the time of the Reformation and was translated by the Lutheran hymnist, Paul Gerhardt, as *O Haupt voll Blut und Wunden*.[22] It was later made famous by J. S. Bach in his Passion Oratorio. Listen to this selection from the hymn:

---

[20]Gerhard, Meditation I on "True Confession of Sin" in *Sacred Meditations*, 14.
[21]Gerhard, Meditation I on "True Confession of Sin" in *Sacred Meditations*, 15.
[22]"O Sacred Head, Now Wounded," *Lutheran Service Book* (St. Louis: Concordia, 2006), 449, 450.

Salve, caput cruentatum
totum spinis coronatum
conquassatum, vulneratum,
arundine verberatum
facie sputis illita
Salve, cuius dulcis vultus
Immutatus et incultus
Immutavit suum florem
Totus versus in pallorem
Quem coeli tremet curia.


Dum me mori est necesse
Noli mihi tunc deesee;
In tremenda mortis hora
Veni, Jesu, absque mora,
Tuere me et libera.
Cum me jubes emigrare,
Jesu care, tunc appare;
O amator amplectende,
Temet ipsum tunc ostende
In cruce salutifera.


Hail! O bloody head,
Completely crowned with thorns,
Beaten and wounded,
Whipped with cords,
Smeared on the face with spit.
Hail! O sweet face of Him
So changed and disfigured
It has changed his bloom
Wholly to a color pallid and white,
Which the hosts of heaven feared.


When the time has come for me to die,
Do not will at that time to desert me;
At the fearful hour of death
Come, Jesus, without delay
To help me and to deliver me.
When you demand that I depart,

Dear Jesus, at that time be near,
O Lover, enfold me,
And may You show Yourself
In the cross that brings salvation.

We might well wonder whether Gerhard had such a hymn in mind when he wrote his Second Meditation, "An Exercise of Repentance from Our Lord's Passion." Certainly the beginning words express the same piety. Addressing his own soul, Gerhard wrote:

Behold, O faithful soul, the grief of your Lord upon the cross. His gaping wounds as He hangs there, and the awful agony of His death. That head, before which the angelic spirits bow in reverential fear, is pierced with crowded thorns; that face, beautiful above the sons of men, is defiled by the spit of the ungodly; those eyes, more luminous than the sun, darken in death; those ears, accustomed to the praises of the angelic hosts, are greeted with the insults and taunts of sinners; that mouth which spoke as never man spoke, and teaches the angels, is made to drink the vinegar and the gall; those feet, at whose footstool the profoundest adoration is paid, are pierced with nails; those hands, which have stretched out the heavens, are extended upon the cross and fastened with spikes; that body, the most sacred abode and the purest habitation of the Godhead, is scourged and pierced with a spear.[23]

The immensity of the event is a revelation of the divine wrath: "If this be done to the Just and Holy One, what shall be done to sinners?" But the immensity of the event is also a divine plea to the sinner that he repent. Out of his deep agony Christ speaks to us:

Let us hear our Savior, O my beloved soul, crying aloud to us. . . . From His cross He cries, 'Behold, O sinful man, what I am suffering for you; to you I cry, because for you I am dying. . . . Though my

[23]Gerhard, Meditation II on "An Exercise of Repentance from our Lord's Passion" in *Sacred Meditations*, 16–17.

outward sufferings are so great, far greater is the agony of My heart, because I find you so ungrateful.'[24]

Sin is not in the first instance a matter of false belief; nor in the first instance is sin even a stubborn will. At bottom sin is a cold heart toward the love of God. From the cross the Savior makes a plea for repentance. The cry of the Savior is for an answer from the heart of the sinner. Thus, Gerhard concluded this Second Meditation with a prayer: "Have mercy upon us, have mercy upon us, O You who are the only God of mercy, and turn our stony hearts to You!"[25]
The work of the cross is not to enflame a love that has grown cold. The work of the cross is to "turn our stony hearts" and so to give to us a love that has been extinguished. "The very foundation and principle of a holy life is godly sorrow for sin," wrote Gerhard at the beginning of his Third Meditation.[26] Without such sorrow in the heart there is no salvation: "Christ's satisfaction is of no effect except in the heart of the truly contrite."[27] A stony heart cannot engender the flame of love. And, therefore, Gerhard ended his Third Meditation with the prayer: "May God work true repentance in us through his Holy Spirit."[28]
The hymn, *Salve, caput cruentatum*, addressed Christ as one who loves us: *O amator, amplectende*—"O Lover, enfold us." Yet, although

---

[24]Gerhard, Meditation II on "An Exercise of Repentance from our Lord's Passion" in *Sacred Meditations*, 19–20.

[25]Gerhard, Meditation II on "An Exercise of Repentance from our Lord's Passion" in *Sacred Meditations*, 20.

[26]Gerhard, Meditation III on "The Benefits of True Repentance" in *Sacred Meditations*, 21.

[27]Gerhard, Meditation III on "The Benefits of True Repentance" in *Sacred Meditations*, 22. Of course, this statement is a conclusion to a line of thought: "Where there is true penitence there is forgiveness of sin; where there is forgiveness of sin there is the grace of God; where the grace of God is there is Christ; where Christ is there is Christ's merit; where Christ's merit is there is satisfaction for sin; where there is satisfaction there is justification; where there is justification there is a glad and quiet conscience; where there is peace of conscience there is the Holy Spirit; where the Holy Spirit is present there is the ever blessed Trinity; and where the Holy Trinity is there is life eternal. Therefore where there is true penitence there is life eternal." *Sacred Meditations*, 21.

[28]Gerhard, Meditation III on "The Benefits of True Repentance" in *Sacred Meditations*, 26.

the language is that of passionate love—*amator*—the occasion is the hour of death. It is difficult to describe the love of God for us as that of the passionate Lover, for God's love for the sinner is that of mercy and sacrifice. The embrace of Christ at the hour of our death is not the embrace of a young lover seeking a kiss. It is the embrace of a love that seeks to comfort and uphold. The union of that embrace seeks to bring the sinner over into the life of God through an embrace that is stronger than death. In the Ninth Meditation, "On Loving God Only" (*De amando Deo solo*), Gerhard first spoke of God's love for us, for which he used the terms *dilectio* and *diligo*. These are not terms of passionate love but indicate more the high value placed upon someone or something. One may recall the words of Luther in his Small Catechism: "not with gold or silver, but with His holy, precious blood and with His innocent suffering and death" (SC II, 2). However, when Gerhard spoke of our love for God, he used the term for passionate love, *amo*. The purpose of God's mercy in the sufferings of his Son is that we might love God with all our heart. He is to be the sole object of our love, the only object of our joy. Founded upon true repentance, this love can be expressed in terms of passion and the union such love brings: "What your love is, that you yourself are, because your love changes you into itself; love is the strongest bond (*summum vinculum*), because the lover and the object loved become one." "What is it," Gerhard then asked, "that has joined together a righteous God and lost sinners, so infinitely removed from each other?" He answered, "Infinite love."[29] Love unites and transforms. If you love God and divine things, you shall become divine. Faith itself, the sole cause of our justification, is not true faith if the love for God is absent. Faith comprehends God's love and so begins that transformation whereby we love God, a transformation that will be perfected and completed in the life to come: "The love of God is the delight of the mind, the paradise of the soul; it destroys the power of the world, conquers the devil, shuts the mouth of hell, and opens wide the gate of heaven."[30]

St. Augustine had written that we are made for God and that our souls are restless until they find their rest in him. In Johann

---

[29]Gerhard, Meditation IX on "Loving God Alone" in *Sacred Meditations*, 52.
[30]Gerhard, Meditation IX on "Loving God Alone" in *Sacred Meditations*, 53.

Gerhard, St. Augustine met the Reformation doctrine of justification of the sinner. The soul's restlessness is due to the attacks of Satan and its own sin; but the love of God has been poured into our hearts through the Holy Spirit. The sinner, therefore, is at rest. As Gerhard said, "The love of God is life and rest to our souls. . . . There is no peace of conscience except to those who are justified by faith; there is no true love except in those who have a child-like trust in God."[31]

---

[31]Gerhard, Meditation IX on "Loving God Alone" in *Sacred Meditations*, 54.

# Language Matters

## Speaking the Words of Faith into Daily Life

*Andrew Pfeiffer*

Language matters. Words matter. They matter in the church, and they matter in the world. Anyone who has tried to buy a train ticket in Germany without knowing German, or attempted to speak with a deaf person without knowing sign language, has quickly realized the significance of having clear communication. For the church, however, the stakes are much higher. Language matters for an articulate and truthful confession of faith. It matters for preaching, prayer, pastoral care, and witness. And language matters when the church and individual Christians seek to communicate the gospel wherever God has placed them in the world.

This essay looks briefly at some different types of *words of faith*. It then highlights the necessity of understanding the *words of daily life*, the language of the culture in which we live. Finally, it tentatively suggests a few examples where the words of faith and the words of life might have a meaningful dialogue, and encourages the reader to continue to engage in that task.

There is no privileged position given to the words of the culture. We do not start from the point of view that if the church simply used and reflected the language of the surrounding culture then it would find the key to its communication and its growth. For one reason, it does not matter what language the gospel is spoken in—the message of Christ crucified will always be a stumbling block and foolishness for some (1 Cor 1:23). The church can use careful and culturally insightful language when proclaiming the truth that fallen humanity wants to live an autonomous existence, but the reality is that ours is not the first generation that does not like to hear about sin. That deafness is part of the human condition. So while we do need to understand and analyze the words of the culture, that process serves more as a diagnostic tool to assist with clear communication, rather than as a means of determining the message.

In addition, social researcher Hugh Mackay reminds us that learning the "tribal language" is part of developing a sense of belonging and a sense of identity in any group, and that includes the church.[1] There is a faith language and a liturgical language. Part of Christian discipleship is learning that language, and then seeking to pass on both the faith and the language of the faith. At the same time, it is necessary to try and understand the words of the culture in which the church finds itself. That assists the church in speaking the words of faith in a way that invites others to join the conversation and even to consider those words of faith for themselves.

## The Words of Faith

Eugene Peterson devoted much of his writing to addressing what he called bilingualism. He encouraged consistency and integrity when it comes to language and Christian communication. Peterson stated:

> I want to eliminate the bilingualism that we either grow up with or acquire along the way of growing up: one language for talking about God and the things of God, salvation and Jesus, singing hymns and going to church; another language we become proficient in as we attend school, get jobs, play ball, go to dances, and buy potatoes and blue jeans.[2]
>
> There is no "Holy Ghost" language used for matters of God and salvation, and then a separate secular language for buying cabbages

---

[1]Hugh Mackay, *What Makes Us Tick? The Ten Desires that Drive Us* (Sydney, New South Wales: Hachette Australia, 2010), 172.

[2]Eugene H. Peterson, *The Word Made Flesh: The Language of Jesus in his Stories and Prayers* (Colorado Springs: Eerdmans, 2008), 267.

and cars. "Give us this day our daily bread" and "pass the potatoes" come out of the same language pool.[3]

Not only did Peterson have the goal of eliminating such bilingualism, but as a gifted communicator he also contributed to that goal.

Peterson distinguished three types of language in the church: preaching, teaching, and more informal conversation.[4] To this I would add liturgical language. Churches call specific people to preach and teach, and those people operate mainly in the public and communal realm. They function with a commitment to speak faithfully the truth of God and the teaching of the church in group settings. Their language, therefore, is measured and considered. The church prepares and trains its leaders in some depth for preaching and teaching. Pastoral candidates learn the original biblical languages as well as the theological language of the church in its historic creeds, confessions, and systematic theologies. They learn homiletical and pedagogical skills that enable them to convey effectively and clearly the content of their studies to their hearers.

These biblical, theological, and historical learnings are critical for the church to be a church of the word. They are to be learned and used by those who would claim to be spiritual authorities. The difficult words, concepts, and truths of the faith need to be received and taught even if the culture of the day is unreceptive (at least initially). To do so takes wisdom.

In addition to preaching and teaching, however, Peterson drew our attention to a third language of the faith to which all Christians are called. This he described as "informal conversational give and take."[5]

Preaching begins with God: God's Word, God's action, God's presence. Teaching expands on what is proclaimed, instructing us in the implications of the text, the reverberations of the truth in the world, the specific ways in which God's Word shapes in detail the way we live our daily lives between birth and death. But unstructured,

---

[3]Peterson, *The Word Made Flesh*, 2.
[4]Peterson, *The Word Made Flesh*, 13.
[5]Peterson, *The Word Made Flesh*, 13.

informal conversations arise from incidents and encounters with one
another that take place in the normal course of going about our lives
in families and workplaces, on playgrounds and while shopping for
groceries, in airport terminals waiting for a flight and walking with
binoculars in a field with friends watching birds. . . . Most of the
words that we speak are spoken in the quotidian contexts of eating
and drinking, shopping and traveling, making what we sometimes
dismiss as "small talk."[6]

When it comes to informal conversations, Christians are encouraged
to listen attentively to those around them, to learn the language of
the world they live in, to be interested in other people, and to be
interesting people themselves. But they also need to continue being
equipped in the language of the faith if such interactions and atten-
tiveness are going to serve as an opportunity for communicating the
gospel.

Peterson explored the use of the language of the faith—the
words of Jesus to be specific—in these informal unstructured conversations. For example: the Good Samaritan story becomes a
springboard to reflect on a personal response to the challenge to go
and love;[7] the story of the owner giving his fig tree a good dose of
manure becomes an opportunity to thank God for his patience;[8] and
the story of the lost brothers becomes a call for people to think about
the ways they themselves might be lost rather than about how they
are finding those who are.[9]

In a similar way, but with preachers in mind, Jacob Preus speaks
of using language and metaphors in such a way that the gospel is
heard as a dynamic and eventful word in people's lives. For example,
Preus demonstrates: how the fifth petition of the Lord's Prayer might
be a resource for ministry to someone who has found themselves
in overwhelming debt;[10] how Jesus the bread of life might speak

---

[6]Peterson, *The Word Made Flesh*, 14.
[7]Peterson, *The Word Made Flesh*, 32–43.
[8]Peterson, *The Word Made Flesh*, 65–74.
[9]Peterson, *The Word Made Flesh*, 85–98.
[10]Jacob A. O. Preus, *Just Words: Understanding the Fullness of the Gospel*
(St. Louis: Concordia, 2000), 99–103.

to those who are feeling unfulfilled in life while seemingly having everything;[11] and how reflecting on the rich metaphor of marriage in the Old and New Testaments—especially in contrast with the world's understanding of marriage—might strengthen those who are struggling in their own relationships.[12]

This is all rich reflection, but it relies on an understanding of the stories of faith. The task of linking these words to daily life is not completed simply when a connection is made. It requires study of the word and of its stories for effective gospel communication. The metaphors need to be explained and unpacked. The language and words of the faith need to be well known so that God's message may be spoken into people's daily situations where fear, guilt, and alienation are realities.

Even while defending the need to work on cultural language connectors, Norma Cook Everist is clear about the prerequisite for Christians to learn the words and language of the Christian faith.

> People need to learn about the stories, concepts and truths about God from the Scriptures, the language of the liturgy and the confessions of the church. Biblical illiteracy and ignorance about church history and theology undermines the life and mission of a congregation.[13]

The first appeal of this essay is that if the church wants to speak the faith meaningfully into the market place, the so-called public square, and if it wants its people to speak the faith meaningfully to family or friends, to neighbor or workmate, then the starting point is not the world, but the word. The starting point is to learn the language of the faith.[14] Absorb the biblical stories, study church history, know the

---

[11]Preus, *Just Words*, 71–76.

[12]Preus, *Just Words*, 157–63.

[13]Norma Cook Everist, "Learn to Share Christ in the Language of People's Daily Lives" in *Christian Education as Evangelism* (ed. Norma Cook Everist; Minneapolis: Fortress, 2007), 123.

[14]For a useful resource that includes a glossary of basic Christian language, an introduction to the church year, and a brief explanation of the liturgy, see David Strelan, *God For Us: An Introduction to Lutheran Teaching* (Adelaide, South Australia: Lutheran Publishing House, 1988), 53–62. For an excellent description

teachings of the church, become familiar with the language of the liturgy, memorize the Ten Commandments, the Creed, and the Lord's
Prayer such that these all become integral to everyday thinking and
living.[15]

With a series of questions, Paul gave expression to one of the
challenges facing the church: "How then will they call on him in
whom they have not believed? And how are they to believe in him
of whom they have never heard? And how are they to hear without
someone preaching? And how are they to preach unless they are
sent?" (Rom 10:14–15). To build on this thought, we might ask,
how can they learn the faith unless they are taught it? And how
can they be taught the faith without someone teaching? And
how are they to teach unless they are properly prepared?

## The Words of Life

Sometimes people make a well-meaning appeal for the church to
be "relevant" and "accessible" to the predominant culture of the day.
Cultural relevance is the catchword. After all, who would not want to
be culturally relevant? The appeal, however, needs some clarification.

On the one hand it has merit. We cannot ignore that fact that
the church always exists within a specific cultural setting, and the
daily life of any Christian is lived in a specific life situation. Nobody
ought to defend the church leader who deliberately ignores that reality, or who refuses to discuss the danger of being irrelevant or inaccessible to outsiders, or who even uses the language of the church to
restrict people as though the church were an exclusive club.

---

of the church seasons and liturgical colors, see *Lutheran Hymnal with Supplement*
(Adelaide, South Australia: Lutheran Publishing House, 1989), 3–5.

[15]I am reminded of this need every time I offer adult instruction to new
members. Sometimes when I try to introduce a theological or liturgical concept in "everyday language," I flounder around using many words when one
would do if the meaning were known. Sometimes those within the group will
say, "How does the church describe that idea? What word or words does it
use?" Then we can participate in the conversation with more understanding.
And so as a group we inevitably discover the helpful resources that our church
has given us for just this task—that is, we discover the language of the faith.

On the other hand, the role of culture can be overstated. One's contemporary culture can never determine the Christian message. The core content of the faith is received and passed on, from one generation to the next (1 Cor 11:23–25; 15:3–7; Jude 3). As the church receives the faith and passes it on, it seeks the guidance of the Holy Spirit with the intention of receiving the truth of Christ (John 14:25; 15:26; 16:12–15). To that extent Christian teaching develops over the centuries; but while the culture might raise significant questions, the church seeks its spiritual guidance not from the culture but from divine revelation: the Bible.

Missionary and theological educator Greg Lockwood notes the challenge that is sometimes raised when speaking difficult words and foreign concepts in the mission field. He is aware of the temptation to ignore or give limited attention to aspects of the faith in light of the specific culture.[16] Just because the book of Romans might seem to be more meaningful to the Western ear, does that mean it is not taught in Africa? Idolatry might present itself in different ways across various cultural settings, but at the bottom line all people share the same need for repentance and faith. Building on Gerhard Maier's response to Rudolf Bultmann, Lockwood challenges the idea that each culture is so unique, so different, that in effect it needs its own type of theology.

> We need to beware of the myth of the thoroughly different Hispanic [person] or Melanesian [person]. The longer the missionary stays in another culture, the more he realizes that under the surface configurations of our differing culture and language are all basically the same. All human beings, for example, are concerned for their own reputation and honour, their own name.[17]

The challenge for the church is to explore how idolatry, for example, reveals itself in different cultures, which is one of the reasons cultural

---

[16]Gregory Lockwood, "The Role of the Sacraments in Gospel Communication" in *The Role of the Laity in Gospel Communication: A Booklet of Essays Delivered at the Seventh Annual Missions and Communications Congress, Concordia Theological Seminary, Fort Wayne, Indiana, October 23–25, 1991* (ed. Eugene W. Bunkowske and Paul W. Mueller; Fullerton, Calif.: R. C. Law & Co., 1992), 108.

[17]Lockwood, "The Role of the Sacraments in Gospel Communication," 108.

and language studies remain significant for the church and the missionary. To recall the opening sentences of this paper, it is difficult to communicate in depth—certainly spiritual depth—without speaking the so-called heart language of the people around you.[18]

This idea of heart language can be looked at from two different perspectives. There are cultural heart languages and more personal heart languages.

When politicians want to point out a social problem or denounce a specific action, they sometimes say, "That is un-Australian." Recently when a politician in the United States suggested it should close its borders to particular people, that pronouncement was condemned by some commentators as an un-American way of thinking and speaking. What they mean is that there exists a certain way of thinking and acting, as well as a certain language, recognizable by those who align themselves with that particular society. By implication, there are also ways of speaking or acting that are considered inconsistent with the core values of that same culture. Of course, the label "un-Australian" or "un-American" can be used as a political ruse simply to demean an alternate opinion. But when the vast majority of the population signals its agreement with the point made by receiving it without dissent, then the speaker has tapped into the cultural heart language.

In his study of Australian spirituality, Gary Bouma has taken this a step further and noted what could be called a cultural spiritual heart language. Australians, he says, have certain ways of thinking and expressing themselves when they reflect on religious and spiritual things. These include a certain spiritual shyness, a wariness of high-demand religion, a distancing from authoritarian leaders, a

---

[18]Eugene Bunkowske introduces this topic in his essay, "Booting Up for Receptor-Oriented Gospel Communication" in *Receptor-Oriented Gospel Communication (Making the Gospel User Friendly): A Booklet of Essays Delivered at the Fourth Annual Missions and Communications Congress, Concordia Theological Seminary, Fort Wayne, Indiana, September 28–30, 1988* (ed. Eugene W. Bunkowske and Richard French; Fullerton, Calif.: R. C. Law & Co., 1989), 11–34, where he explains the significance of encoding and decoding the message if accurate communication is to take place. He shows how any "cultural skin" is complex and that cross-cultural communication is more involved than merely learning a few jargon words or phrases so as to "connect" with people.

suspicion towards spiritual "gatekeepers," valuing the ability to laugh at oneself, and a serious commitment to life in the here and now.[19]

If the church is to speak in the public square, it needs to reflect on these findings. That does not mean the church works out what it is to say by being a weather vane and simply trying to see what the world wants to hear. But it does mean that when it speaks the church needs to reflect on the way Australians see and listen to "religious talk." Further, it means to back up the words of faith with the actions of faith, to be committed to the local parish but not in such a way that it leaves no time to serve in the world, to be self-deprecating, to respond in repentance and humility when the church has been wrong.

Everist explores what might be called more personal heart languages. She explains that when we think about words and language we need to move beyond the obvious. Language issues are not limited to whether we are speaking English or German or Spanish or Cantonese. These barriers are significant, and speaking only one language immediately limits the ability to connect to the wider world. The challenge Everist raises, however, is for educators to help people think about the language they use in daily life, and how they can begin to "translate the Bible and the theology of the church into phrases and concepts that prepare them to think, feel, relate and make decisions in the languages they speak all week."[20]

Through a variety of workshops, Everist asked people to reflect on the languages they spoke in the arena of their daily life, and she then categorized them under four umbrella terms: vocation, relationships, location, and outlook.[21] The first three are clearly the language of everyday life. For example, if someone begins a conversation with a new neighbor or a relative's friend at a Christmas party, it will not be long before the topics of workplace, family, and location arise. What do you do? Whom do you know here? Where do you live? Yet the final category of "outlook" may not be so easy to access. It refers to what might be called personal worldview or personality. One

---

[19]Gary Bouma, *Australian Soul: Religion and Spirituality in the Twenty-First Century* (Port Melbourne, Victoria: Cambridge University Press, 2006), 45–47.

[20]Everist, "Learn to Share Christ in the Language of People's Daily Lives," 124.

[21]Everist, "Learn to Share Christ in the Language of People's Daily Lives," 125.

person can speak the language of humor, another of tears, another of passion and enthusiasm for new things. Someone else can speak the language of art or imagination or discernment.

These personal heart languages are the way people typically speak with and relate to each other. Everist suggests that if the church wants to communicate the faith it needs to pay close attention to these categories of language and assist people to speak them in a faith-filled way. The challenge for the church is to:

> [Equip] all Christians educationally for sharing the gospel in words that connect to people where they are . . . it is not a question of convincing people to speak/preach/proclaim, but first of all seeing what it is people are already proclaiming in daily conversations. Do people understand the faith undergirding the decisions they make?[22]

This task will be easier to understand and also more likely to bear fruit when it is explored within the context of people's stations and vocations. The way in which faith undergirds decisions is not a generic question but a specific one. How does faith inform the choices we make as a father/mother, son/daughter, employer/employee, neighbor, or church member?[23] For example, I can now speak the language of grandparent, but what does it mean to do so as a Christian?

Once again, the challenge for the church is to study these cultural and personal languages in whatever situation it finds itself. These do not determine the message, but assist with its communication. They begin to alert us to when and where a culture and its people might be open or resistant to the core elements of Christian teaching.

---

[22]Everist, "Learn to Share Christ in the Language of People's Daily Lives," 123.

[23]For more on this point of the connection between station, vocation, and gospel communication, see Andrew Pfeiffer, "Christian Vocation and the Mission of God: A Missing Link?" *Lutheran Theological Journal* 48 (Dec. 2014): 160–71.

## Words in Faith and Life

What language, then, will the church use as it is involved in the likes of pastoral care, Christian witness, and corporate prayer? First it needs to know well the words of faith and not be afraid to use them. The church must also identify the vernacular of the particular culture it attempts to reach and serve with the word and sacraments. What topics do people tend to talk about and in what ways? What questions interest and concern them? What stories enliven them? The church can then act as a translator, bringing the words of faith and the words of life into conversation with each other. As the native speaker of the faith, the church invites others to participate in that same language of faith.

A few specific challenges to the church's success in these endeavors can be found in Australian culture (and perhaps in other Western cultures as well, such as the United States and parts of Europe). Mackay suggests there are ten desires that drive us, two of which will be explored in terms of what aspects or emphases of Christian teaching might speak to those desires. In doing so, the reader is invited to continue to explore this type of cross-cultural communication.

In Mackay's estimation, people are driven by *the desire to be taken seriously*. He suggests that most everyone wants to be recognized and acknowledged as a unique individual, and that much of what people do—both in a conventional sense in terms of work and interests, and also in the unconventional sense of non-conforming or aberrant behavior—is lived out of that desire.[24] Mackay therefore makes an interesting case that listening is the greatest gift to give another person because it demonstrates that someone actually cares.[25] He also suggests that one of the reasons counseling seems to work for some people is because counsellors are committed, even paid, to treat every client as a valued person and to listen attentively and sympathetically.[26]

Bernard Salt, in his thought-provoking social commentary on Australian society, describes what he calls "praise inflation" and how

---

[24]Mackay, *What Makes Us Tick?*, 2.
[25]Mackay, *What Makes Us Tick?*, 29.
[26]Mackay, *What Makes Us Tick?*, 32.

it can have significant consequences.[27] Whereas genuine praise is
rightly offered to those who earn it and readily received by those who
want to be taken seriously, "praise inflation" refers to the phenomenon of offering undeserved praise—that is, praise for things that in
themselves are not that noteworthy, like showing up to work on time
or doing the job you are paid to do. Such undue acclaim can hinder
people from reflecting on personal growth areas as well as existing
strengths, which in turn impedes professional growth and contribution to the wider workforce. "Praise inflation" can also result in an
inability to receive negative feedback or to be self-critical. Salt maintains that this form of mollycoddling has led to an entire generation
which perpetually needs to be validated and will struggle when such
affirmation is not forthcoming.[28]

Whether Mackay or Salt are entirely correct or not, such social
analyses challenge the church to reflect on what it has to say to
people who either seek to engage life as a serious pursuit, or who
struggle when receiving constructive criticism. When thinking of
*the desire to be taken seriously,* Christians know that their sense
of worth and value is directly related to their belief that "God has
made me and all creatures" (SC II, 1). They know the joy that comes
from finding out their choices in life do not make them God's children but his choice of them does. They know that in the death of
Jesus Christ God took sin and sinners seriously—he seriously dealt
with sin and he seriously loves sinners. And yet there is still work
to be done for clear gospel communication. What might be the best
language, the best images, the best metaphors to communicate these
truths to others? And how are the words best spoken?

---

[27]Bernard Salt, *The Big Tilt: What Happens When the Boomers Bust and the
Xers and Ys Inherit the Earth* (Prahran, Victoria: Hardie Grant Books, 2011),
170–72.

[28]Interestingly, he does not blame that generation for the problem. "The
baby boomers are to blame for praise inflation. If they hadn't continually
praised their generation Y offspring as kids, we wouldn't have a 20-something
workforce in a perpetual state of anxiety, seeking recognition and feedback for
what preceding generations regarded as merely doing their job." Salt, *The Big
Tilt,* 170.

People who want to be taken seriously sometimes have different questions, different concerns, and different contributions.
Preus suggests that when those questions end up in confusion,
there might be wisdom in exploring the metaphor of light and in
issuing an invitation to consider what it means that Jesus is the
light of the world.[29] Light offers a way through the darkness;
the "light at the end of the tunnel" is a reason for hope. There are
also those whose life situation has brought them to a place where
they think they have no one to turn to and no one to listen to them.
Preus thinks it might be helpful for them to explore the thought of
Christ as an intercessor, someone who not only listens but speaks
on people's behalf and in their defense.[30] When the challenges of
life lead someone to feel as though they do not belong anywhere,
and cannot seem to find their niche in life, Preus suggests giving attention to the notion of adoption and what it means to be
adopted as a son or daughter in the family of God.[31]

How did Jesus work with people who came to him with serious
questions, people who valued being taken seriously in his day? Jesus
interacted with them in various ways. For him, to take people seriously meant both to listen to their questions and to seek to engage
them in conversation, but also to move the conversation in a direction of discovery about one or more of God's truths. In Matthew
19:16 Jesus is asked, "What good thing must I do to inherit eternal
life?" The conversation ends with the questioner at the crossroads
of his life. While he thinks he has kept all the Ten Commandments,
Jesus challenges him with the thought that he has actually fallen at
the hurdle of the First Commandment, and still clings to another
god. This is a serious challenge to a serious question. In daily conversations in our world, people may not ask specifically what they
need to do to inherit eternal life, but they do have beliefs or thoughts
about eternity. Perhaps there is no eternity and this life is all there is,
or perhaps everyone is going to heaven and the way to get there
is to do the best you can with what you have. The second of those

---

[29]Preus, *Just Words*, 63–69.
[30]Preus, *Just Words*, 117–21.
[31]Preus, *Just Words*, 123–27.

assumptions, for example, is not far from the starting point of the inquiring man in Matthew 19.

In Luke 10:25 an expert in the law effectively asks the same serious question: "What must I do to inherit eternal life?" Again Jesus treats the man with respect and answers him, but this time Jesus tells a story and then asks the man to reflect on it. The man comes to his own conclusion and begins to discover the role of faith, love, and mercy in the big questions of life. The point for the believer, however, is not that the church must always have immediate answers for authentic people with weighty queries. Rather, the challenge is to find ways to receive people's serious questions seriously, to listen to people and their concerns for life, to invite them to explore life from within the worldview of the faith and with the language of faith, and perhaps even to learn Christ for themselves (Eph 4:20–21).

We close with a brief reflection on a second desire Mackay mentions: *the desire to be useful*.[32] Mackay explores what it might look like to be useful for others in human relationships and to find meaning in employment.[33] He also suggests it is important for people to have evidence that they are being useful, which is why people tend to set modest short-term goals so that at least something is achieved.[34] Of particular interest is the observation that this desire can also propel people to want to make the world a better place.[35]

This latter point seems to be a good place to begin when we think about words of faith to speak into this desire. Mackay says: "Anything we do to make the world a better place is useful; anything useful makes the world a better place. Civil societies don't just happen; they are a sum of countless useful acts by well-meaning people."[36]

Christians can immediately recognize here that the doctrine of vocation might speak to this desire to be useful. For example, this teaching enables the church to affirm that the good done in the world

---

[32]Mackay, *What Makes Us Tick?*, 129.
[33]Mackay, *What Makes Us Tick?*, 133–40.
[34]Mackay, *What Makes Us Tick?*, 140–43.
[35]Mackay, *What Makes Us Tick?*, 146.
[36]Mackay, *What Makes Us Tick?*, 149.

is for the benefit of all. We see such acts of civil righteousness at times of crises, as people help their neighbors, support their families, and even work with civil authorities in a way they normally do not.

However, the teaching also invites people to reflect more deeply on how God is always at work in daily life, and the meaning and purpose this gives to seemingly mundane activities. The idea of vocation—a divine calling—shifts the focus of life from simply performing kind and generous actions to the reality that God is at work as his people serve those around them wherever he has placed them. The sense of usefulness comes not just from participating in an act of kindness, but from serving as God's hands in the callings he has given in marriage, family, workplace, community, and even congregation.[37]

## Summary

Speaking the words of faith into daily life is not an easy task. It is a task of cross-cultural communication, requiring the church to learn the faith and the language of the faith (its confessions, its prayers, its pastoral wisdom), and to invite new generations to do the same. The words of life—that is, the language of the culture of the day—must also be learned. Yet this latter undertaking remains difficult since a culture's preferred or sanctioned language can change just when Christians think they have rightly comprehended it. (Indeed, social commentators are increasingly reluctant to make prophecies that extend too far into the future.) But the attempt to understand well contemporary cultural language and the personal languages of other people demonstrates a willingness to take the world seriously, to communicate the gospel cross-culturally as honestly as possible, and to invite others to consider the words of faith in a thoughtful and respectful way. Meaningful dialogue between these two words or languages will undoubtedly aid the church in its attempt to proclaim the good news of Jesus Christ to every creature under heaven.

---

[37]See Chad E. Hoover, *Vocation: God Serves Through Us* (St. Louis: Concordia, 2010).

# Mercy Work and Pastoral Care in Times of Tragedy

## An Introduction to Lutheran Practice

*Ross Edward Johnson*

Lutheran Christians have a long and active history of helping in times of tragedy. For example, Martin Luther and Johannes Bugenhagen are known for their benevolent work of comforting the sick and dying during the plague of 1527; and in the mid-1800s there was also C. F. W. Walther who led the Lutheran Church—Missouri Synod (LCMS) in opening numerous orphanages for children without hope. By the last half of the twentieth century, however, the emphasis on human care faded within confessional Lutheran congregations. Some of this was due to the rise and popularity of the Social Gospel Movement after World War I, which de-emphasized salvation by faith alone in Christ and instead emphasized ethics. Its focus, therefore, was not on preaching and receiving the sacraments, but rather social activism that improved the quality of life in the community. Unfortunately, in their effort to disassociate themselves from this bad theology, many Lutheran pastors "threw the baby out with the bathwater" and inadvertently removed themselves from works of compassion in times of tragedy.

Another significant factor in this decline of mercy work was the increased influence of the United States government's social welfare system. When the government began to do social work, the church at large slowly handed over her role of providing temporal care. Federal and state authorities began to give aid to the needy, bring relief during catastrophic disasters and tragedy, and take responsibility for abandoned or displaced children. Regrettably, this led to a decrease in congregational involvement in the community: the mindset of some pastors was that congregational charity should be confined to its members within, and clergy were to engage in word and sacrament ministry alone, nothing more.

By the twenty-first century, mercy work performed by the LCMS had waned throughout the world. People often met times of tragedy by sending checks to organizations like Lutheran World Relief or Lutheran Disaster Response, the Evangelical Lutheran Church in America's relief organization. The support was welcome, but the practice did distance churches from delivering care firsthand. Some Lutherans began to recognize that a vital aspect of congregational life had been lost and wondered how the shift had occurred. Why did pastors and laity go from reaching out to the sick and dying in Luther's day, and helping the orphaned and widowed during Walther's time, to merely supplying monetary support to organizations? When did churches lose sight of the intrinsic nature of the congregation's role of personally providing care and compassion? Why did so many in the LCMS overlook words in Scripture such as 1 John 3:16–18, which says, "By this we know love, that he laid down his life for us, and we ought to lay down our lives for the brothers. But if anyone has the world's goods and sees his brother in need, yet closes his heart against him, how does God's love abide in him? Little children, let us not love in word or talk but in deed and in truth"?

In short, the LCMS needed to reevaluate its practices of showing mercy and compassion through good works. Thankfully, an overhaul was deemed necessary and a renaissance has begun. President Matthew C. Harrison, former Executive Director of Lutheran World Relief and Human Care, helped raised awareness for mercy work in large part by drawing attention to our heritage. He wrote on historical topics such as how the early church performed acts of mercy; he reprinted works from both our Lutheran forefathers and the early church fathers on the topic; and he demonstrated to pastors that Lutherans have always cared for people in both body and soul. Harrison's work was principally inspired by his experiences following the terrorist attacks of September 11, 2001, which revealed the need for greater mercy work at the congregational level. Additionally, John Fale, currently the Executive Director of the Office of International Mission, traveled the world as Associate Director for Mercy Operations learning how best to reach out to the sick, downtrodden, and afflicted with both the gospel and material resources. These men, and others, revolutionized the way mercy work within the LCMS is understood today.

There is still much to be done. In a fallen world full of terrorism, natural disasters, hunger, disease, and various sources of despair, pastors have the opportunity to bring the good news about Jesus, coupled with mercy and compassion, to those who are hurting. To do so effectively, Lutheran pastors should be aware of the biblical basis and historic precedent of mercy work, including the heritage of their own church body. Accordingly, the first part of this essay will briefly cover the foundation laid in the New Testament, the example of the early church, and what preceded the aforementioned decrease and increase of activity in the LCMS. More importantly, however, those who are called to serve in Christ's stead *must* keep the gospel front and center in all their attempts to care for people's spiritual and temporal needs. The second part of this essay, then, will succinctly emphasize how pastors can bring comfort by staying focused on God's revealed will in his Son, by being theologians of the cross, and by presenting Christ himself through the word and in the divine service.

## New Testament Illustrations of Care for Body and Soul

Christian mercy work was not an invention of the Lutheran Reformation, nor was it even a creation of the early church; rather, its origins are found in Scripture. Mercy was especially exemplified in the life of Christ. By his incarnation, Jesus entered a broken, hostile world; in his ministry, he healed the sick, exorcized those afflicted by demons, and preached good news to the poor; by his passion and death, he suffered in the stead of every last person. Harrison, commenting on the use of a particular Greek term in the New Testament, emphasizes the love and care that drove Jesus to do these things:

"Mercy makes something happen. For Jesus, *splanchnizomai*, the verb form of *splachnon*, is always 'compassion giving birth to action.'"[1] The compassion that Jesus had for his people—the gut-wrenching concern that drove him to take action and help those in need—serves as a model for all Christians. An example of this is when Christ fed the 4,000 in the Gospel of Mark. Because the crowd had been so enamored and engrossed with Jesus' teaching, they failed to secure provisions for themselves. Knowing their plight, Jesus said, "I have compassion (*splanchnizomai*) on the crowd, because they have been with me now three days and have nothing to eat. And if I send them away hungry to their homes, they will faint on the way" (Mark 8:2–3). He did not continue to preach, nor did he separate himself from them. Rather, Christ took action to meet their physical need just as he had their spiritual need: "And they ate and were satisfied" (Mark 8:8).

The ministry of St. Paul contains both examples of caring for people in every need and exhortations to bear the burdens of others (Gal 6:2). For instance, Paul calls for congregational compassion without limits in his encouragement to the Galatian Christians: "Let us not grow weary of doing good. . . . So then, as we have opportunity, let us do good to everyone, and especially to those who are of the household of faith" (Gal 6:9–10). What is more, Paul not only instructs others to give and serve but did so himself, such as when he spent years gathering funds in Macedonia and Corinth for the poor in Jerusalem. As Mark Seifrid, an expert on Pauline studies, observes, "Paul regards the collection for Jerusalem not merely as service to relieve need (although it does do precisely that) but, more fundamentally, to bring about common thanksgiving to God and interchange among the churches."[2] The Macedonians were thus commended by Paul, "for in a severe test of affliction, their abundance of joy and their extreme poverty have overflowed in a wealth and generosity on their part" (2 Cor 8:2). He purposely identified them as an

---

[1]Matthew C. Harrison, *Christ Have Mercy: How to Put Your Faith in Action* (St. Louis: Concordia, 2008), 41.

[2]Mark A. Seifrid, *The Second Letter to the Corinthians* (Pillar New Testament Commentary; Grand Rapids: Eerdmans, 2014), 317.

example of Christian generosity, love, and charity for those suffering in the midst of severe persecution and tragedy.

The writings of St. James also contain a reminder of how Christians are to treat one another. He asserts: "If you really fulfill the royal law according to the Scripture, 'You shall love your neighbor as yourself,' you are doing well" (Jas 2:8). James thus sums up the Old Testament law into a phrase of love, in this case toward one's neighbor.[3] Therefore, if one is to be a Christian and bear Christ's name, he must be Christ-like in his love for others.[4] James stresses this point further:

> What good is it, my brothers, if someone says he has faith but does not have works? Can that faith save him? If a brother or sister is poorly clothed and lacking in daily food, and one of you says to them, "Go in peace, be warmed and filled," without giving them the things needed for the body, what good is that? So also faith by itself, if it does not have works, is dead (Jas 2:14–17).

In his book, *James the Apostle of Faith*, David Scaer helpfully explains that these verses speak to the practical problem James was seeking to correct—namely, that "deference to the rich and the criminal ignoring of the poor contradicted God's generous attitude to all men in Christ."[5] It is not possible to be a follower of Jesus and intentionally ignore the destitute, especially if they are members of the household of faith. Although helping those in need does not merit salvation, charity and love are fruits of the Christian life and the natural outgrowth of faith (Eph 2:10).

---

[3]Cf. Matt 22:36–40.

[4]So Luther: "Although the Christian is thus free from all works, he ought in this liberty to empty himself, take upon the form of a servant, . . . to serve, help, and in every way deal with his neighbor as he sees that God through Christ has dealt and still deals with him" (*LW* 31:366).

[5]David P. Scaer, *James the Apostle of Faith: A Primary Christological Epistle for the Persecuted Church* (St. Louis: Concordia, 1983), 89.

## Ministry to the Needy in the Early Church Era

Christian care for all humanity continued after the apostolic age, especially through works of mercy for the poor, slaves, prisoners, and the infirm. Coupled with the preaching of the gospel and the planting of churches, these charitable deeds done in the name of Christ helped the church to grow significantly. Historian Adolf Von Harnack explained that when the unbelieving community publicly witnessed Christian love in action, "people glorified the Christians' God, and, convinced by the very facts, confessed the Christians alone were truly pious and religious."[6] Correspondingly, generous aid and care for the poor is a common theme in the works of many prominent early church fathers, such as Clement of Alexandria, Tertullian, Cyprian, and Augustine. That charity was viewed as an essential part of the Christian faith "from the apostolic counsels down" was observed by Harnack:

> Cyprian develops alms into a formal means of grace . . . representing alms as a spectacle which the Christian offers to God. . . . But so far from being satisfied with private almsgiving, early Christianity instituted, apparently from the first, a church fund (Tertullian's *arca*), and associated charity very closely with the *cultus* and officials of the church.[7]

From one such fund, in AD 250 the church in Rome supported 100 clergy and 1,500 additional people who were in need.[8]

Before modern medicine, severe illness was much more prevalent and people often lived with excruciating pain and debilitating

---

[6]Adolf Von Harnack, *The Expansion of Christianity in the First Three Centuries* (ed. and trans. James Moffatt; vol. 1; New York: G. P. Putnam's Sons, 1904–1908), 215.

[7]Harnack, *Expansion of Christianity in the First Three Centuries*, 191–93. Although Cyprian was correct in emphasizing charity and its benefits, charity is not viewed as a sacrament in the traditional sense. "Baptism, the Lord's Supper and absolution (which is a sacrament of Repentance) are truly Sacraments" (Ap 13.4).

[8]Ross Edward Johnson, *Mercy in Action: Essays on Mercy, Human Care and Disaster Response* (St. Louis: The Lutheran Church—Missouri Synod, 2015), 78.

illnesses. Local congregations were aware of their communities' needs and used deacons, deaconesses, and widows to oversee the work of aiding the sick, disabled, and poor. This care and sacrificial giving extended to both believers and unbelievers, providing Christians with a strong reputation for meeting the needs of those living in tragic situations. Hence Tertullian, when confronted with the charge that Christians were the cause of revenue falling off in pagan centers of worship, pointed out the well-known fact that "our compassion spends more in the streets than yours does in the temples."[9] He even went so far as to make the sarcastic suggestion that if Jupiter were truly in need he should ask the church for alms, for then he would receive them.

Early church fathers were also concerned for the treatment of the working poor. Slavery was common, and many of the Roman slaves were indentured servants and prisoners of war. In his commentary on the Book of Philemon, John Nordling explains that the quality of life for slaves varied from being treated as family by some slave owners to receiving frequent beatings from others.[10] Harnack documented five areas where Christians influenced the secular culture toward a more compassionate treatment of slaves.

1. Slaves that converted to Christianity were considered full brothers and sisters in the faith.
2. Slaves were allowed to have membership in the highest offices of the church as clergy and bishops.
3. Christians taught that female slaves should be treated the same as free females and were not allowed to be exploited as sexual objects. Sexual abuse of females was not permitted by the church.
4. Masters and mistresses were strictly charged to treat their slaves humanely and slaves were taught to respect them.
5. Christians would often buy the freedom of other Christians, especially those enslaved by abusive masters.[11]

---

[9]*Apology* 42.8 (*ANF* 3:49).

[10]See John G. Nordling, *Philemon* (Concordia Commentary; St. Louis: Concordia, 2004), 57–59.

[11]Johnson, *Mercy in Action*, 85–87.

Indeed, these moral practices of the early church in many ways surpass those of certain Christian slave-owners in more recent times.

Life under the Roman Empire was often harsh; there were no
substantial government social welfare nets to help the sick, dying,
and destitute. The church, however, rose up to aid the ill, nurture the
dying, and sustain the disabled. Deacons and deaconesses oversaw
the mercy work to these people and the widows were charged with
prayers for the poor. During much of the early church era, there were
very few large church buildings. Church structures were rather humble and the majority of the tithes and offerings were designated as
poor-funds. The focus was on proclaiming the word and providing
aid for both Christians and non-Christians. While congregational
offerings were primarily distributed to the Christian poor, sickly, or
disabled, believers also generously gave to destitute non-Christians
in the streets.[12]

## Ministry to the Needy by Lutherans

Such mercy work was certainly not confined to the early church
era. In the late 1590s, Germany and many parts of Europe were
struck by the plague, and some estimates indicate that as much as
one-third of the total European population died. In 1597 the plague
decimated a German town named Unna. In the month of July alone,
over 1,000 people died and Pastor Philipp Nicolai, a Lutheran, buried 300 members.[13] Critical to Lutheran spiritual care was to minister to the sick and dying, despite the possibility of clergy also dying
from infection.[14] In the midst of this devastating catastrophe, Pastor
Nicolai found his comfort in the cross, Scripture, the divine service,
and hymnody. During the worst parts of the plague he wrote the
book *Freudenspiegel* (*Mirror of Joy*), as well as what would eventually become known as the queen and king of the Lutheran chorales,
"Wake, Awake, for Night is Flying" and, "O Morning Star, How Fair

---

[12]Johnson, *Mercy in Action*, 81.

[13]Johnson, *Mercy in Action*, 135–36.

[14]For further reading on pastoral care in times of the plague, see Martin
Luther, "Whether One May Flee from a Deadly Plague" in *LW* 43:113–38.

and Bright."[15] With the introduction of congregational singing during the Lutheran Reformation, hymnody became one of the primary ways for Christians to articulate the joys of the cross and the hope of heaven to come, even in the direst of circumstances.

The Lutheran Church—Missouri Synod in particular has a long tradition of congregational mercy work and human care, even from its very inception. There is little question that Walther, its first president, staunchly defended that the primary work of the pastor is to preach the word of God and administer the sacraments. The boundaries of pastoral work, however, are not confined only to distributing the means of grace. Walther wrote,

> Although a preacher above all has concern for the spiritual needs of the members of his congregation, concern for the physical well-being, particularly the needs of the poor, the sick, widows, orphans, the infirm, the destitute, the aged, etc., are within the scope of the duties of his office.[16]

Hence, pastors are not acting outside of their role when encouraging their congregations to show mercy to fellow members and their communities during times of tragedy.

A powerful example of both the immediate and long-term benefits that can result from providing such care is found in the work of Pastor John Frederick Buenger. As a young candidate for the office of holy ministry, he traveled with Walther from Germany and settled in Missouri where he served as a parish pastor. During Buenger's life there, he experienced enormous personal tragedies including the death of his wife and five children.[17] Despite these setbacks, Pastor Buenger worked closely with Walther and oversaw the formation of Lutheran hospitals in St. Louis and a large orphanage in the nearby city of Des Peres. As F. Dean Lueking explains,

---

[15]Johnson, *Mercy in Action*, 137; *Lutheran Service Book* (St. Louis: Concordia, 2006), 516 and 395, respectively.

[16]Quoted in Johnson, *Mercy in Action*, 229.

[17]F. Dean Lueking, *A Century of Caring: The Welfare Ministry Among Missouri Synod Lutherans, 1868–1968* (St. Louis: Board of Social Ministry, The Lutheran Church—Missouri Synod, 1968), 2.

> John Frederick Buenger's 35 years of pastoral ministry . . . left a pro-
> found influence upon the benevolent ministry of the young Synod.
> His work in founding the Lutheran Hospital and the Lutheran
> Orphanage set a pattern in theory and practice of social ministry that
> continued long after his death.[18]

In truth, mercy ministry exploded during the first 100 years of the
LCMS's history. By 1928 there were 72 Lutheran hospitals, orphanages, child welfare societies, homes for the aged, and institution missions. In 1950, the LCMS Board of Social Welfare was established to
help increase the 2,500 people serving in Lutheran Social Ministries
to approximately 100,000 people annually. By the 1960s each district of the Synod had a board or commission for social welfare and
70 percent of the LCMS congregations had mercy committees.[19]

The introduction noted that the LCMS is currently experiencing a fledgling renaissance after a recent dearth of mercy work. If this
resurgence in Lutheran churches is to continue, faithful pastors must
perform and encourage works of charity while preventing a depar-
ture into a graceless social gospel and an overreliance on govern-
mental aid. With the word and presence of Christ at their disposal,
they are well-prepared to provide spiritual care even to those who
suffer horrific disasters.

## Certain Promises vs. Speculative Answers:
## How to Handle the Question of "Why?"

"If God is so loving, then why do bad things happen to good people?"
This perennial question contains the unstated assumption that most
suffering is undeserved because people are basically good. Yet the
Bible is clear that people are not spiritually good or worthy of God's
favor. Scripture teaches that "all have sinned and fall short of the
glory of God" (Rom 3:23) and "the wages of sin is death" (Rom 6:23).
Even after conversion, Christians remain sinners who regularly fail
to do what is right according to God's standard (Rom 7). This is why

---

[18]Lueking, *Century of Caring*, 5.
[19]Lueking, *Century of Caring*, 45, 70, 74.

we regularly confess in the divine service, "We justly deserve God's present and eternal punishment."

There will always be aspects of our all-knowing, all-powerful, and all-loving God that humans can never understand. In the face of horrific events and heartrending experiences, fallen humanity tends to assume the worst of God and condemn him as uncaring. People even believe they somehow have the right to demand that God explain and justify his actions. Instead, we should trust in his love and good character even if we fail to grasp the reasons for what is happening to us or around us. What we *do* know, with utmost certainty, is that God is at work to redeem, restore, and save those who are suffering the very real consequences of sin. The love of God is clearly evident in this: he sent his Son into our flesh to die on the cross as payment for our sins and to conquer the grave. Thus, all who die in the one true Christian faith will be rescued from this vale of tears and live in the perfection of heaven.

In times of tragedy, instead of speculating about God's nature or demanding he do our will, the proper response is repentance and faith. In Luke 13, Jesus is asked about an incident where Pilate slaughtered the pious, an evil and senseless act. Instead of offering an explanation of why this occurred, Jesus directs his audience's attention elsewhere: "Unless you repent, you will all likewise perish" (Luke 13:3). Repentance turns a prideful, self-centered sinner from reliance on himself to trusting solely in God's goodness and mercy. Suffering, then, is not to be met with conjectures or accusations. "For my thoughts are not your thoughts, neither are your ways my ways," declares the Lord (Isa 55:8); and as St. Paul points out, "Will what is molded say to its molder, 'Why have you made me like this?'" (Rom 9:20). Instead, suffering is to be met with confidence in the all-loving God who promises not clear answers to our problems but the ultimate solution in his Son.

Lutheran pastoral care can provide the proper context for understanding suffering even when the details of individual tragedies remain unknown. The biblical narrative creates a worldview that, at least in a general way, helps make sense of why disasters and miseries occur. In the beginning, the entire creation was made and declared to be good by its Creator. As part of this good creation God gave Adam and Eve the choice to obey him or not, also giving them an explicit warning of what would happen if they defied his words. They chose to be disobedient, which brought death and brokenness into the world and plunged all of humanity into sin. This world will remain fallen until the its final day, with countless cases of tragedy and heartbreak. Shortly after the fall, however, God began his work of redemption (Gen 3:15); he actively rescued the world from sin, death, and the devil through Christ; and he continues to care for those whom he has created, both through specified means and in ways that are not always obvious.

Pastors are to focus on these clear, loving acts of God when caring for those who are hurting or confused. Far more important than finding an answer to the "Why?" of suffering is hearing the good news that Jesus suffered in our place and will rescue us forever from our broken world and sinful selves. To meditate on the incomprehensible hiddenness of God, however, questions God and what he is doing behind the scenes of our lives and this world, which only invites despair.[20] We are not assured of all the answers; rather, everything that is necessary to know about God and salvation is clearly revealed in the Scriptures.

Moreover, it is always important to remind those suffering that when evil occurs it is not necessarily directly related to a particular sin that they have committed. In this fallen world, our bodies betray us and we get sick and die, or others betray us and cause great problems and misfortune. And at times there are spiritual attacks by the devil and his demons who like to harass people and cause misery (as in the case of Job). To be sure, we often do go through personal agony because of the sinful choices that we ourselves have made (Ps 51). Regardless of the exact cause, however, offering pastoral care also entails reminding people that God often brings amazingly good things out of tragic situations. Joseph's sufferings led to the saving of many lives (Gen 50:15–21), Job was eventually blessed after his time of tragedy (Job 42:10), and the murder of God's own dear Son

---

[20]Thus Luther's distinction: "[W]e have to argue in one way about God or the will of God as preached, revealed, offered, and worshiped, and in another about God as he is not preached, not revealed, not offered, not worshiped. To the extent, therefore, that God hides himself and wills to be unknown to us, it is no business of ours" (*LW* 33:139).

resulted in salvation for the whole world. That said, it must also be maintained that there is no promise that believers will always directly see or understand the good that comes out of particular trials and tribulations. This is why what God has revealed about himself in the person and work of his Son must predominate and direct the words and actions of every pastor when caring for others. There is simply no other basis for assurance that we have been reconciled to our heavenly Father and that nothing can separate us from his love (Rom 8:38–39).

## Take Courage: Shepherding with the Theology of the Cross

Martin Luther famously explained, "A theologian of glory calls evil good and good evil. A theologian of the cross calls the thing what it actually is" (*LW* 31:40). Times of tragedy break down people's false walls of pride and show that the comfort they receive from their own achievements, intelligence, and self-sufficiency is fleeting. Being diagnosed with terminal cancer, having an uninsured house flood, or the sudden loss of a loved one is shocking and humbling; it is a reminder of what Job learned: "The Lord gave, and the Lord has taken away; blessed be the name of the Lord" (Job 1:21). When this world strips away all that this life has to offer, the Christian is left with two choices: to struggle alone or to seek refuge in Christ. Pastoral care can provide refuge in the midst of life's storms; yet what sort of shepherding will the pastor provide?

Theologians of glory try to candy-coat the sting of sin with shallow spirituality like, "If you just have enough faith, things will turn out okay." A theologian of the cross says, "I can see how difficult this is. This is completely normal. But take courage! Jesus suffers with you. He knows the pain that you are going through," and continues to point the person to the mercies of the incarnate God. Only by shepherding with the theology of the cross is the pastor's ministry and care guaranteed to be Christ-centered and a source of consolation. When the focus is on Jesus and his saving work, it allows him to increase and the pastor to decrease (John 3:30); when the focus is elsewhere, it becomes difficult—if not impossible—to make it through the struggles of this life (see Heb 12:1–2).

Theologians of glory seek to affirm their members with their own optimism and positivity. Thus, the teachings of many mega-churches over the past few decades have emphasized the so-called practical theology of optimism and self-worth. Popular evangelical Christian books have been written specifically about experiencing your best life now or a victorious Christian life.[21] But a theologian of the cross centers people's self-worth in the fact that the same God who made them also redeemed them with his own shed blood. This directs their hope forward to the resurrection, where the best life is yet to come. As Jesus said, "Do not lay up for yourselves treasures on earth, where moth and rust destroy and where thieves break in and steal, but lay up for yourselves treasures in heaven" (Matt 6:19–20).

A theologian of the cross brings comfort by reminding the person how compassionate Jesus was in his suffering in this world—for sinful humanity. Jesus was lied about, lied to, betrayed, hungry, beaten, and killed so that he could fulfill the law perfectly for our salvation. Pastors can lead those who are hurting to take comfort in the fact that they live their lives in the shadow of Jesus' cross where they do not suffer alone. St. Paul wrote, "I have been crucified with Christ. It is no longer I who live, but Christ who lives in me. And the life I now live in the flesh I live by faith in the Son of God, who loved me and gave himself for me" (Gal 2:20). This status as a new creation in Christ allows Christians to have joy amidst sorrow, knowing that they are God's own dear children and reckoned as perfect in his sight because Christ has taken all of their sin and shame, and has given his perfection, active obedience, and righteousness to them (2 Cor 5:21).

When Christians feel as if they are going "through the valley of the shadow of death" (Ps 23:4), they have a sure and certain promise that the troubles of this world are only temporary.

Truly, truly, I say to you, you will weep and lament, but the world will rejoice. You will be sorrowful, but your sorrow will turn into joy.

---

[21]Joel Osteen, for example, has numerous such books, including: *Your Best Life Now: 7 Steps to Living at Your Full Potential* (New York: FaithWords, 2004); *It's Your Time: Activate Your Faith, Achieve Your Dreams, and Increase in God's Favor* (New York: Howard Books, 2009); *Think Better, Live Better: A Victorious Life Begins in Your Mind* (New York: FaithWords, 2016).

When a woman is giving birth, she has sorrow because her hour has come, but when she has delivered the baby, she no longer remembers the anguish, for joy that a human being has been born into the world. So also you have sorrow now, but I will see you again, and your hearts will rejoice, and no one will take your joy from you (John 16:20–22).

For the one who does not belong to Christ, this life's sorrows *are* his best life, and his future will be utter destruction. But for the one who believes in Christ, this world will not compare to what God has prepared for him in the world to come (Rom 8:18). Despite the catastrophes suffered in the present age, the greatest tragedy that could ever happen is to die outside of the one true Christian faith. It is thus ideal that congregational mercy be connected to the gospel message whenever possible so that spiritual healing can happen while earthly needs are being met.

## The Comforting Presence of Christ in Times of Crisis

Christ's presence after his resurrection demonstrates the power he has to console and comfort the needy. He dispelled the darkness of fear and the uncertainty of the future by moving the disciples from the tragedy of death to the triumph of life. This serves as a paradigm for our ministry of mercy. That same power of the resurrection is realized today when pastors stand in Christ's stead to transcend the critical events that affect people's lives. For Lutherans, the response is a clear testimony of the gospel, bringing the word of Christ's forgiveness to people both at church and in the community.

Peace for the brokenhearted is more than vague talk about the love of God or a passing allusion to Jesus. Rather, pastoral care is given when the truth about the severity of law and the promises of the gospel are declared with clarity and confidence. While the pastor will ideally establish this foundation for his people before a tragedy strikes, Christians will still be tempted to look to pop-psychology, false beliefs, and false promises about God and his nature when going through crises. Faithful pastors have the opportunity to correct God's people with his word when the world and their flesh attempt to lead them astray. This requires patience, visitation, kindness, and

teaching, just as Christ took the time to shepherd his people by walking and living among them (Matt 4:18–23).

There will likewise be various opportunities to proclaim the gospel and bring Christ to the unchurched. Through charity work in the
community, connections through parishioners, or visitors at church,
pastors will invariably be brought into contact with those who are
suffering and searching for peace that the world cannot give. Tragic
events—a family member's death, a grave medical diagnosis, or a catastrophic natural disaster—allow people to see the destructiveness of
a fallen world and sin's consequences. Yet it is precisely to those who
recognize their brokenness that Christ gives this invitation: "Come
to me, all who labor and are heavy laden, and I will give you rest"
(Matt 11:28). After the terrorist attacks on September 11, 2001, for
example, American church attendance swelled for a few months.
People flocked to hear God's word and receive hope. At such times
of tragedy, pastors need to preach the law even if death and destruction is all around them, even if they are surrounded by caskets; and
they also must preach the gospel to believers and unbelievers alike,
assuring them that God's promises of forgiveness, eternal life, and
the resurrection remain true. In this way pastors can comfort all
people with Jesus' presence since, as Luther said, preaching is not
only talk *about* Christ, but "an offering and presentation of Christ"
in accordance with God's mercy (*LW* 39:183).

Indeed, it is in the divine service that people are in the presence of
Christ as he descends to bless his people through the means of grace.
One of the simplest and most eloquent explanations of this was written
by Dr. Norman Nagel in the preface of the hymnal, *Lutheran Worship*:

> Our Lord speaks and we listen. . . . The rhythm of our worship is
> from him to us, and then from us back to him. He gives his gifts, and
> together we receive and extol them. We build one another up as we
> speak to one another in psalms, hymns and spiritual songs.[22]

The pastor stands in front of the sheep at the start of the service,
which is a powerful visible reminder of God's comforting presence

---

[22]*Lutheran Worship* (St. Louis: Concordia, 1982), 6.

amidst the storms of this world. After the corporate confession of sin, the word of absolution is pronounced by the one called to serve in Christ's stead. There is nothing sweeter for a repentant sinner to hear than the unconditional love, grace, and mercy of God spoken into his or her ears. This declaration of forgiveness brings comfort and peace, and assures God's people that he is with them no matter what hardships they may be experiencing. The same can be said of the spoken gospel in the sermon, and especially of the sacrament of the altar. By receiving Christ's body and blood, his people are truly connected to him (1 Cor 10:16–17). The Lord's Supper, then, is where God himself is present to bestow forgiveness, life, blessing, strength, comfort, and encouragement in the midst of chaos and destruction.

Throughout the divine service, Lutheran hymnody provides songs of substance that bring hope and consolation. The word is at work as Christians sing scriptural truths, and afterward as they remember simple yet profound lines, such as "Nothing in my hand I bring, Simply to Thy cross I cling."[23] At the close of worship, the entire congregation is reminded once more that they are blessed and at peace with God. The last words they hear are pure grace to them: "The Lord bless thee and keep thee. The Lord make His face shine upon thee and be gracious unto thee. The Lord lift up His countenance upon thee and give thee peace."[24] Once again the believers are passive recipients: the Lord is the one blessing them and reminding them of his love. Virtually the entire experience is meant to give comfort and confidence to the believer through Christ's merciful presence in a fallen world.

## Conclusion

Although works of mercy may seem like a common-sense practice, faithful pastoral care in times of tragedy is often neglected. The deceptive theologies of self-reliance, optimism, speculation, and glory fail to speak the truth about evil, suffering, and God himself. This either causes people to have a misplaced confidence or leaves them with

---

[23] *The Lutheran Hymnal* (St. Louis: Concordia, 1941), hymn 376.
[24] *The Lutheran Hymnal*, 31.

despair. Yet calamities and heartbreak have a way of bringing people to their knees and exposing the flaws in their theological assumptions. When tragedy occurs, Lutheran pastors are well-equipped to combat the world, the devil, and false teachings. They have the examples from the New Testament, and the encouragement and wisdom found in the historic practices of the church. Especially, pastors have the revealed word that centers on Christ and him crucified, who is present wherever his gospel is preached and his sacraments are administered. These gifts are as much for use in times of disaster as on an ordinary Sunday. Moreover, this care is not limited only to a pastor's own flock, nor is it only meant to meet people's spiritual needs. By being present and active in the community, the pastor and congregation position themselves to tend to the needs of this body and life, and to point all people to the Christ who has promised to be with them always, even to the end of the age (Matt 28:20).

## Suggestion for Further Reading

Harrison, Matthew C. *Christ Have Mercy: How to Put Your Faith in Action*. St. Louis: Concordia, 2008.

Johnson, Ross Edward, ed. *Mercy in Action: Essays on Mercy, Human Care and Disaster Response*. St. Louis: The Lutheran Church—Missouri Synod, 2015.

Lindberg, Carter. *Beyond Charity: Reformation Initiatives for the Poor*. Minneapolis: Fortress, 1993.

Lueking, F. Dean. *A Century of Caring: The Welfare Ministry Among Missouri Synod Lutherans, 1868–1968*. St. Louis: Board of Social Ministry, The Lutheran Church—Missouri Synod, 1968.

Scharlemann, Martin H. *The Church's Social Responsibilities*. St. Louis: Concordia, 1971.

Uhlhorn, Johann. *Christian Charity*. New York: Charles Scribner's Sons, 1883.

# Of Dinosaurs and DOXOLOGY

## Philosophy for Pastoral Care in the Twenty-First Century

*Gregory P. Schulz*

"And whereas we work to teach pastors to think like Lutherans, Dr. Schulz has the unenviable job of teaching his students to *think* in the first place." It is always a privilege to be introduced by Harold Senkbeil. Lately, however, he has been adding a change-up pitch to his repertoire by introducing me to brother pastors at DOXOLOGY events as "a dinosaur." It turns out that he has been referring to himself in the same fashion; so to be a dinosaur, it seems, is a good and salutary thing.

In what respect then is Senkbeil, a twenty-first-century pastors' pastor, a dinosaur? He is a throwback in respect to his education and thus to the subsequent erudition he brings to the ministry. His undergraduate and seminary training was in the liberal arts tradition along the lines articulated by Philip Melanchthon and the first-generation Lutherans in the sixteenth century. The training received by our younger generations of Lutheran pastors generally is not.

Senkbeil is from a different age—a Paleolithic era in contrast to the technically-oriented training of seminary graduates of the last forty years or so. Indeed, sixteenth-and seventeenth-century Lutheran professors can all be classified as dinosaurs when judged by the common core of standards in our century, if we can even say that there are such standards. This is a view of pastoral training from the Lutheran Paleolithic Era:

> It is a great mistake to imagine that ministers can be carved from any wood, and that the teaching of religion can be grasped without erudition and without long training. . . .
> No one hands an oar to someone in a small boat if that man has not learnt to row. No one can cultivate fields without a guide—not to speak of other, more complicated, skills. How much less could one who has not learnt to do so be an interpreter of heavenly teaching and a leader of the Church? . . . The general sense [of divine Scripture] can be communicated in brief, but the knowledge of divine things must become clearer, little by little, through meditation on, and comparison of, the words of the Prophets and Apostles, for all the pious, whether they have erudition or not. This cannot be done without reading and interpretation and, as I have said above, extensive and varied teaching is necessary for interpretation.[1]

In other words, the pastor who embodies the *ethos, pathos*, and *logos* of classical rhetoric in his writings, sermons, and conversations is engagingly erudite as he brings Christ to hurting souls. In contrast, the pastor who cannot do this tends to fundamentalism, carelessness, and rudeness—all of which are potential stumbling blocks for hearers of the gospel and of the whole council of God. This is the conceptual archeology of the term "erudition" that Melanchthon expressed here, and it is this erudition that makes Senkbeil a dinosaur. It is what he has been laboring to pass on through *DOXOLOGY: The Lutheran Center for Spiritual Care and Counsel*. Think of it as a deeply *philosophical* education in the service of the office of the ministry.

He has been working to make dinosaurs of us pastors—for the good of the office of the ministry and for our faithful care of souls. His is an urgent task. To be sure, the gates of hell cannot prevail against the kingdom of God (Matt 16:18). Notwithstanding, the

---

[1]Philip Melanchthon, *Philip Melanchthon: Orations on Philosophy and Education* (ed. Sachiko Kusukawa; trans. Christine F. Salazar; Cambridge: Cambridge University Press, 1999), 15–16.

office of the ministry among us, that is, the Lutheran doctrine and practice of the-means-of-grace, the law-and-gospel ministry of the Confessions and of Scripture, *can* be lost to us. Luther prophesied that the gospel would, like a rainstorm, pass on to other regions. Melanchthon wrote in detail that this passing on would be the result of our failure to cultivate a properly educated clergy. Without erudition, dinosaur pastors will become extinct and the light of the gospel will be extinguished.

To see why we pastors ought to become erudite philosophical dinosaurs, let us consider Martin Luther's 1536 *Disputation Regarding Man* for the reformer's philosophical anthropology. My essay consists of two main parts, followed by a pastoral wrap-up. In Part One, I posit that we need to understand Aristotle in order to follow Luther's approach to understanding the human being. We will also see how Luther's view surpasses the inadequate view of Aristotle. In Part Two, I elaborate how Martin Heidegger, a major twentieth-century German philosopher, utilized Luther's definition of the human being to show that humans are unique in that they care about their very being. Indeed, they care about it so much that they cannot but seek to be justified, either by their own works or by Christ. This will help us to recognize and utilize the bridge that Luther provided between a view of the human being that is both intellectually substantial and Christological, on the one hand, and those individuals to whom we provide pastoral care in person, on the other hand.

## Part One: Luther and Aristotle on Human Being

"What is man?" the psalmist asks (Ps 8:4). In terms familiar in contemporary philosophy, we call Luther's way of understanding our human kind of being "phenomenology."[2] Yet Luther's phenomenological approach was robust: unlike Aristotle, his understanding of what it means to be human (his "ontology") was ultimately based

---

[2]For an explanation of phenomenology (including how it is distinguished from ontology), see David Woodruff, "Phenomenology," The Stanford Encyclopedia of Philosophy (Summer 2018 Edition), ed. Edward N. Zalta, https://plato.stanford .edu/archives/sum2018/entries/phenomenology/.

on the text of Scripture. Indeed, the central proposition of Luther's disputation is, "32. Paul in Romans 3[:28], 'We hold that a man is justified by faith apart from works,' briefly sums up the definition of man, saying, 'Man is justified by faith'" (*LW* 34:139). Before we can see how this definition applies to the pastoral office, especially via the work of Heidegger, we first need to lay some groundwork.

## *Philosophy for Doing Theology*

Luther's opening propositions exhibit his own familiarity with and use of Aristotle, which he took for granted in his readers as well. It is a qualified use of Aristotle, to be sure, but it remains easy to see how different the training of Luther (and of many other dinosaurs) was from that of various Christian pastors today.

1. Philosophy or human wisdom defines man as an animal having reason, sensation, and body.
2. It is not necessary at this time to debate whether man is properly or improperly called an animal.
3. But this must be known, that this definition describes man only as a mortal and in relation to this life.
4. And it is certainly true that reason is the most important and the highest in rank among all things and, in comparison with other things of this life, the best and something divine.
5. It is the inventor and mentor of all the arts, medicines, laws, and of whatever wisdom, power, virtue, and glory men possess in this life.
6. By virtue of this fact it ought to be named the essential difference by which man is distinguished from the animals and other things (*LW* 34:137).

First, notice that the entire format of the disputation is philosophically erudite. A disputation was one way of having a thoughtful discussion and dialog concerning a critical topic in mediaeval universities such as the University of Wittenberg. To be a Lutheran pastor today is to be one of the latest heirs of a *university* theology. The online *Stanford Encyclopedia of Philosophy* (*SEP*) explains that this type of teaching by disputation is essentially an academic form of philosophical dialog (the sort of teaching that Plato did in dialogues such as his *Republic*). It is also significant that this disputation form "comes into the classroom as an outgrowth of the *lectio*, the careful reading and commentary on authoritative texts"[3] such as Holy Scripture in the first place, but also academic texts such as the writings of Aristotle. Luther's thinking and writing display an authentic liberal arts education.

As the *SEP* explains in detail, disputation "is centered on a systematic rather than a textual question, and the supporting and opposing arguments are supplied by students."[4] What Luther called "theses" are what we in philosophy today refer to as "propositions," statements of fact to be judged as either true or false. In the traditional, pre-Cartesian Western way of talking and writing, this was known as the *Second Act of the Mind*, the exercise of our distinctively human capacity for judging. Each proposition is an open invitation to say either, "This is true" or "This is false." Then the dialogue begins.[5]

Thus, the disputation format required some philosophical training. But what of the ecclesial myth that Luther wanted to erect a Berlin Wall between theology and philosophy, with philosophy cast as the enemy at the gate? It is of course possible to cull a few quotes from a cursory reading in support of this notion: "[I]f philosophy or reason itself is compared with theology, it will appear that we know almost nothing about man" (*LW* 34:137); "Theology to be sure from the fullness of its wisdom defines man as whole and perfect" (*LW* 34:138); and so on. A careful and extensive reading, however, shows that Luther had an "open border policy" toward philosophical logic and rhetoric.

---

[3]Eileen Sweeney, "Literary Forms of Medieval Philosophy," The Stanford Encyclopedia of Philosophy (Summer 2015 Edition), ed. Edward N. Zalta, http://plato.stanford.edu/archives/sum2015/entries/medieval-literary/.

[4]Sweeney, "Literary Forms of Medieval Philosophy."

[5]Paul Vincent Spade and Mikko Yrjönsuuri, "Medieval Theories of Obligationes," The Stanford Encyclopedia of Philosophy (Winter 2014 Edition), ed. Edward N. Zalta, http://plato.stanford.edu/archives/win2014/entries/obligationes/.

Look, for instance, at the formal aspect of his disputation. Luther followed the summa-style of the universities of his day, listing and then responding to anticipated objections to his position, providing his own reasoned response, and so on. He adopted the Four Causes of the Western tradition, the familiar four questions needed to vet anyone's claims to knowledge of any thing, as established by Aristotle. Furthermore, he deployed Aristotelian logic in his responses to anticipated objections. Among educated persons in pre-modern centuries or pre-seventeenth-century writing and debating, this was known as the *Third Act of the Mind* or the use of our human capacity for providing reasons as to why our judging something to be true or false stands up. It seems clear, therefore, that while Luther superseded the content of Aristotle's philosophy, he nevertheless did so according to the philosophical forms.[6]

Second, Luther exhibited his own philosophical literacy in Aristotle, put to use for the pastoral purposes of the dissertation. By opening with Aristotle's definition of man, he followed the *First Act of the Mind*, the use of our faculty for understanding, in order to define clearly the term at issue such that everyone would understand. In the opening of this disputation, for example, Luther exhibited his familiarity with Aristotle's definition of *man* or the human being as *zōon logon echon,* or "a type of being or a species characterized as fitting under the category of *animal,* rather than *nonliving* or *vegetative,* and being essentially differentiated by its demonstrated potential for *logos.*" The definition is assembled from Aristotle's *Politics,* Book I. Call it a minimum definition of the human being for educated discussions.

---

[6]See, for example, *The Disputation Fragment* (*LW* 34:140) and his anticipation of objections to his thirteenth and fourteenth propositions. Luther did not take issue with the (Aristotelian) demand that to know our essence we must be able to account for man's efficient and formal causes. He objected to the objector's assertion that God can *ever* be known as either our efficient cause (our Creator) or our final cause (the one by whom and for whom all things are created) apart from biblical revelation.

## Aristotle's Definition of Man

Do we twenty-first-century Lutheran pastors know Aristotle's definition? Luther did. He gave no time to irrelevant and fictional evolutionary narratives or eliminative materialistic theories—just an open-eyed and clear-minded way of categorizing human beings as what they are. It is minimalist, and Luther was not satisfied with it philosophically. As he wrote, "6. By virtue of this fact it ought to be named the essential difference by which man is distinguished from the animals and other things" (*LW* 34:137), he maintained that reason (*logos* in Greek, translated *ratio* in Latin) is the essential difference because we are *zōon logon echon*, as Aristotle said. Luther continued, "19. But as this life is, such is the definition and knowledge of man, that is, fragmentary, fleeting, and exceedingly material" (*LW* 34:138). Aristotle's minimalist definition—his grasp of our human being—is inadequate for understanding ourselves and for pastoral care. This is due to his restricted field of research: Aristotle gave no serious consideration of human immortality, nor did he conduct any study in God's own personal words to us on the subject.

Before one hurries off to the biblical anthropology that our triune God teaches in places like Psalm 8 and Hebrews 2, let me point out another aspect of Luther's fluency in Aristotle that we seldom acquire in our pastoral education today: Aristotle's *Four Causes*. In our disputation, Luther matter-of-factly wrote,

9. Nor did God after the fall of Adam take away this majesty of reason, but rather confirmed it.

10. In spite of the fact that it is of such majesty, it does not know itself *a priori*, but only *a posteriori*.

11. Therefore, if philosophy or reason itself is compared with theology, it will appear that we know almost nothing about man,

12. Inasmuch as we seem scarcely to perceive his <u>material cause</u> sufficiently.

13. For philosophy does not know the <u>efficient cause</u> for certain, nor likewise the final cause,

14. Because it posits no other <u>final cause</u> than the peace of this life, and does not know that the efficient cause is God the creator.

15. Indeed, concerning the <u>formal cause</u> which they call soul, there is not and never will be agreement among the philosophers.

16. For so far as Aristotle defines it as the first driving force of the body which has the power to live, he too wished to deceive readers and hearers.

17. Nor is there any hope that man in this principal part can himself know what he is until he sees himself in his origin which is God.

18. And what is deplorable is that he does not have full and unerring control over either his counsel or thought but is subject to error and deception therein.

19. But as this life is, such is the definition and knowledge of man, that is, fragmentary, fleeting, and exceedingly material (*LW* 34:137–38).

In other words, Luther argued, we do not and cannot know our own nature, *human nature*, innately or automatically. We can know what it means to be a human being only *after the fact*—that is, after the fact of the incarnation. Only in the person of Christ do we learn who and what we really and truly are as human beings.

What has this to do with the *Four Causes* of Aristotle? We Lutheran pastors ought to know.[7] A significant portion of our Lutheran patrimony remains inaccessible or unintelligible to us if we do not know these basic things from Aristotle. Read, for example, the Table of Contents in the recent translations of Johann Gerhard's theological writings. In the first volume of *Theological Commonplaces*[8] he writes at length about the *causes*, notably the *efficient cause* of Holy Scripture. When the apostle Paul writes in Colossians that all things are made by Christ and for Christ, he is giving the answer to the efficient and final causes of human beings. The apostle knew Greek

---

[7]Please see my interview with Bryan Wolfmueller on this subject (conducted on January 27, 2016) at Around the Word, http://www.whatdoesthismean.org/master-metaphors-of-philosophy/aristotles-cross-examination-of-nature-aka-the-four-causes-master-metaphor-2.

[8]Johann Gerhard, *On the Nature of Theology and on Scripture*, vol. 1 of *Theological Commonplaces* (ed. Benjamin T. G. Mayes; trans. Richard J. Dinda; 2d ed.; Concordia: St. Louis, 2009).

philosophy, as Luke reports in Acts 17. So should we—its forms, its common nomenclature, its limits—as Luther demonstrated in *The Disputation Concerning Man.*

So: biblical content, but philosophical form. What are the implications for our pastoral thinking? Luther was not being schizophrenic in his handling of reason and revelation; nor was he being a fundamentalist. On the contrary, he was an integrated thinker who used philosophy and theology in a clear, traceable relationship. There is a temptation to scavenge his biblical insights to provide sermon illustrations or a requisite Luther quote or two for a conference paper; but here in the *disputatio*, Luther, in light of Romans 3:28, was working out his exegetical discovery regarding human being *philosophically*—that is, critically and at some logical and Aristotelian length. To hark back to Senkbeil's dinosaur metaphor, Luther was being philosophically erudite rather than acting like a rube. He made the case, carefully and logically, beginning with the best available understanding and explaining why and how we all must move on to a better understanding—just as he had learned to do from Aristotle's writings.

### Luther's Superior Definition of Man

Now let us turn to the payoff proposition in Luther's disputation on the human being. What emerges from a philosophical analysis of Luther's text is that he did not rudely trump Aristotle's philosophical view of man with his own theology, nor did he offhandedly dismiss Aristotle's anthropology in favor of a favorite Bible passage of his own. Rather, it is the case that Luther delivered a philosophical critique of Aristotelian/Scholastic theory of man and thus argued in the public space of debate for the wider explanatory reach, for the "thicker account" (as a philosopher would say) of his theological theory of the human being.

Luther's way of thinking about human being is theologically bold, but it is also logically persuasive. It is intelligible. This is to say that Luther's theology of man affects not only *what we believe about ourselves*, but also *how we think about the way we think of ourselves* as human beings. Here again is his central thesis, his *Hauptartikel* proposition: "32. Paul in Romans 3[:28], 'We hold that a man is justified by faith apart from works,' briefly sums up the definition of man, saying, 'Man is justified by faith'" (*LW* 34:139).

In other words, while we have grown up learning to think of the human being as *homo sapiens*, on the basis of the "thicker," more authoritative biblical anthropology it would be more accurate to think of the human being as *homo justificans*. That is, we are the kind of being that seeks to be justified: Either we acknowledge that we are justified by God's grace alone in Christ or we spend our time of grace seeking to justify ourselves apart from Christ—an inherently undoable and unsettling project—a project that comes from the very bottom of our being!

Since this thesis is definitional (that is, doing *First Act of the Mind* work), we would do well, as Oswald Bayer says, to translate Luther's proposition as "The human being is human in that he is justified by faith." Bayer explains,

> The human being is human *insofar as* he is justified by faith. . . . Justifying faith for Luther is not something *about* a human being, no qualitative element, which comes only secondarily, as that which is accidental to the substance. *Hominem justificari fide* (a human being is justified by faith) is, instead, a *fundamental* anthropological thesis.[9]

Writing in traditional philosophical terminology, Luther was arguing *against* the traditional essential definition of the human being. In so doing, he was making the case for a radically different way of thinking. He did not dismiss Aristotle and the Greek philosophical tradition uncritically or out of ignorance (Professor Luther taught and translated Aristotle, after all!), but for philosophical reasons. He criticized Aristotle (at least in part) on philosophical grounds to argue for a new, more-than-Aristotelian way of thinking about man. In effect, Luther was arguing that our basic minimum definition from Aristotle is that we human beings are *animated beings characterized by* logos. However, this definition is hampered by Aristotle's narrow field of inquiry. He restricted his definition to the brief time of our

---

[9]Oswald Bayer, *Martin Luther's Theology: A Contemporary Interpretation* (trans. Thomas H. Trapp; Grand Rapids: Eerdmans, 2008), 155–56; emphasis original. See also Bayer's description of how the world is Word-dependent on pages 100–101.

own experience before death. In light of what God has revealed about his incarnation and resurrection for us all, we have to upgrade our understanding to include *justification* as more essential and to-the-point than unfocused *logos* as the essence of being human.

Luther turns out to be, in effect, a sixteenth-century Einstein in the philosophy of human nature. As the result of the return to the text of Scripture, which is God's communion with us, we now know that there are *two dimensions* that constitute our being (or *ontos*) as human beings: There is our vertical relatedness to God and there is our horizontal relatedness to this populated universe. Luther's anthropology accounts for both; Aristotle's does not, and is thus incomplete.

Crucially, the kind of thinking we need to do in order to know ourselves is only achievable *sola scriptura*, that is, *solus Christus* or exclusively by virtue of the revealed word. For example, we can know God in the praying of Psalm 8:4: "What is man that you are mindful of him . . . ?" and thus we can begin to know ourselves. It is only through contact with the divine word that we can sensibly ask what it is about our relatedness to God that gives us life, movement, and our very being. This is of the essence for coming to realize why we cannot ever know ourselves by ourselves. To put it in terms of the famous Delphic oracle: We cannot *gnothi seauton* (or know ourselves by ourselves) because we cannot know ourselves apart from knowing God. The Greeks, even with all their philosophical openness toward the gods or even a putative singular god, did not have the Hebrew Scriptures and thus they could not know God. This was why their philosophical anthropology dead-ended.

What we get from this argument is not "another worldview" that accounts for human persons objectively, but rather a reformation of our thinking *about our thinking of ourselves* such that we can at last speak sensibly of our *ontic* being. Bayer summarizes Luther's thinking this way:

> As a created being, human existence is "justified-through-faith" existence. As "justified-through-faith" existence, it is created existence. For Luther, teaching about creation is to teach about justification, and teaching about justification means to teach about creation.[10]

---

[10]Bayer, *Martin Luther's Theology*, 156.

And so, it is important for us to grasp that Luther was not merely tweaking the standard philosophical thinking of his day regarding the human being; on the contrary, he was proposing an entirely new kind of philosophical anthropology. This is on the basis of his biblical insight regarding our *Hauptartikel* of justification.

In summary, then, the *being* of the human being—the *enosh* (Hebrew) or *anthropos* (Septuagint) of the psalm—is essentially knowable to us human beings. But it is knowable only in terms of the human's active relationship with the personal God who is active for him in the person of Christ.

So, what about Luther's disputation in the twentieth and now in our twenty-first century? As I have said above, one reason that Aristotle, as philosophically interesting and important as he is otherwise, failed to deliver the essence of the human being is this: Aristotle was alert to the horizontal dimension of our being ("Man is a political or social animal" he stated in *Politics* Book 1), but he was fatally inept when it comes to the vertical, God-ward dimension. Aristotle's prime mover is, if one is to be charitable, a wafer-thin abduction of a final cause, an intellectually boring embarrassment, in contrast to the personal Yahweh of the Jewish and Christian Scriptures. The rejection of Aristotelian philosophy on this point and for this reason is a noteworthy chapter in history and in the history of ideas,[11] but I am not aiming to do an historical study here. Instead, my concern is with our pastoral care as Lutheran pastors.

---

[11] I would suggest for this reason, to use a ready-at-hand example, that we remember to read Robert Preus's fine narrative on the relation of philosophy to theology and his assessment of "Gerhard's attitude toward and use of philosophy as a theologian" as a study in the history of ideas and not a definitive word on the relation of theology to philosophy. Holding to the "normed and normative" character of our Confessions and then granting for the sake of discussion that the methodology and terminology of Lutheran dogmatics today are influenced by classical Lutheran orthodoxy, it does not follow that our attitude toward the use of philosophy ought to be the same as the attitude of our post-reformation forebearers for the obvious reason that philosophy today is not the philosophy of Aristotle. See, for example, Robert D. Preus, *The Theology of Post-Reformation Lutheranism*, vol. 1, *A Study of Theological Prolegomena* (St. Louis: Concordia, 1970), 122–34.

## Part Two: Luther and Heidegger on Human Being

Although Aristotle (whom Luther ultimately opposed in the disputation) is "out" in modernity, it does not follow that everything has become congenial to Lutheran theology! Notwithstanding, there is a case to be made for the influence of Luther on contemporary philosophy. This in turn may motivate us to pay more and deeper attention to what the British refer to as one's "duty of care" and thus, more attention to pastoral care. I have in mind a notion regarding *Sorge*, which is perhaps part of our understanding of *Seelsorge*—a thought I will return to momentarily.

### The Revealed God

Of great interest to us as confessional Lutherans is the fact that this sea change from Aristotle to non-Aristotelian anthropologies available today is due, at minimum, to the impact of Luther's thought on at least one major intellectual figure in twentieth-century philosophy, namely, Martin Heidegger. For example, we know that Heidegger (whose philosophical phenomenology I have been adapting for my analysis of Luther's disputation) possessed and studied the Erlangen edition of Luther's works. In the 1920s, the decade in which he published his hugely influential *Being and Time*, Heidegger referred frequently and intensely to Luther's thought in conversations with philosophers such as Karl Jaspers, in lectures on Luther's influence on Kant's philosophy, and in a planned journal publication on "The Ontological Foundations of Late Medieval Anthropology and the Theology of the Young Luther."[12] The case of the early Heidegger thus suggests how Luther's thinking has had a profound influence on contemporary philosophy, at least via Heidegger's early philosophy, in the area of so-called Continental thought and phenomenology.

Put into more philosophical terminology, I have pointed out that this is a "field theory" in that it begins with our being-in-the-world as a necessary condition for understanding our human kind of

---

[12]See John van Buren, "Martin Heidegger, Martin Luther" in *Reading Heidegger from the Start: Essays in His Earliest Thought* (ed. Theodore Kisiel and John van Buren; New York: State University of New York Press, 1994), 159–74.

being. Descartes, on this recognition, was fundamentally mistaken. We do not first think and thus exist as mental substances. On the contrary, we first exist in the world, and then we begin to think about things. The field, we may read Luther as saying, cannot be arbitrarily limited to the here-and-now in front of our noses, but must extend far enough to include God, the God whose words are the very words of Holy Scripture. Luther highlighted this in his disputation.

> 35. Therefore, man in this life is the simple material of God for the form of his future life.
> 36. Just as the whole creation which is now subject to vanity [Rom. 8:20] is for God the material for its future glorious form.
> 37. And as earth and heaven were in the beginning for the form completed after six days, that is, its material,
> 38. So is man in this life for his future form, when the image of God has been remolded and perfected.
> 39. Meanwhile, man lives in sins and daily is either justified or becomes more polluted.
> 40. Hence, Paul does not even deign to call that realm of reason world, but rather calls it the form of the world [Gal. 4:3] (*LW* 34:139–40).[13]

The *image of God* is the Trinity's imprint on our very being, our *human* kind of being. The starting point for our understanding this is not Genesis by itself but Jesus himself, as indicated in passages like Colossians 1:15: "He is the image of the invisible God, the firstborn of all creation."

To be crystal clear, God prohibits us from dealing with him according to speculative reason. He wants us to have nothing to do with him except "as far as He is clothed in, and delivered to us by, His Word,"[14] or *nisi per verbum*.[15] This is what Luther intended by

---

[13]Notice Luther's Aristotelian terminology in his use of "form."

[14]Martin Luther, *The Bondage of the Will* (trans. Henry Cole; Peabody, Mass.: Hendrickson, 2008), 125.

[15]"But God cannot be treated with, God cannot be apprehended (*nisi per Verbum*) except through the Word" (Ap IV, 67).

coming back again and again in the disputation to the impossibility of knowing God, and hence the impossibility of knowing the
essence of the human being, apart from God's self-revelation in
the word. This is why Luther was prone to speak here and elsewhere
of philosophy as law. According to his experience, philosophy is
Aristotelian and Scholastic. It is speculative—a merely human
rationality that presumes to think what human rationality cannot
think, namely, God himself. But the written revelation of the word
changes everything. Now we know God as he desires to be known.

### Heidegger and a Lutheran Theological Anthropology

We as twenty-first-century thinkers need to get caught up with the
relevant philosophical developments that have taken place in philosophy in the centuries since Luther, in particular in nineteenth-
and twentieth-century philosophy. We must do this in order to think
well—even as *a necessary condition* (a prerequisite, if you will) of
thinking well. Philosophical anthropology is no longer Aristotelian;
nor has it been for most of modernity. This does not mean that philosophy's understanding of the human being is better in our day and
age. But where our anthropology today is an advance on Aristotle's
definition of the human type of being, it has to do with the impact
of Luther's thought on Heidegger.[16] Recharged now with a proper
Lutheran goodwill toward philosophy, let us return for a few para-
graphs to a philosophical reading of Luther's sixteenth-century disputation by the twentieth-century Heidegger that may help us better
to appropriate Luther in Lutheran ministry today.

In the so-called First Division of *Being and Time*, Heidegger
pointed out that there is a two-part problem with Aristotle's definition of the human being: (1) it makes us think that life (*zōon*) is
something objectively present in the human being; and (2) the *logos*
is some sort of obscure "higher endowment" possessed by human
beings. Heidegger went on to say that our Western or "Christian
theological anthropology" has swallowed this Aristotelian theory,
hook, line and sinker, although with the added feature that the life
and *logos* we possess are piously said to be "a gift from God," thereby

---

[16]See van Buren, "Martin Heidegger, Martin Luther," 159–74.

hopelessly muddying the waters.[17] Notice that "Christian theological anthropology" is not the same as "Christological anthropology" or "Lutheran theological anthropology."

As inheritors of what Heidegger called "the Christian theological anthropology," we may well require the critical push and the "Oh, is that really so?" question that comes from philosophy in order to wake us up to how radical (and *theo*-logical) Luther's view is. He urged us to rethink our thinking about ourselves as human beings, to think about the uniquely *human* kind of being that we are by reflecting on exactly how we human beings are implicated in the very question that we are asking. It is a sort of philosophy by catechesis of our fallen nature.

Bayer, you will recall, says that Luther viewed the human being in effect as *homo justificari fide*, taking the human being as the kind of being that is justified by faith. In respect to the human being's relationship to God this is crucially true, as we have seen. The passive *justificari* of Luther's definition of man in contrast to the active participles in the Aristotelian and popular science definitions is an indication of this. The human being is the kind of being that is in need of justification and *can be made aware of* this fundamental stratum to our existence. This brings to light a question with implications for us as preachers and *Seelsorgers*: What kind of being is the human that we are able to hear the *evangel* of our justification *Solum Christum*—not in terms of merely existing, as a rock exists, but by virtue of being *homo justificari*?

One response to this question provides the title of a book by one of Martin Heidegger's students, Karl Rahner: *Hearer of the Word*. Rahner argued that the human being is the kind of being who is able to hear and thus is open to the possibility of God's revelation.[18] This sort of study is philosophical in that it is pre-theological, a rigorous ontological disclosure of the kind of being the human being is. A more accessible, Thomas-free introduction to Heidegger has become

---

[17]Martin Heidegger, *Being and Time: A Translation of* Sein und Zeit (trans. Joan Stambaugh; New York: State University of New York Press, 1996), 45–46.

[18]See Karl Rahner, *Hearer of the Word: Laying the Foundation for a Philosophy of Religion* (ed. Andrew Tallon; trans. Joseph Donceel; New York: Continuum, 1994), 53: "This openness is the condition for the possibility for every single knowledge. . . . To be human is to be spirit [*Der Mensch ist Geist*], i.e., to live life while reaching ceaselessly for the absolute, in openness toward God."

available with the relatively recent publication of *Justifying Our Existence: An Essay in Applied Phenomenology* by Graeme Nicholson. In a nutshell, Nicholson unpacks one intriguing outcome of Heidegger's ontology in a practical way. In the next section let me paraphrase a point from Heidegger and then make one point from Nicholson's work with an eye on its cash value for Lutheran pastors.

### *Seel, Sorge,* and Justification

Phenomenology is a philosophy that, in a manner of speaking, is tailor-made for pastors who see themselves as *Seelsorgers:* According to the phenomenological description or *ontology*, each human being is an individual who is an utterly unique sort of being (a *Seel*), one who is fundamentally characterized by care (*Sorge*). The intriguing outcome of Heidegger's ontology is the discovery that human beings do not merely exist in anything like the sense that rocks or frogs exist; on the contrary, human beings are a kind of being for whom being is a concern. We do not just *have* existence; rather, the unique character of our existence is that we are capable of *caring about* our existence. This is the essence of the human being. As Heidegger argued in his early writings, concern is *constitutive* of human being. It is what we do. Human beings are never truly *care*-less about death and facing God. And this essential care, if it remains bereft of the gospel of Christ, leads to despair. The *only* answer is Christ himself brought to despairing human beings by the means of grace.

Now, this philosophical understanding of human beings as caring beings is pre-religious, which is to say there is no moral or theological work being done here. My point is that this philosophical thinking supports Luther's biblical insight that man is *homo justificari* by bringing to light that human beings, unlike any other beings in creation, are the kind of beings who care about being and are thus in their very nature needy for justification. It is worth pointing out that we are speaking about the justification of the complete human being, not merely the justification of some action or inaction. Further, this need for justification is an essential[19] need that human beings are universally prone to fill with self-justifications of one sort or another.

---

[19]That is, essential in the philosophical sense, not in some Maslovian sense.

There is no predisposition to faith; indeed, we are predisposed to justify ourselves, in defiance of God.

So then, in what follows from Heidegger's ontology of the human being, how exactly are we open to justification? Nicholson says, "Justifying oneself is an *a priori* disposition, rooted in our existence."[20] This follows logically from the ontology of the human being that we meet in the twentieth-century philosophy of phenomenology. If care or *Sorge* is how we fundamentally relate to being in the world, to other human beings, and to our own being, then it follows that, in respect to our care or concern for our own being, we are *homo justificari fide*, just as Luther argued in his disputation. But clearly, everything hinges on whether or not we have Christ as the object of faith, or whether we are anxiously searching for justification of our being *incurvatus se*, turning inward, looking to ourselves and our rationalizations for salvation.

In order to avoid any misunderstanding, let me reiterate that philosophical thinking does not *per se* deliver the gospel. Philosophy does not save human beings; but it does save human beings from thinking of one another as donkeys, as mere animals. It can help pinpoint the place in human being where the law gains its purchase. Luther's theory of the human being is a theological anthropology in that it depends on biblical revelation (Rom 3:28 in this case), but it is philosophical as well. Luther did not simply announce his position; he used his acquaintance with Aristotle and his logical acumen to *make an argument* for everyone to join in.

In the course of my philosophical analysis of Luther's *Disputation Concerning Man*, I offered some critical thinking of my own to indicate that the twentieth-century philosophy of phenomenology not only does not contradict Luther's theological anthropology, but also in fact appears to support Luther's new fundamental anthropology with an *ontology* of the human being. This ontology reveals human beings to be an utterly unique kind of being in all of creation: The *human* being does not merely exist; rather, the human being *cares* about being—its own being and the being of others. In fact, the human being cares *so deeply* that, absent Christ, he inevitably falls to justifying himself.

---

[20]Graeme Nicholson, *Justifying Our Existence: An Essay in Applied Phenomenology* (Toronto: University of Toronto Press, 2009), 78–79.

This, of course, is the purpose of the pastoral office: to placard Christ and to deliver Christ as the one who justifies, for to know and possess him is to know and possess his benefits. With the erudition that comes from a theological *and* philosophical understanding of human being, we pastors are better equipped to accomplish this task.

## Closing Vignette

It seems to me that you may have two kinds of objection to my essay. You may think that this is entirely too academic and, well, *too philosophical* for our work in congregations. In that case, let me just point you back to Luther's obviously philosophical *Disputation Concerning Man* from 1536. Or, you may think that this essay is fine for professors but has little practical value for pastors and missionaries. In that case, do I have a story for you:

> The gospel must reach my country *in the universities*! The people in the churches do not read the Bible. Neither do the pastors, who are uneducated, and so they have no doctrine to teach. But in the universities the students want to know. They read. They ask questions. They listen and then they ask more questions. The gospel of Jesus Christ must reach my country in the universities.

The professor, a philosopher and friend whose name and university I will not credit here as it may put him in danger back home, was lecturing about mission work in China. Over dinner that evening we talked philosophy: Wittgenstein, Gregory of Nyssa, and Kierkegaard; East and West. A couple of months later, on the way to teaching a course at Asia Lutheran Seminary in Hong Kong, I was able to lecture a group of mostly non-Christian graduate philosophy students and professors at his university in mainland China.

My lecture had to do with truth theories, in particular with a notion of truth-as-revelation from Martin Heidegger. As a formal lecture, I explained in some detail how Heidegger described the human being as *Dasein*, a spatiotemporal being whose existence is essentially characterized by *Sorge* or care, with this concern about being making humans unique. I began by rehearsing the available truth theories as commonly discussed in Western philosophy. Then I proposed a necessary condition—an indispensable ingredient for knowing truth. The dictum is *veritas non cognoscitur, nisi amatur*, "truth is not known unless it is loved," from Gregory the Great (540–604). I presented my version of Heidegger's philosophical elaboration of the Greek term for truth, *aletheia*, then concluded by demonstrating that Jesus, who claims to be the Truth (John 14:6), uniquely satisfies this necessary condition, namely, that to be known truth must be loved.

A number of the graduate students knew Heidegger. They listened, asked me questions, then listened further and asked more questions. We argued philosophically about capital-T Truth, about truth theories, and about Jesus the Truth. A number of students were furiously writing down every single definition and proposition I had introduced, some even before my key terms had been translated into Mandarin. There were smiles and audible "aahs" when I characterized Jesus as the Truth incarnate, known because he first loved us (1 John 4:10, 19). One student who had received word that day that he had passed his Masters exams told me quietly, "I think that I should tell you that I am not a Christian yet, *but I think I am going to be*." So you see, philosophy can indeed be practical and in service of the gospel.

Now that I have warmed your pastoral heart with this philosophical mission story, I trust that we will be more fully engaged in the effort to become Paleolithic, philosophically erudite pastors. In order to be Lutheran *Seelsorgers*, according to Luther's own biblical understanding of the human beings for whom we care, we need to be at least modestly conversant with traditional Western philosophy and twentieth-century philosophy.[21] Thus, the story of the gospel and the proper care of souls in our twenty-first century is, I think, a narrative of dinosaurs and DOXOLOGY.

---

[21]Lutheran Pastors with little to no training in philosophy might begin with Diogenes Allen and Eric O. Springsted, ed., *Philosophy for Understanding Theology* (2d ed.; Louisville, Ky.: Westminster John Knox, 2007), or Jennifer Hockenbery Dragseth, ed., *The Devil's Whore: Reason and Philosophy in the Lutheran Tradition* (Minneapolis: Fortress, 2011). For a more general introduction to the field, see Norman Melchert and David R. Morrow, *The Great Conversation: A Historical Introduction to Philosophy* (8th ed.; Oxford: Oxford University Press, 2018).

# Form and Purpose of Clergy Vestments in the Lutheran Tradition(s)

*Wilhelm Torgerson*

*This essay was originally prepared as an oral presentation for a Lutheran Conference in Riga, Latvia, in 2006.*

## I. Introduction

"Is this really important?" That was my first reaction when asked to present a paper on the topic of vestments in the Lutheran tradition. Should we not instead be talking about issues touching the very existence of the church (*esse ecclesiae*) and its continued wellbeing (*bene esse ecclesiae*)? Ought not our focus be on texts instead of textiles? After all, the varieties in clergy vestments are great and the differences in their usages considerable, according to national, regional, historical, and church-body traditions. What is more, when one looks at photos depicting clergy vestment usage in various Lutheran church bodies in North America, the Baltic states, Scandinavia, and Germany, no single rule seems to apply or prevail—save one: *there is no rule, everyone does his own thing.*

If one takes note, however, of the intense discussion—even the discord—that can arise when the longstanding clergy vestment usage *has been changed*, either for an entire church body or at the level of a local parish, it is clear that the topic of vestments and their use is of some significance to people in the church, at least emotionally. Indeed, the preaching of false doctrine or heresy in the pulpit can be received with more charity and can cause less of a stir than the use of "new" clergy vestments at the altar—particularly when "*what we've always done*" is no longer done. For some people, clergy vestments have become something of a denominational hallmark, a sign of recognition, a mark of identification. Nevertheless, things are not quite that simple.

## II. Lutherans and Vestments

The Augsburg Confession reminds us: "The chief purpose of all ceremonies is to teach the people what they need to know about Christ" (AC XXIV, 3–4). The vestments of the officiating minister are ceremony; as such, they primarily serve a pedagogical purpose for the benefit of the laity. Further, the Apology of the Augsburg Confession speaks clearly of the spirit that pervades, or at least ought to pervade, the worship of the Lutheran church: "We gladly keep the old traditions set up in the church because they are useful and promote tranquility" (Ap XV, 38).[1]

Vestments have been used in the church virtually from the beginning.[2] No one starts with himself—everyone has been influenced by his particular learning and experiences, as well as by the (singular) tradition of the church catholic. Further, national, regional, and denominational churches have their own traditions (plural) according to their individual historical contexts—and in the latter case these traditions may be of various age, from ancient to recent. No one can do without such traditions; something must be worn that is deemed decent and appropriate by some standard, and tradition is often the chief arbiter. This fact alone indicates that vestments are not entirely unimportant.

---

[1] See the entire section as well: Ap XV, 38–44.

[2] Raymund James, *The Origin and Development of Roman Liturgical Vestments* (Exeter: Catholic Records Press, 1934), 3; Herbert Norris, *Church Vestments: Their Origin and Development* (New York: E. P. Dutton & Co., 1950; repr., Mineola, N.Y.: Dover Publications, 2017), 8–9; Arthur Carl Piepkorn, "What about Vestments for Pastors?" *Concordia Theological Monthly* 30 (July 1959): 483–84; John T. Pless, "The Leaders of Worship" in *Lutheran Worship: History and Practice* (ed. Fred L. Precht; St. Louis: Concordia, 1993), 219.

This paper will focus strictly on the usage of vestments in the Lutheran traditions. Note the plural form. There is no such thing as the one Lutheran vestment. This requires emphasis because in Luther's homeland there are many people who think otherwise. For example, it is a widely held opinion in Germany that the Lutheran minister (and by "Lutheran" most really mean *evangelisch*—that is, Protestant) properly wears and is recognized by the black gown with tabs (*Talar* and *Beffchen*). A valid regional exception, however, would be the two-part black gown with round ruffle collar still customary in some of the former Hanseatic cities, such as Hamburg or Lübeck, or in areas of Denmark and Norway. Yet this comes from the 1811 mandate of the King of Prussia, Frederick William III, which ordered the use of the black gown with tabs as the professional garment for all Lutheran pastors, Jewish rabbis, and judges. This was the king's right since they were civil servants and government employees. The Prussian government felt it necessary to issue the vestment instruction because many of these professionals had begun wearing what was *en vogue*—the fashionable fad of the moment—which caused more than a little irritation among the population.

This government mandate subsequently led to the situation that wherever Lutherans of German background planted their churches and parishes in other places in the eighteenth and nineteenth centuries, the black gown with tabs became the usual garb for the Lutheran officiant at worship. Succeeding generations of theologians followed the familiar example of their predecessors. For instance, it is not uncommon to see black clergymen in southern Africa wearing what seems to be eminently "German" vestment as gown and tabs. This is what they had learned from the missionaries and it became part of their church tradition. Moreover, for some of them this usage has become a sign of theological faithfulness to what they had been taught.

The usage of vestments in the churches of Scandinavia is different, at least in part. Some pastors in Denmark and Norway normally wear black gown with ruffle collar during the worship service; but in both countries, and almost everywhere in Sweden, the old traditional priestly garments of alb and chasuble are in use—something that in Germany by and large is associated with the papists.

It seems evident today that clergy vestments are determined by the following factors: personal taste, historical usage, liturgical tradition, ethnic influence, and regional considerations. At St. Peter's Parish in Edmonton, Alberta (a congregation of the Lutheran Church—Missouri Synod, where both German and English worship services were retained), the long-time pastor who confirmed me always wore a simple black gown: Geneva style; v-neck. However, most of the pastors in neighboring congregations in the 1960s had begun wearing what I now call "Anglican" vestments: black cassock (*Soutane*) with white surplice (*Chorrock*) and a colored stole. And in the years after World War II and well into the 1970s many of the older people considered this to be "rather catholic." For them, it took some getting used to this "new" attire.

On one occasion our congregation at St. Peter's was invited to a mission presentation held at another congregation. A film was shown about mission work in Tanzania, a place where a significant part of the Christian outreach work is of Swedish origin. I remember there being a rather lively and displeased reaction on the part of the audience when an African Lutheran bishop was shown in alb, cope, mitre, and bishop's staff. To use Queen Victoria's phrase, "We were not amused." This was popish excess in the minds of most of those present. But the point is this: No clergy vestment is universal, neither in time nor in place nor in circumstance.

In my own ministry this has been quite obvious. When I was ordained in 1971 at St. Paul's in Edmonton, Alberta (a German-speaking congregation), I wore, and kept wearing for some years after that, a black gown with tabs. Eventually I began to wear this only for the German services during my ministry in Canada, much to the appreciation of our German parishioners. For the English services I started wearing the "Anglican" garb mentioned above. Now as I serve parishes in Hamburg and in Berlin, with celebration of Holy Communion every Sunday, and with the festive liturgy of the old-Lutheran tradition, I usually wear alb and chasuble. Yet on Good Friday, during Lenten services, and for other non-communion worship occasions, I still wear what to this day many consider "German garb"—that is, black gown with tabs. This again illustrates the point that no clergy vestment has universal or exclusive validity. Ceremonies can change in time and in place and for different occasions.

It may be helpful to look at how Lutherans have historically dealt with vestments in the church or looked upon their usage.

I believe Dr. Arthur Carl Piepkorn was right when he distinguished four general attitudes[3]:

a. *Negative Symbol*

   To begin with I refer to those who see in the traditional pastoral/liturgical vestments, especially those of the ancient church, a sign for popish tyranny and excess; thus they should not be tolerated. For such people, colorful vestments indicate a lack of Christian *simplicity* and biblical *purity*. This view was not only held in times past by the Anabaptists, the Enthusiasts (*Schwärmer*), and the Sacramentarians, those who did not want the one presiding at the worship service to wear any garb different from that of the worshipers. To this day there are still those who consider the old vestments quite *immodest* at best on the part of the one wearing them, and *distracting* at worst to the worshipers. Thus they are deemed unacceptable within the churches of the Reformation.

b. *Not Illegal but . . .*

   Secondly there are those who do not look upon old-church vestments as illegal or contrary to the commandments. Rather they are considered to be a sign of temporally limited tradition or of merely local historical origin. In that sense they are looked upon as an understandable connection with the past. The implication is: They are *backward*-looking and should in time be "overcome." This seems to be a widespread attitude toward vestments among not a few Protestant (*evangelisch*) Germans even today.

c. *Absolute Adiaphoron*

   What about Luther and the fathers of the Reformation? Luther did not think such things either good or bad in and of themselves; he considered them truly "middle

---

[3]See Arthur Carl Piepkorn, *The Survival of the Historic Vestments in the Lutheran Church After 1555* (St. Louis: Concordia Seminary School for Graduate Studies, 1956), 8–10.

things" (*adiaphora*). The head pastor in Wittenberg and Luther's confessor, Dr. Johannes Bugenhagen, concurred. In a letter from 1530 to Martin Görlitz, he wrote:

> There is a twofold doctrine on chasubles. . . . one is the truth, namely, that chasubles can be used; this does not give scandal to those who are accustomed to hearing the Gospel. The other is a Satanic lie out of the doctrines of devils, namely, that it is never lawful to use chasubles; this gives scandal to the people where they hear and believe such lies from the ministers.[4]

The rule here is obvious: Do whatever you will—but let love and good order prevail in this matter.

d. *Indicative Adiaphoron*

According to this fourth view the old traditional vestments may indeed be called "middle things"; but their use, especially their reintroduction where they have fallen into disuse, is a strong indication of a specific message. And this message expresses the view that regular and normal use of the old vestments is one outward sign for the unbroken continuity of the church of the Augsburg Confession with the one holy catholic and apostolic church in its Western tradition.

Oddly enough, this to be the exact reason why in a considerable part of Lutheranism the old vestments fell into disuse! Remember, especially in areas of Europe where Roman Catholic rulers held sway, they at times issued decrees prohibiting the continued use of old-church vestments by the Lutheran clergy within their dominion. The claim here is quite clear and obvious: You, the Lutherans, are a new sect; you have severed yourself from the true church, so you better not "look like the church."

---

[4]Quoted in Piepkorn, *Survival of the Historic Vestments*, 9.

Despite the fact that Luther considered vestments to be in the category of "Absolute Adiaphoron," it may prove helpful to consider the question: What vestments did Luther actually wear? Pictorial representations of the great reformer often show him preaching in a black gown. It would be incorrect, however, to deduce from such pictures (often woodcuts or paintings) that Luther wanted this to be the minister's garb for worship or that this should now be a sign identifying the preachers of Reformation theology. There is instead a rather simple explanation for many of these representations: Luther is pictured in the black monk's habit of the Augustinian Eremites, just as one of his chief opponents, Johann Tetzel, was normally pictured in a white monk's habit because he was a Dominican. Both are shown wearing the habit of their monastic community, which was also the preaching and teaching garb. Later Luther stopped wearing the monk's habit and usually wore his professor's gown. At one time he commented that if a Spaniard would come to Wittenberg he would see and hear in the liturgical forms of the services nothing unusually different.

And in a letter to Georg Buchholzer, Dean (*Propst*) in Berlin, Luther wrote: "And if for your lord, the Prince Elector, one cope or one surplice which you wear as dean is not enough, then start wearing three of them. . . ." This is usually where the quotation ends. Frankly, that sounds as if Luther thought the whole issue of vestments is at best something *unimportant*, at worst something rather *silly*. But the sentence continues: ". . . as Aaron the high priest wore three vestments one over the other, which were wonderful and beautiful (*herrlich und schön*)."

One of the clearest statements on Luther's view of pastoral vestments is to be found in his *Table Talks*:

> Among the enthusiasts (*Schwärmer*) they are considered the best preachers, who are well able to do these four things: one, don't wear a surplice; next, no chasuble; thirdly, think nothing of confession; and fourthly, that in the sacrament of the altar there is nothing but bread and wine.

The question, then, as to what Luther wore when officiating at the altar can be addressed quite simply. As a monk from an Erfurt monastery, a priest in the church of his day, and a professor of biblical studies serving at a university of some importance, why should he have worn anything but the then-customary priestly vestments as he had been taught and to which his parishioners were accustomed? This is in fact what he did.

## III. The Bible and Vestments

Lutherans have always insisted and maintained that the ministerial office (*Predigtamt*) is not derived from the Old Testament priesthood. Melanchthon said: "Priests are not called to make sacrifices that merit forgiveness of sins for the people, as in the Old Testament. . . . As the Epistle to the Hebrews teaches clearly enough, we do not have a priesthood like the Levitical" (Ap XIII, 10). No Lutheran minister, therefore, can legitimately claim a direct and lineal connection to the priesthood of the old covenant. This means that any rules governing that ancient priesthood *do not apply to*—and certainly *do not govern*—the office of the ministry in the new covenant. The former, like the other rules, regulations, and provisions in the Old Testament, are "a shadow of things to come" (Col 2:17). The ministerial office is authorized by Christ himself (John 20:21) and an outflow of the apostolic ministry following Christ's ascension and Pentecost (Matt 16:19; 28:18–20; Acts 2).

Nevertheless, something can be learned by considering the vestments from the Old Testament in regards to their use in worship. The most obvious fact is that a great deal of time and an amazing amount of detail are involved in the question of priestly vestments. Clearly, then, the issue could not have been unimportant for the old covenant. "The vestments shall be upon Aaron, and upon his sons, when they go into the tent of meeting, or when they come near the altar to minister in the holy place . . . for glory and beauty" (Exod 28:43). Indeed, the entire chapter of Exodus 28 deals with the garments of Aaron and his sons as priests of the Most High God. It is by the Lord's command, after all, that they are to stand in his holy presence in the stead of his people, representing God to them and, in turn, representing their own flock to him. Only the very best, only the most carefully prepared attire, is good enough as the priest stands before the Most High and in his service.

And in Lutheran churches today? Where do we consider ourselves to be when celebrating—let me stress that word again: *celebrating*—the liturgy? Indeed, *where* exactly do you pastors think you are? Does not the *Gloria in Excelsis* in the holy mass remind us of the hymn of the angels of Bethlehem (Luke 2:14)? And do we not in the *Sanctus* join in the seraphim's chorale of praise and adoration at the very throne of God (Isa 6:1–4)? But most of all, we are (or at least, should we not be?) full of wonder and awe at the blessed altar miracle of *the real presence of Christ's true body and blood* given for the sinner's redemption! The Virgin Mary wrapped her Son in ordinary swaddling clothes back then and over there; yet God, by the power of his creative word, wraps Christ's body and blood in ordinary bread and wine here and now. So then, this principle remains: Only the very best and only the most carefully prepared attire is good enough for the service in the presence of the Most High.[5]

There is a popular German saying worth considering here: "*Kleider machen Leute*" ("Clothes make the man"). Initially this is a dreadful thought if you understand it to mean that the way people see you—the way you appear on the outside—amounts to your standing in society. Horrible! But if instead you understand this to mean that the way you are on the inside reflects on the way people see you—or more significantly, that what you have received you can in turn pass on to others—this is far more agreeable and even splendid. Regarding vestments in the New Testament, a similarly positive connotation is conveyed by two significant images for understanding worship garments under the new covenant: the appearance of Christ at his transfiguration and the notion of being clothed in baptism.

The transfiguration is recorded in both Matthew and Luke, with similar terms found in both accounts:

> And he was transfigured before them, and his face shone like the sun, and his clothes (*himatia*) became white (*leuka*) as light (Matt 17:2).

---

[5]The Old Testament presents a rich symbolism of garments and vestments which is outside the scope of this paper. Among other scriptural references, see Psalm 30:11; 132:9, 16; Isaiah 61:10.

> As he was praying, the appearance of his face was altered, and
> his clothes (*himatismos*) became dazzling white (*leukos*) (Luke
> 9:29).

The divine lordship and glory of Christ becomes momentarily visible to human eyes, as indicated by the dazzling whiteness of his garments.

The author of Revelation also speaks of such white garments when referring to the redeemed:

> Yet you still have a few names in Sardis, people who have not soiled
> their garments (*himatia*); they shall walk with me in white
> (*en leukois*) (Rev 3:4–5).
> I counsel you to buy . . . white garments (*himatia leuka*) to clothe
> you and to keep the shame of your nakedness from being seen
> (Rev 3:18).
> Twenty-four elders on thrones "clad in white garments (*en himatiois
> leukois*)" (Rev 4:4).
> A great multitude . . . clothed in white robes (*stolas leukas*)
> (Rev 7:9).
> And they washed their robes (*stolas*) and made them white
> (*eleukanan*) in the blood of the Lamb (Rev 7:14).

Whatever else these verses may mean, an inescapable point is this: none of the redeemed stands naked before God.[6] Nakedness, after man's fall in paradise, is a sign for depravity, shame, and sinfulness. The redeemed are covered by the righteousness of Christ in the light of God's justice, washed in the blood of the Lamb, vested in whiteness and brightness. This is what their garments symbolize and indicate.

In relation to the baptized children of God here on earth, Paul often uses the word *enduo*. This means as much as "getting dressed, putting on a garment, vesting yourself." Particularly striking are the following passages:

---

[6]Richard Bauckham, *The Climax of Prophecy: Studies On the Book of Revelation* (Edinburgh: T&T Clark, 1993), 104–5, 107; G. K. Beale, *The Book of Revelation* (New International Greek Testament Commentary; Grand Rapids: Eerdmans, 1998), 279, 403, 837–38, 942.

FORM AND PURPOSE OF CLERGY VESTMENTS 235

But put on (*endusasthe*) the Lord Jesus Christ, and make no
provision for the flesh, to gratify its desires. (Rom 13:14)
For as many of you as were baptized into Christ have put on
(*enedusasthe*) Christ (Gal 3:27).
. . . and to put on (*endusasthai*) the new self, created after the
likeness of God in true righteousness and holiness (Eph 4:24).
You have put on (*endusamenoi*) the new nature (Col 3:10).
Put on (*endusasthe*) then, as God's chosen ones, holy and beloved:
compassion, kindness, lowliness, meekness and patience
(Col 3:12).

Here also the point is this: the baptized are *covered up, vested* in the
righteousness of Christ their Savior through faith. Thus, "clothes
make the man" is not a biblical message. How one is seen by others or appears to others does not reveal one's true Christian identity.
Outward garments, rather, are signs and symbols for something that
has happened to a person; they are indicative of an inner process, of
something that was given to them, bestowed upon them by Christ,
their Lord and redeemer.

There may be reservations about this kind of symbolism
because too much can be read into it. But the thought is not new and
certainly not odd. In one of the popular hymns attributed to Count
Zinzendorf, it is put this way:

Christi Blut und Gerechtigkeit, das ist mein Schmuck und
Ehrenkleid,
damit will ich vor Gott bestehn, wenn ich zum Himmel werd eingehn.

John Wesley's translation[7] reads:

Jesus, Thy blood and righteousness My beauty are, my glorious dress;
Midst flaming worlds, in these arrayed, With joy shall I lift up my
head.

To make the point, one might say that by wearing vestments the pastor is "covered up" in the sense that he is "de-personalized." He is

---

[7]*Lutheran Service Book* (St. Louis: Concordia, 2006), 563.

not officiating as a privateer, possibly because he is so highly gifted or so greatly talented, and not even because he is elected by popular choice. The worshipers are not to see in him a charming neighbor, a dear friend, or their paid employee. The pastor stands there to represent Christ; he is doing what he does and saying what he says *not* because he is obeying the consistory, a parish council, or a synod, but because *the Lord himself has commanded and authorized* pastors to do and to speak thusly.

## IV. Conclusions

The Rev. Dr. Charles Evanson once told me a little story that is indicative of our topic, "Why vestments?" While visiting a small Lutheran parish in Ontario, Canada, the officiating minister explained why he wore no special garb during the divine service but just an ordinary suit. "We don't wear costumes," he succinctly declared. And indeed, he is correct. At whatever time, during whatever function, in whatever capacity, *Lutheran clergymen do not wear costumes!* That is, we do not put on garments to indicate that we are putting on a "show," or that we are pretending to be someone other than we are. Costumes are for actors as a form of pretense, to separate or differentiate the person from the role he plays.

That is precisely **not** the purpose of clergy vestments. They are not for pretense or a charade; rather, the contrary is the case. He who legitimately appears in vestments—that frail sinner who shepherds the flock entrusted to his care in the stead and by the command of the Lord—unites the human person he is and the divine charge entrusted to him. First of all, vestments "cover" his human nature and his sinful state. And secondly, vestments "uncover" insofar as they point to the heavenly reality of redemption that has now broken into the earthly realm in the divine service in the name and by the authority of him who acts through the words and actions of his servant.

That is what vestments are "saying," that is their message. It is also the reason why we—the church as a whole, local congregations, all the ministers of God—ought to be careful and attentive as we make decisions about the use of vestments. If everything is a "text" of some kind, then I am convinced that the aphorism, "Actions speak louder than words," certainly applies to clergy vestments. At the least, one's appearance speaks *as* loud as his words.

One of the major factors for any church to consider regarding clergy vestments is its own historical background and the tradition(s) it has adhered to so far. But this raises an obvious question: Which tradition? The Evangelical Lutheran Church in western and central Europe, for example, is clearly a descendent of the (Latin) Church of the West. If it is part of that historical tradition, how is this reflected in its theology, in its worship, and in the appearance of its clergy as seen by the public? If in some way—properly understood—everything starts with Rome, then in another sense—properly understood—we all originate in Wittenberg. But these two points of derivation (as suggested above) are not opposed to one another in terms of the outward appearance of ministers.

In regard to pastoral vestments, the larger context of (western and central European) history and tradition will be tempered and influenced by what has been the practice in a particular church in recent times and how vestment usage differed from place to place. Two examples may serve to make the point.

First, if it is true that a Lutheran church body has been heavily influenced by a post-Reformation, perhaps nineteenth-century German background, then obviously black gown and tabs (*Talar* and *Beffchen*) have come to be something of a mark of recognition for the Lutheran officiant. But as a Canadian who spent most of his life in Germany, I say: By general consensus it may be held that the catholic church is the Roman Church; *but the Evangelical Lutheran Church is not the German church!*

Second, Lutherans for many years—some of them since shortly after the Reformation—have been proclaiming the gospel and ministering the holy sacraments in an environment where the old Latin Church never took hold, in an area and amongst people not "Western," and certainly not German. I am thinking of Russia and the Ukraine, of Kazakhstan or Moldavia, and other places. There Christianity originally appeared in its Byzantine "orthodox" form and their clergy were recognizable in the garb of that tradition. I claim that it is not a legitimate ministry of the Lutheran Church in such an environment to persuade converts to become "westerners," nor should the Lutheran pastors there indicate by word, action, or appearance that Western traditions are in any way superior to practices that hitherto were not in any way considered inimical or offensive to the pure gospel. As the Jerusalem Council of the Apostles (Acts 15) ruled, one need not become a Jew before becoming a Christian; so, too, no one must become a westerner before becoming a Lutheran.

What, then, are the appropriate clergy vestments to wear as you serve in the function to which Christ has called you? And what is suitable in the particular place where the church has placed you as an ordained minister of the gospel? As the church at large, local churches, pastors, and parishioners all try to answer such questions properly, perhaps the following attitudes will be helpful:

- abiding love for and loyal commitment to your church
- high regard for the office of the ministry
- deep appreciation for the liturgy
- ready willingness to learn from Christian history
- preparedness to teach your people with gentleness and respect about worship and ministry

In my estimation, members of a congregation ought to be able to recognize some of these traits in their pastors.

Please don't misunderstand: I am not saying that while riding the bus or the bicycle, while sitting in the restaurant or going to the movies, the clergyman must wear garb identifying him as such. What I am pleading for and proposing is that while officiating in his capacity, while engaged on "official business," so to speak, while speaking by the command and in the stead of Christ—preaching, absolving, consecrating—it is not only helpful to others but a reminder to oneself, that the pastor/priest/minister should be seen as more than just Mr. X. In my view, vestments are eminently suitable for this task and they are appropriate in helping to achieve this goal, certainly more appropriate than wearing a common business suit and infinitely more appropriate than casual attire.

One final example to make the point: The soldier of a regular army is readily known by his uniform, the military officer so gives an indication of his rank. These are marks for recognizing one's legitimate office and task. Similarly, dressing up in a policeman's uniform when not so authorized is illegal (not to mention dangerous) if one attempts to direct traffic, make arrests, or do any number of things reserved for the specific authority granted to that particular vocation. Even in the case of an ambassador who presents his credentials to a foreign head of state, the attire serves to identify his position and gives an indication of the importance of his task.

Nothing less ought to be the case as we stand at the altar and in the pulpit. The apostle Paul reminds us: "We are ambassadors for Christ, God making his appeal through us" (2 Cor 5:20). Wearing church vestments as Lutheran clergymen is therefore not a question of fad or fashion, of personal choice and preference, nor of what someone has called the *Seven Last Words of the Church*: "But we've never done it that way!" Vestments are tools to aid in the work of the ministry, reminding the one who wears them of the importance of his position and task, and helping the congregation more easily to recognize the undershepherd of the flock and thus be somewhat more receptive and attentive to his words and actions. Thus, vestments are not essential for the existence (*esse ecclesiae*) of the church, but they helpfully serve an orderly ministry and are important for the wellbeing (*bene esse ecclesiae*) of the church.

# Guardians in Christ

## The Gospel Moves to Europe

*Harald Tomesch*

More than a decade ago in a radio broadcast for Issues, Etc. entitled, "The Hijacking of the Church's Mission," I proposed that Matthew's Gospel was hopelessly misunderstood and had been completely co-opted by well-intentioned Christians seeking a platform to expand evangelical interests.[1] This sounds rather arrogant and critical, but I felt that the evangelical voices of our time needed a new perspective. In brief, I maintained that the canonization of Matthew into the larger context of the New Testament had made Jesus' words in the Great Commission, "to teach *everything* I have commanded you" (Matt 28:18–20), inclusive of all the Gospels and Epistles. The Great Commission understood in the way of those evangelicals did not point to Matthew's fine and systematic treatment of Jesus' teachings within this Gospel; rather, for them the Great Commission became a kind of self-directed, let-me-provide-for-you method of discipleship, falling broadly under the themes of accelerating multiplication, equipping movement makers, pursuing the next disciples and releasing them to continue the cycle.[2]

---

[1] This interview took place on February 18, 2004, but is no longer available online at the time of this Festschrift's publication.

[2] A sampling of these books would include: Alan Hirsch, *The Forgotten Ways: Reactivating the Missional Church* (Grand Rapids: Brozos, 2006); Alan Hirsch and Dave Ferguson, *On the Verge: A Journey into the Apostolic*

## The Great Commission as Recapitulation

In the 2004 radio exclusive, I made an observation that evangelism was being reinvented and re-imaged in man's image, rather than an image of Jesus' will for the church. I maintain to this day that the Great Commission is not the eschatological prime directive for the church. Rather it is the recapitulation of the entire Gospel of Matthew itself and its contents. I might add, as seems only logical in retrospect, that Matthew wrote his Gospel without thought of its inclusion into the larger canon. Therefore, Matthew intended his Gospel to be by its very design the sum of Jesus' commission, and it was an invitation to be catechized!

Jesus' Great Commission includes listening to the *vox viva*, the living voice of Jesus. Thus does Matthew believe that his witness to Jesus is best accomplished by preserving the Lord's voice in the five extended sermons of this Gospel, so that its hearers may listen to Jesus again and again. Moreover, by Matthew's design these sermons alternate between the instructional voice of Jesus himself ("everything I have commanded you"), and life's lessons in which Jesus' words are shaped in us by faith and failure. Just as Luke recapitulates by describing the "way" of his entire Gospel by means of the journey made by the two disciples going to Emmaus (Luke 24:13–35), and John recapitulates his Gospel with his repeated and final words concerning the beloved disciple (John 21:23–24), so Matthew does the same by means of the Great Commission.[3]

---

*Future of the Church* (Grand Rapids: Zondervan, 2011); Larry Osborne, *Sticky Church* (Grand Rapids: Zondervan, 2008); Hugh Halter, *AND: The Gathered and Scattered Church* (Grand Rapids: Zondervan, 2010); Brandon Hatmaker, *Barefoot Church: Serving the Least in a Consumer Culture* (Grand Rapids: Zondervan, 2011); Darren Patrick and Matt Carter, *For the City* (Grand Rapids: Zondervan, 2011); Helen Lee, *The Missional Mom: Living with Purpose at Home & in the World* (Chicago: Moody, 2011); Jim Putman, *Disciple/Shift: Five Steps That Help Your Church to Make Disciples Who Make Disciples* (Grand Rapids: Zondervan, 2013).

[3]There are more examples of such recapitulation in the New Testament. Revelation 1:12 begins with a grand description of Jesus: he is described as the Son of Man enthroned and on high, holding the seven lampstands and wearing a golden sash! What follows this description are seven separate messages

The *vox viva* in Matthew can be readily seen in the red-letter editions of our Bibles. The alternation between red-lettering and black-lettering is quite stark. Listed below are the five sermons which form the pillars of Matthew's Gospel, for which we can provide the proper themes:

| | | | |
|---|---|---|---|
| Sermon 1 | Matt 5–7 | The Sermon on the Mount | Christ's Alien Righteousness is Given: "Be Perfect as Your Father is Perfect" |
| Sermon 2 | Matt 10 | The Great Commission to the Jews | Absolute Dependence on Jesus |
| Sermon 3 | Matt 13 | The Mysteries of the Kingdom | Not Flesh and Blood but by the Spirit |
| Sermon 4 | Matt 18 | The Sermon for the Church | Hosanna to Jesus, Your Brother in Christ |
| Sermon 5 | Matt 24–25 | The Sermon on End Times | Beyond the Abomination: Now and Not Yet |

Time does not permit me to demonstrate the relationship between the five living sermons of Jesus and the life experiences shaped in the events portrayed by Matthew between these same five sermons. In fact, the network and tangible connections are many and acute between the sermons and the life events that follow. The

---

where Jesus' living voice (*vox viva*) addresses their needs. The seven churches of the Apocalypse, as we know them, are apportioned one part of the grand description of Jesus found beginning with Revelation 1:12. As Jesus addresses each of the seven congregations the original image of Jesus is apportioned to the specific needs of each. To give another example, Hebrews 1:1–4 serves as an outline for the entire epistle. See Harald Tomesch, *Genre and Outline: The Key to the Literary Structure of Hebrews* (Ph.D. diss., Concordia Seminary, St. Louis, 1994).

sermons always prepare the disciple for the lessons learned immediately afterward. A most prominent example is Peter's confession (Matt 16:13–20) of Jesus as Christ and Lord found between
Sermons 3 and 4. Note how Jesus is, in effect, saying, "Peter, flesh and
blood have not revealed this to you, but the Spirit," (harking back to
Sermon 3 about the Mysteries of the Kingdom) and, "Peter, upon
your confession I will build my church!" (the message anticipated in
Sermon 4 on the church).

Similarly, it can be argued that critical editions of the New
Testament placed an enumeration system in the Greek text of
Matthew from 0–170 in the margins of codex Vaticanus (B, also a[52],
579).[4] These divisions corresponded to the Sedarim (lectionary) of
the Hebrew Torah, thus further supporting the notion that Matthew
wanted his Gospel to be divided in such a manner that the living voice
of Jesus continues within the church to the present day—namely, as
a voice that alternates weekly in our experience between faith and
failure as we listen to Jesus. This means, in effect, that the Sunday
sermon continues the "everything I have commanded you," and the
hearer's life in vocation continues in life's lessons. In brief, it means
that Matthew wrote his Gospel to pattern the life of the Christian in
faith (hearing) and love (doing).

After that radio interview I placed my reflections and research
into Matthew onto a back burner, so-to-speak, but there was this

---

[4]The divisions are also found in X and in at least the first seven pages
of Matthew in Siniaticus. See W. D. Davies, "Reflections on Archbishop
Carrington's 'The Primitive Christian Calendar'" in *The Background of the
New Testament and Its Eschatology: Studies in Honour of C. H. Dodd* (ed.
W. D. Davies and D. Daube; Cambridge: Cambridge University Press, 1964),
145. Davies continues, "But Von Soden pointed out that even in the case of the
non-B manuscripts only an increased knowledge of the liturgical practice of
the Early Church can further enlighten us on the purpose of some of the divisions. That lines as those found in B, etc., to divide the text, may well go back
to the earliest days of the Church despite the lack of actual textual evidence
in manuscripts of the New Testament, may be suggested by the Isaiah scroll
from Qumran. The dissident sect which used the scroll, used lines in their text
which are very similar, if not identical, with those found in B, etc. These lines
were noted by Millar Burrows who apparently takes them to refer to lections
(as does Carrington)."

kind of nagging, a hounding in my soul, that asked, "Was I the only one to understand the Great Commission correctly? Would not the Holy Spirit nurture the church into a true understanding of the Great Commission?" I mused, "How could the church be so misguided in evangelism, that no one wanted a personal rabbi/teacher like Jesus?" In short, would the import of the five sermons of Jesus in Matthew be forever eclipsed in modern-day evangelism?

Slowly, I began to add other things to my list of mysteries as I explored Eric Werner's *The Sacred Bridge*,[5] describing our bridge from Judaism to Christianity, and James Burtchaell's *From Synagogue to Church: Public Services and Offices in the Earliest Christian Communities*.[6] I had come to believe in this general principle: canonization innocently moved Matthew into a new theological constellation. Matthew was now being read alongside other Gospels rather than shining in a solar system by itself. I also began to explore the notion that the movement from Judaism to a Gentile world—including Europe—also shifted theological perspectives away from Matthew's vantage point. The Lord's Prayer, for example, though frequently recited by Christendom today, plays relatively little importance in the rest of the books of the New Testament. Additionally, there is a shift away from "Rabbi" to "Pastor," and from "Synagogue" to "Church." This shift may well be expressed in the Scriptures themselves:

> But you are not to be called rabbi, for you have only one Master and you are all brothers. And do not call anyone on earth father, for you have one Father and he is in heaven. Nor are you to be called teacher, for you have one Teacher, the Christ (Matt 23:8–10).

It is an interesting progression—from rabbi, to father, to teacher.

---

[5]Eric Werner, *The Sacred Bridge: The Interdependence of Liturgy and Music in Synagogue and Church During the First Millennium* (2 vols.; repr., New York: KTAV Publishing House, 1984).

[6]James Tunstead Burtchaell, *From Synagogue to Church: Public Services and Offices in the Earliest Christian Communities* (Cambridge: Cambridge University Press, 1992).

While it is clear that Jesus welcomed the term "rabbi," W. H. Mare has noted that the title is frequently used in the Gospel by those who do not know Jesus as Lord.[7] The Church Fathers do not use the term "rabbi" at all, and the term "teach" is limited to "Jesus our only Teacher"[8] and Jesus our "famous Teacher."[9] Some have suggested that the term "father" is the most frequently used and preferred word for "pastor" in the New Testament. And of course, who of us would deny the use of the term "teacher" or "professor?" More than one commentary has lamented the fact that Matthew 23 has been used to justify or to deny our use of titles today, when, in fact, it speaks of service in church life. In my schematic of things, Matthew 23 places the references to rabbi, father, and teacher right after Jesus' sermon on the church (Matt 18) and thus instructs the church on service to our Lord.

## The Gospel Moves to Europe

Mike Breen notes that even the word "disciple" disappears from Acts after chapter 21, stating that once the church moves beyond the "cultural heartland of the Holy Land" in Galatia's synagogue there seems to be a shift. He observes that the implied rabbi/disciple relationship is going through a transition and that this metaphor is no longer the main paradigm.[10] Rather, he advocates a "Parent/Child" or "Father/Son" image as Paul's solution. Breen states that discipleship does not emphasize information as in the teacher/rabbi model, but imitation and innovation. This innovation for Paul comes as he leaves Asia and is summoned by the Spirit to move into Europe: the apostle makes a shift in terminology precisely when he leaves the synagogue model in the rear-view mirror. When he enters Europe, and what I might call the "synagogue-free" zone, he now comes upon the "households"

---

[7]W. Harold Mare, "Teacher and Rabbi in the New Testament Period," *Grace Theological Journal* 11 (1970): 11–21.

[8]Ignatius, *Epistle to the Magnesians* 9.

[9]Polycarp, *Martyrdom of Polycarp*, 14.1.

[10]Mike Breen, "Anglican 1000—Michael Breen on Outward Focus of Discipleship," VirtueOnline, http://www.virtueonline.org/anglican-1000-michael-breen-outward-focus-discipleship.

of Europe. Here, remarkably, Paul shifts his imagery to formalize the parent/pedagogue model which he advocates in 1 Corinthians 4:14–17.

In spring 2012, I attended my third Exponential Conference at First Baptist Church in Orlando, Florida. Having interacted with such influential evangelicals like Alan Hirsch, Dave Ferguson, Rick Warren, Neil Cole, and Larry Osborne, I looked for balanced and mature theologians which were few and far between. Larry Osborne had opened new avenues for my work in my vacancy congregation in Franklin, Wisconsin, with his book *Sticky Teams*,[11] and Mike Breen in his book, *Launching Missional Communities*, opened a doorway for me to the New Testament that for years I had feared was hijacked and hidden from the church.[12] The doorway was this: the New Testament conceives of two different ways of preparing pastors. Breen's observations opened a new vista into the New Testament, though there is much in his evangelical theology that is foreign to me.

Breen argues that Paul moved the church not only from Judaism into the Gentile world, but Paul also moved discipleship from a rabbinical model of the church, from one at home in the synagogue, to a model at home in the *oikos*, the household of faith![13] This model was well-suited for the "economy" of Roman households with its emphasis on "guardians and fathers," "sons and daughters," and "imitators and innovation." Furthermore, Paul's innovation is advanced at precisely that point in Acts when synagogues are limited or exhausted and Paul moves into Europe with its opportunities for the Gentile world. As a child in the Roman world was weaned, writes Breen, a pedagogue (teacher, guardian) would then teach the child the basics (the necessary catechesis; so Luke 1:1–4) to move to the next level.

---

[11]Larry Osborne, *Sticky Teams: Keeping Your Leadership Team and Staff on the Same Page* (Grand Rapids: Zondervan, 2010).

[12]Mike Breen & Alex Absalom, *Launching Missional Communities: A Field Guide* (Myrtle Beach, S.C.: Sheriar Press, 2010).

[13]James D. G. Dunn, *Romans 9–16* (Word Biblical Commentary 38B; Dallas: Word, 1988), 900. Dunn notes at least five different missional communities operating within Rome. Note also Philippians 4:22, which mentions that saints are found in the household of Caesar, and 1 Peter 2:5: "you yourselves like living stones are being built up as a spiritual house."

At the age of 12 there was then a ceremony for the household and the child was presented for imitation to their parents; boys to fathers and girls to mothers, to carry on their vocations as set by family tradition from generation to generation.[14]

Breen continues:

> A girl would be placed at the shoulder of her mother and from then on, she would learn the incredibly complex task of running a Roman household. The Roman household is the center of life: both social and commercial. When she marries, she knows how to run a Roman household. From the age of 12 to the point of marriage, she imitates and learns from her mother.

In terms of a son, Paul makes the relationship clear in 1 Corinthians 4:14–17 (emphasis added):

> I am writing this not to shame you but to warn you as my dear children. Even if you had ten thousand *guardians* in Christ, you do not have many fathers, for in Christ Jesus I became your *father* through the gospel. Therefore I urge you to imitate me. For this reason I have sent to you Timothy, my *son* whom I love, who is faithful in the Lord. He will remind you of my way of life in Christ Jesus, which agrees with what I teach everywhere in every church.

Breen continues:

> A son is taken to the shoulder of the father and taught a task to use in adulthood. We are pretty sure Paul was trained to be a tentmaker. He knew how to make rope and create structures for all kinds of weather conditions. Years of imitation. "Lots of people," says Paul, "function as a pedagogue. But you need to grow up and graduate from paidagōgeō to parent. Your life is to be about information and imitation." Then he gives the perfect example, saying, "I am sending you my son, Timothy."

---

[14]Breen, "Anglican 1000." [*The editors have taken the liberty of modifying Breen's original text in the interests of grammar and clarity.*]

Timothy's mother and grandmother are spoken of in high words earlier in the New Testament. They hand Timothy over to Paul for training. Look at how he speaks about Timothy—almost the same terms as the Father speaks of Christ at his baptism. If you look at him, he'll remind you of my way of life. What you see and what you heard. Imitation.

## Imitation of Christ

Now other passages in the New Testament began to make sense to me. Until this point I had never embraced the New Testament "imitation" passages because of my Lutheran ethos grounded in John the Baptist, that demanded that I must become less and less, and Jesus must become more and more (John 3:30). Now, the imitation of Paul and others was rooted in pastoral formation.

> Be imitators of me, as I am of Christ (1 Cor 11:1).
> What you have learned and received and heard and seen in me—practice these things, and the God of peace will be with you (Phil 4:9).
> In the name of the Lord Jesus Christ, we command you, brothers and sisters, to keep away from every believer who is idle and disruptive and does not live according to the teaching you received from us. For you yourselves know how you ought to follow our example. We were not idle when we were with you, nor did we eat anyone's food without paying for it. On the contrary, we worked night and day, laboring and toiling so that we would not be a burden to any of you. We did this, not because we do not have the right to such help, but in order to offer ourselves as a model for you to imitate (2 Thess 3:6–9).

The author of Hebrews, identified as a friend of Paul's close companion, Timothy, twice makes the exhortation to imitate.

> We do not want you to become lazy, but to imitate those who through faith and patience inherit what has been promised (Heb 6:12).

> Remember your leaders, who spoke the word of God to you.
> Consider the outcome of their way of life and imitate their faith
> (Heb 13:7).

Hence, I now speak of imitation and our apprenticeship for pastors in the New Testament this way: Apprenticeship to Jesus Christ, under the direction of the revealed Word of God and the administration of the Holy Spirit in sacraments, is the single most powerful and beneficial transformational process known to humankind. Suffering turns away "lukewarm Christians," but those who face suffering and death on Jesus' behalf will without doubt be his intensely devoted apprentices. The individual in today's world is highly time-intensive, yet character remains costly; only choice and experience through time can produce movement forward in Christlikeness. Apprenticeship to Jesus in the "koinonia" of his people is the only assured path or "odos" of life under God. We on that path in the Missouri "Syn-odos" move from faith to more faith, and from grace to more grace.

Let me now return to the implications of this disciple-shift! Has the Gospel of Matthew really been hijacked? The answer is yes and no! Yes, in the limited sense, the "rabbi/disciple" model was hijacked already in the first century as the church reached out to the Gentile world. However, with Paul's innovation the "way" of the Christian may now freely focus on an imitation of Christ found in the baptismal model of Christ. The Son of God, in whom the Father is well pleased, begins his mission, post-baptism, with the Spirit of the Lord upon him. A comparison can be made with Paul's words and sentiments regarding Timothy (Phil 2:19–22). In effect, the apostle says, "I send you my son, Timothy, in whom I am well pleased, for he was trained by imitating me, his father in the faith." This is certainly a fine way to envision evangelism. The gospel imperative, if one can speak that way, has shifted from Matthew to Paul, from the rabbi/disciple model to a model of father/son as well. Hence the Great Commission has not been hijacked but rerouted for the sake of the Gentile church.[15]

---

[15]See Kenneth Bailey, *Paul Through Mediterranean Eyes: Cultural Studies in 1 Corinthians* (Downers Grove, Ill.: InterVarsity, 2011).

## Conclusions

The practical implications of 1 Corinthians 4:14–17 and the father/son model resonates with me on many levels, especially as we honor Dr. Harold Senkbeil's accomplishments among us. Who of us cannot say that we have loved to learn by imitation from him? Indeed, much of what Harold has proposed and initiated in our beloved DOXOLOGY[16] is patterned after the father/son relationship found in 1 Corinthians 4. This imitation has been designed into the very framework of DOXOLOGY. Guardians (pastors) in Christ have embraced the care of souls and shared Christ's gifts with their people not only by immediate instruction (via Matthew) but also by imitation (via Paul).

The ramifications for discovering two models within Scripture for preparing and forming pastors is significant. New questions emerge as to how long it takes to model a pastor into a servant within a church. One might ask this question of the traditional formation of pastors within a seminary, "Where in pastoral formation is one best placed into a father/son relationship?" Perhaps here too, DOXOLOGY has provided a valuable and much-needed answer for the formation of young pastors and missionaries! DOXOLOGY teaches by imitation. For this the church is grateful and our studies now are beginning to demonstrate the benefits of DOXOLOGY for the long-term health of the church.

I also ask, "How is this imitation best conceived, especially since we often live in distant/lonely/loveless communities?" Here, the retreat settings of DOXOLOGY, in live, face-to-face interaction have built long-lasting and vibrant friendships, built tested methods of care of souls within the church.

Time does not allow me to explore all the ramifications of an "imitation of Christ" offered in this paper but one final observation is noteworthy. Does 1 Corinthians 4 also speak of the relative strength of the church in Corinth in Paul's days? I think so! Paul's

---

[16]Following his service as parish pastor and seminary professor, Senkbeil has served as co-founder (along with Dr. Beverly Yahnke) and Executive Director of Spiritual Care for DOXOLOGY: *The Lutheran Center for Spiritual Care and Counsel.*

description of 10,000 guardians in Christ is not simply a metaphor in hyperbole, but rather an accurate comment about the size of Christendom at the time! Imitation had brought strength and growth to the church in his day, just as it still does in ours. Exciting, isn't it? The Great Commission is alive and ongoing, moving from one generation to another, as the living voice of Jesus continues to be heard.

# To Serve or Be Served?

## The Good Samaritan in Context

*Daniel T. Torkelson*

It is difficult to think of a single text of Scripture that has more importance for the Christian life than the parable of the good Samaritan (Luke 10:25–37). This beloved story appears to set forth the fairly simple argument that the Christian life is to be a life of good works—that is, works of mercy done for the neighbor in need. Certainly there can be no denying that this is a teaching of the parable: the genuine follower of Jesus should seek to be a neighbor to all in need. In *Mere Christianity*, C. S. Lewis called attention to the meaning of the word "Christian" as a "little Christ,"[1] a little doer of good for the neighbor and, ultimately, for the world. As such, the good Samaritan can be interpreted as Christ himself who serves as an example of love and good works that the Christian ought to imitate. To become a "little Christ," however, means to have received him as he comes to us in his gifts of forgiveness and life. It

---

[1] C. S. Lewis, *Mere Christianity* (repr., New York: HarperOne, 2000), 177, 192–93, 199, 225. Martin Luther likewise stated that, because our heavenly Father freely came to our aid in Christ, "each one should become as it were a Christ to the other that we may be Christs to one another and Christ may be the same in all, that is, that we may be truly Christians. . . . Surely we are named after Christ, . . . because he dwells in us, that is, because we believe in him and are Christs one to another and do to our neighbors as Christ does to us" (*LW* 31:367–68).

means to have passively tasted, seen, and heard Christ in his word and sacraments. While Jesus is indeed the good Samaritan, one cannot perform the good work of serving others without first having been served in the ultimate good work of Christ's suffering, death, and resurrection for the forgiveness of sins.

In the text directly following this parable, Jesus seemingly contradicts the now-conventional interpretation that the narrative is primarily about good works: he extolls Mary's passivity while gently scolding Martha for her "busy-ness" (Luke 10:38–42). This would suggest that Luke has either set up the two texts in deliberate contrast with one another, or that there is greater harmony between them than is often ascertained at first glance. Immediately before the parable Jesus reminds his disciples that they are extraordinarily blessed, for "many prophets and kings desired to see what you see, and did not see it, and to hear what you hear, and did not hear it" (Luke 10:24). Such words reconcile easily with the account of Mary and Martha, but not so with the parable in between according to many modern commentaries.[2] This raises the question of whether the good Samaritan story is merely about performing good works for the neighbor.

This essay will explore the Christian life through a "second look" at the parable of the good Samaritan. It will be shown that the context of the parable emphasizes not only the doing of good works as central to Christian identity but also the receiving of Christ, which is in fact more important and must precede the former. Indeed, this is a major theme stressed throughout the entire tenth chapter of Luke: the Christian life is first a matter of being served by Christ, then, as a result, it is a matter of serving others through works of mercy. This study will demonstrate that the good Samaritan tale does not break this unity.

---

[2]Examples include Luke Timothy Johnson, *The Gospel of Luke* (Sacra Pagina 3; Collegeville, Minn.: The Liturgical Press, 1991), 171–75; Darrell L. Bock, *Luke* (InterVarsity New Testament Commentary; Downers Gove, Ill.: InterVarsity, 1994), 195–99; and John T. Carroll, *Luke: A Commentary* (New Testament Library; Louisville: Westminster John Knox, 2012), 242–46.

## The Preceding Context: Hearing, Seeing, and Receiving Jesus (Luke 9:51–10:24)

The arrangement of Luke's account reveals both chronological and theological considerations.[3] Luke 9:51 introduces a major section of the Gospel when it declares that Jesus had "set his face toward Jerusalem." This unit, commonly deemed the Travel Narrative, begins with Jesus' rejection in a Samaritan village and his encounters with those who prove themselves unworthy of being his disciples (Luke 9:52–62). Whether he sends out messengers or gives a firsthand invitation to "Follow me," Jesus is either rebuffed or given inappropriate responses. The overall point of this early section of the Travel Narrative, then, is that Jesus remains committed to saving people who are not nearly as committed to him in return. How Jesus is received becomes the driving theme as the Gospel moves into chapter 10.

Jesus' commissioning of the 72 in Luke 10:1–16 is his third instance of sending out disciples in a little more than a chapter (9:1–6; 9:52). His instructions to them flow seamlessly from the emerging topics of rejection and false discipleship in the preceding verses at the end of chapter 9. Jesus tells the 72 to pay close attention to how they are treated when they come to a village. If they are received well in the village's homes, then they are to let their blessing remain on these places and continue to preach the arrival of the kingdom of God in Christ. If not, they are to shake the dust from their feet in protest to their rejection. Jesus then pronounces woes upon the predominantly Jewish communities of Chorazin and Bethsaida for their refusal to repent and believe in him, and explains why the 72 can expect to encounter similar hostility: "The one who hears you hears me, and the one who rejects you rejects me, and the one who rejects me rejects him who sent me" (Luke 10:16).

---

[3]N. T. Wright, *The New Testament and the People of God*, vol. 1 of *Christian Origins and the Question of God* (Minneapolis: Fortress, 1992), 373–78, observes that Luke is written more like other ancient histories (such as Josephus) than are the other Gospels. Yet this fact does not fully reveal or explain the deeper, theological/philosophical reasons for the arrangement of Luke's narrative since the configuration of secular histories often remains misunderstood or underappreciated.

The first major break in the chronology of the narrative since the "After this" of Luke 10:1 appears at verse 17 when the disciples return to report their results. Obviously some time had elapsed between verses 1–16 and verse 17. The major theme continues without interruption, however, just as the chronological leap that marks the start of chapter 10 did not disrupt the theme introduced in the last verses of chapter 9. The 72 remark with wonder how the message was received: "Lord, even the demons are subject to us in your name!" (10:17) Jesus redirects their rejoicing to a far greater source of joy—namely, that their names are "written in heaven" (10:20). Since major time breaks in the narrative do not introduce major breaks in the overall theology, this would seem to demonstrate that Luke had theological reasons for arranging this portion of the Gospel the way he did. Indeed, by the end of chapter 10, as will be shown, the chronology of the text seems to be of relatively little importance to the theology of this section.

Then Jesus himself rejoices in the Holy Spirit that the Father has revealed "these things" (which v. 9 identifies as the arrival of the kingdom of God) to the little children and hidden them from the wise and intelligent.[4] The kingdom of God is not received by intellectual pursuit or performing works of the law, but rather by faith. These words introduce Jesus' last public statement before the parable of the good Samaritan, and may act as the pretext for the lawyer's question that precipitated the parable: "What shall I do to inherit eternal life?" What Jesus says before the lawyer's query, however, he says privately to his disciples: "Blessed are the eyes that see what you see! For I tell you that many prophets and kings desired to see what you see, and did not see it, and to hear what you hear, and did not hear it." (10:23–24)

The force of these words for the entire chapter is unmistakable. Jesus once again returns to the subject of reception by hearing and adds the sense of sight for emphasis. This establishes a clear

---

[4]This brings to mind the reason Jesus gave for why he taught in parables in Luke 8:10: "To you it has been given to know the secrets of the kingdom of God, but for others they are in parables, so that 'seeing they may not see, and hearing they may not understand.'"

theological theme for this segment of Luke's Gospel: the kingdom of Christ is meant to be seen and heard, to be received by faith. Neither shifts in the chronological setting of the Gospel nor changes in location can shake this overall message. Presumably, Jesus sets his face toward Jerusalem while in Galilee, sends out the 72 while in or near Samaria, does not receive their report in the exact same place, tells the parable of the good Samaritan in proximity to Jericho, and resides in Bethany near his journey's end. Yet the theology remains constant.

Additionally, Jesus is positioned as the perfect outsider in these opening verses of the Travel Narrative. He and his message of the present kingdom of God are unacceptable in Samaritan villages every bit as much as they are in more Jewish locations such as Chorazin and Bethsaida. Christ rejoices in the astounding truth that the kingdom can only be apprehended by children and not by the wise and the intelligent. Rather, God's kingdom is received only by faith. Only those who hear and see by the ears and eyes of faith can begin to grasp the special working of God as his kingdom becomes present among his people. The true people of God, then, are defined in this section as having ears to hear and eyes to see what the Father is doing in and through his Son (see 10:22).

From the outset of the Travel Narrative (9:51) to the point of the telling of the parable of the good Samaritan (10:25), Luke's Gospel is narrowly focused on people's faithful reception or faithless rejection of the kingdom of Christ, the consummate outsider, either directly or indirectly through his sent messengers. Having established this theme, one would expect Luke either to shift the theological focus of the narrative or to expand on it. The modern understanding of the parable of the good Samaritan, given its emphasis on good works and Jesus as the pattern for them, would support the former. The text itself, however, read in light of its surrounding context, must determine whether or not this is true.

## The Good Samaritan: Giving and/or Receiving?
## (Luke 10:25-37)

The parable of the good Samaritan is introduced in 10:25 by the fairly simple construction, "And behold." Some scholars have argued that this provides a significant degree of separation from the preceding material, introducing a new time and setting, while other scholars have disagreed.[5] As noted above, however, chronological breaks and changes in location have had little connection with Luke's theological themes. It has also previously been mentioned that Jesus' last public words (10:21-22) provide an adequate rationale for the lawyer's inquiry. If he had cause for concern that the kingdom was truly being hidden from him, a wise and learned expert of the law, his question of what he must do seems only natural (and thus perhaps less presumptive than is often assumed).

The most significant part of the exchange in terms of interpreting the parable itself is found in the four questions that surround it: two from the lawyer and two, in response, from Jesus. The impetus for the first question, "What shall I do to inherit eternal life?" has already been discussed. Jesus responds with a question of his own, referring the lawyer to his own specialty, the interpretation of the Torah: "What is written in the Law? How do you read it?" (10:26) The lawyer then truncates the law into its two basic commands: love God and love your neighbor. Jesus affirms this answer, telling him that by loving God and his neighbor he would live. This interchange upholds the lawyer as correct, which emboldens him to press the issue.

The lawyer's second question, "And who is my neighbor?" (10:29) is tied to geographical and ethnic underpinnings which have been visible throughout the Travel Narrative to this point. Jesus has been rejected in Jewish and Gentile locations, thus setting up Luke's theology that salvation is not about nationality but rather comes by hearing and seeing God's words and actions in the incarnate

---

[5]For the argument in favor of a new setting, see Arthur A. Just, Jr., *Luke: 9:51-24:53* (Concordia Commentary; St. Louis: Concordia, 1997), 446. For the opposing view, see Joseph A. Fitzmyer, *The Gospel According to Luke X–XXIV* (Anchor Bible 28A; New York: Doubleday, 1985), 879.

Christ and receiving the kingdom by faith. Jewish sentiment in the first century was otherwise; the lawyer most likely believed salvation was a matter of Jewish identity and works of the law.[6] Unthinkable in his eyes is the notion that the law required him to love anyone other than his "neighbor," that is, his fellow Jew. To him, Canaanites were dogs and Samaritans were half-breed hypocrites. He felt under no compulsion to love them, for they were not his neighbors.

The reader of Luke, on the other hand, should understand by now that Jesus has been proclaiming the gospel without regard for ethnicity. He has been accepted and rejected in both Gentile and Jewish territories; he has shown mercy, performed miracles, preached the present kingdom of God, and been praised and cursed throughout both. Thus, even though Jesus chooses to tell a parable, the reader is primed to recognize a literal component in his answer to the lawyer's second question: his neighbor is a Samaritan, an outsider. Not only does Jesus broaden the definition of the word "neighbor," he also makes the neighbor the actor, not the recipient, of the works of mercy. It is the Samaritan who fulfills the law of love by serving an unclean, dying man on the side of the road. To stress the significance of this, Jesus brilliantly introduces a priest and a Levite—both of whom the lawyer would have readily assumed were "neighbors" and likely sources of aid—who refuse to be neighbors to the half-dead man because the law seemingly prohibits them from doing so. When interpreting the parable, their inaction poses too much of a problem for the lawyer to insert himself in their place. Neither can he trade places with the Samaritan, for he is an outsider while the lawyer is not. The only character remaining with whom the lawyer can identify is the man nearly killed and left for dead.

For the reader, this effectively places Jesus the outsider into the parable as the good Samaritan. While this was the favored

---

[6]The so-called New Perspective on Paul has brought significant attention to the legalism practiced in Jesus' day, and has identified ethnic identity as a significant component of the equation. For an introduction to the New Perspective on Paul, see Charles A. Gieschen, "Paul and the Law: Was Luther Right?" in *The Law in Holy Scripture: Essays from the Concordia Theological Seminary Symposium on Exegetical Theology* (ed. Charles A. Gieschen; St. Louis: Concordia, 2004), 113–47.

understanding of the ancient church[7] and of Martin Luther,[8] some
interpreters have been tempted to find Jesus in other places, particularly as the half-dead man.[9] This may assuage the desire to have
a "theology of the cross" in their reading; nevertheless, viewing Jesus
as the good Samaritan carries with it a cross of its own. The parable
teaches the lawyer—and us—that we need to receive the one who is
all too easy to reject. Indeed, as the outsider, Jesus willingly allows
himself to be rejected even as he reaches out and shows mercy to all
in their afflicted state. He comes to us as our neighbor, though we
do not recognize him as such; he is willing to do whatever it takes
to save us, to pay any price necessary. A theology of the cross is not
diminished in the least if Jesus is the good Samaritan, but rather it is
enhanced.[10]

The parable also gives an answer to the lawyer's initial question of what he must do to inherit eternal life. By first referring the
lawyer to the law, but then enfleshing its fulfillment in the person of
the good Samaritan, Jesus is demonstrating that perfect fulfillment
of the law happens only in him. This adds force to Jesus' departing
words to the lawyer: "Go and do likewise" (10:37)—meaning, you
are to see Samaritans and other outsiders as both faithful givers of
compassion as well as recipients of it. In broader terms, the gospel
is for all people regardless of nationality or situation in life. This is
what constitutes the "outsider nature" of Christ, for he is an equal

---

[7]See Riemer Roukema, "The Good Samaritan in Ancient Christianity,"
*Vigiliae Christianae* 58 (2004): 56–74.

[8]Martin Luther, "The Thirteenth Sunday after Trinity: A Sermon on the
Law and the Gospel, or the Two Greatest Commandments and the Good
Samaritan" in *The Complete Sermons of Martin Luther* (ed. and trans. John
Nicholas Lenker; 7 vols.; repr., Grand Rapids: Baker, 2000), 3:27–31.

[9]See, for example, Robert Farrar Capon, *Kingdom, Grace, Judgment: Paradox,
Outrage, and Vindication in the Parables of Jesus* (Grand Rapids: Eerdmans,
2002), 212.

[10]Throughout the church's history this parable has been allegorized to a
high degree. While assigning its characters to historical referents—principally,
identifying the good Samaritan as Christ—is essential for discerning its overall
meaning, how one interprets the other elements of the story is less crucial. For
example, whether or not one connects the inn to the church and the wine and
oil to the sacraments, the overall meaning is neither helped nor hindered.

opportunity neighbor and lover. Thus, the parable is an invitation for the lawyer (as well as the reader) to be a "little Christ."

The interpretation of this teaching as a lesson in good works is fairly one-dimensional; it places emphasis on a point of the parable, which, although valid, is certainly not its main one. Within the preceding context and throughout Luke 10, Jesus is explaining that he and his kingdom are received passively by faith. The emphasis is not at all on good works, but the parable does help the reader understand the relative importance of such works in the life of the Christian. There is a therefore hierarchy to this message. Of first importance is hearing, seeing, and receiving—that is, being served by Christ. Then, as a matter of secondary importance, the parable encourages the believer to do works of compassion just as Christ has shown compassion to all of us. This order is unavoidable since the only good work is a work done in Christ's perfect fulfillment of the law for the disciple. One cannot even consider good works rightly without first receiving Christ. Once he has been heard and seen, however, good works on behalf of the neighbor will flow naturally from the believer, for it is Christ himself who does them.

The unity of the Travel Narrative becomes lost when the parable of the good Samaritan is interpreted solely or even chiefly as a moral tale. Had Luke intended to change the theme at 10:25, the reader might reasonably expect him to elaborate on the subject of good works in the following episode. Jesus' encounter with Mary and Martha, however, seemingly contradicts any notion that works of the law are to take center stage in the lives of his followers. On the contrary, as Jesus draws closer to Jerusalem the message of this section remains remarkably consistent.

## The Following Context: Faith and Works with Mary and Martha (Luke 10:38–42)

To posit any connection between the chronology and geography of the Gospel of Luke and its theology is a daunting task. From the outset of the Travel Narrative (9:51) through the parable of the good Samaritan (10:25–37), the text only leaves hints that Jesus is steadily approaching Jerusalem. (It is possible that he is even traveling on the very road from Jericho mentioned in the parable.) Moreover, the exact amount of time that has elapsed between Jesus setting his face toward the holy city and his arrival at the house of Mary and Martha is impossible to ascertain. From John 11 we know that Mary and Martha lived in Bethany, a short two-mile walk from Jesus' final destination and one of the last stops along the dangerous road.[11] Again, major changes in time or location do not seem to initiate any significant deviation from the overall message of this portion of Luke's Gospel. The contrast between rejecting Jesus and the gospel on the one hand, and hearing, seeing, and thus receiving them on the other, remains consistent. In fact, this theme only intensifies for readers once Jesus and his disciples have numerous conflicts with the religious leaders in Jerusalem at the end of the journey.

This contrast is clearly evident at Mary and Marth's house and creates conflict as the two sisters give opposing examples of how Jesus is to be received. Martha preoccupies herself with preparing the house, while Mary merely sits at his feet and listens to his teaching. Martha then complains and requests that Jesus encourage Mary to help her: "Lord, do you not care that my sister has left me to serve alone? Tell her then to help me" (10:40). In return, Jesus gently scolds Martha and explains to her that only "one thing is necessary" and that Mary had chosen "the good portion" (10:42). This mild rebuke ("Martha, Martha") from Jesus, effectively reveals some sympathy for Martha's busy-ness. There is a place and a time for labor in the Lord. Mary's portion, however, is the good one. The "one thing needful" is not serving Christ by good works, but rather sitting at the Lord's feet and being served by him.

Luke expects his readers to recall Jesus' recent words to the disciples about the importance of "hearing what you hear" (10:23). Thus Mary, whose priority is to listen to Jesus teach, serves as a powerful and concrete example of what it means to be a faithful follower of Christ. It is not anticipated, however, that Jesus commending her for focusing on "the one thing needful" might encourage readers to conclude that good works are altogether irrelevant for those who

---

[11]For a brief yet vibrant summary of what one would experience when taking the road from Jericho to Jerusalem, see Tom Wright, *Luke for Everyone* (Louisville: Westminster John Knox, 2004), 228–30.

receive the Lord's salvation. Such a deduction would not be honoring the parable of the good Samaritan as a whole, nor would it fully comprehend the encounter at Mary and Martha's house. Jesus' tender handling of Martha still recognizes the importance of getting the house prepared. In fact, such work is so important that only one thing clearly trumps it: hearing the word of God and receiving the Christ proclaimed therein. It is misguided to interpret this section solely as a call to meditate on the word, as if faith can exist without works. Rather, Jesus' words to Mary and Martha preserve the hierarchy of being served first, then serving others.

The major themes of Luke 10 are revisited in its closing narrative when Jesus is at the home of Mary and Martha. When Jesus sent the 72, their reception was determined based on whether their teaching was faithfully heard by their hosts. The disciples were to live in the homes of the villages they entered and be supported out of those homes. This is what occurred later with Jesus when he was received into the home of Mary and Martha. The hosting of the 72 is the closest this text comes to ascribing any sort of good works or merit to the act of receiving the kingdom; yet it also teaches that even when hosting the ultimate outsider, Jesus, hearing his word is the highest good work—the "one thing needful"—that occurs passively by faith.

The theme of hearing the outsider is also found in the account of Jesus and the lawyer. In the parable of the good Samaritan, when Jesus shifts the discussion of the neighbor from recipient of good works to actor, it shifts the lawyer's position in the story from active to passive as well. This is crucial: once he is placed into the position of the half-dead man who is served by his neighbor, the good Samaritan, the meaning of the whole parable changes for the lawyer (as well as for the reader). Jesus the outsider has to reorient his hearer(s) before he preaches the kingdom. This exchange does not constitute a major shift in theological focus in the Gospel, nor does it set up a contrast or chiasm between the preceding or following material. (What amounted to a gentle scolding for Martha, though, probably sounded harsher to the lawyer's ears.)

As a result, the sending of the 72, the parable of the good Samaritan, and the encounter at the home of Mary and Martha all serve as retellings of the same story. The only aspect that fluctuates

is the audience. The gospel is for outsiders and the marginalized: vil-
lagers in small Jewish towns, half-breed Samaritans, and women. For
all people, regardless of station, gender, or nationality, faith is about
receiving Christ by hearing his word. That good works are the fruits
of this reception is still a part of the story, but this aspect receives
little specific attention from this section of Luke. Chapter 10 is a uni-
fied portion of Scripture that teaches the same basic truth found in
Romans 10:17: "So faith comes from hearing, and hearing through
the word of Christ."

## Lessons Learned

What may be gleaned for our understanding of the Christian life and
the cure of souls from such an approach to this section of Scripture?
Does another look at an old favorite give the pastor new insights into
his work of caring for the sheep entrusted to him? Does it help reveal
what the chief end is of his preaching and teaching done in the stead
of Christ? While one might imagine an endless array of possibilities,
for the sake of brevity only a few will be given.

1. *Faith comes by hearing.* This is, quite obviously, the main
   theme of Luke's Travel Narrative to the end of chapter 10
   (though the sub-theme of reception/rejection is closely
   related). Since hearing the gospel is critical to the life of
   the Christian, messengers must be sent whom Christ has
   authorized to preach. Those who do not hear such preaching regularly (whenever offered by those whom Christ has
   sent—that is, pastors) reject Christ. This rejection has two
   sides to it. One, Christ authorizes the pastor to speak on
   his behalf. Two, Christ and his kingdom are the subject of
   preaching in the Gospel of Luke, and of the gospel itself.
   To hear is to receive; to hear and receive the messenger is to
   hear and receive Christ. For Christians, having a pastor is
   critical to faith for this reason. For pastors, it is well advised
   to listen regularly to the sermons of respected peers.
2. *The main goal of preaching is to deliver Christ, not to coax
   good works out of the Christian.* As she sat at Jesus' feet and

listened to his teaching, Mary embodied the reception Jesus had instructed the 72 to look for when he authorized them to preach the presence of his kingdom. Their focus was Christ. Her focus was Christ. While this looks like sloth to Martha (and to the world as well), it is the "one thing needful" for faith. The parable of the good Samaritan may have more to say about good works, but Jesus did not tell it to coax them out of the lawyer. The neighbor's mercy to the half-dead man is a fairly simple matter of seeing the situation for what it is and addressing the man's needs. By taking the good works out of the lawyer's hands and placing them into the loving hands of a Samaritan, Jesus wants the lawyer to see the value of receiving Jesus' own compassion. In other words, preach the gospel of Christ and good works will naturally follow. As it states in Article XX of the Augsburg Confession:

> For without faith and without Christ human nature and human power are much too weak to do good works: such as to call on God, to have patience in suffering, to love the neighbor, to engage diligently in legitimate callings, to be obedient, to avoid evil lust, etc. Such lofty and genuine works cannot be done without the help of Christ, as he himself says in John 15[:5]: "Apart from me you can do nothing" (AC XX, 36–39).

Indeed, the parable of the good Samaritan could carry no better interpretation than the one provided by Jesus in John 15:5.

The old debate about preaching good works is clearly addressed in this section. While many a pastor has succumbed to the temptation to preach good works in his sermons, it should be noted that this often comes at the expense of preaching the present kingdom of God in word and sacrament. Good works are works done by the Christian clothed in the robes of Christ's righteousness, which makes him a "little Christ." The pastor who preaches good works at the expense of the gospel sets the hearer up for the same self-righteousness demonstrated by the lawyer and, to a lesser degree, by Martha.

It is the nature of fallen mankind to want to be told specifically what one must do in the way of good works. In fact, this probably explains why the one-dimensional interpretation of this parable is so readily accepted by most Christians. Christ does not preach, however, to satisfy human desire. He preaches, rather, that people should look beyond their fallen nature to him and his perfect righteousness, a free gift. This is the proclamation that brings good news to Christians, for it delivers Christ himself to them and removes despair over whether they have done enough. Where this comforting teaching is not preached in all its truth and beauty, there is no cure of souls.

3. *Faith itself is the chief good work.* Mary's passive reception of Jesus' teaching is, in itself, the good portion, the one thing needful. Where Christ is, there his church will be. The people of faith gather around Christ, sitting at his feet and receiving all he has to give them. This occurs in the preaching and teaching of the Divine Service, where Christ's gifts of forgiveness and life are given to the faithful, the receivers, the Samaritans, the half-dead people robbed of their righteousness, the women, the Gentiles, and the world. Jesus' good work of fulfilling the law perfectly is then credited to us. All other good works are sourced in the Christ who is at the heart of faith.

## Conclusion

Context is determinative of meaning. The commonly held belief that the parable of the good Samaritan is simply an exhortation to do good works isolates it entirely from its surrounding context. In fact, there is no indication in the Gospel of Luke that the author intended to shift gears or include an excursus with this section. Interpreters, therefore, should read it in light of what comes immediately before and after. When this is done, Jesus is rightly recognized in the parable as the one who serves while we are the ones served, and faith coming by hearing is preserved as the overall point of this unit of Scripture.

As this brief study has signaled, pastors should thoroughly exegete even the most familiar texts when preparing to preach and teach on them. Hearers trust their pastors to engage in this sacred task so that Christ may be delivered with clarity and received with confidence. Although right interpretation is ultimately the Holy Spirit's work, the Lord will reward pastors' efforts. So long as the saving work of Jesus predominates and precedes any talk of doing good works as Christians, believers will be free to act as "little Christs" to their neighbors by walking in those works which God has prepared for them beforehand (Eph 2:10).

# Pastoral Care and the Introvert

*Brady Finnern*

"Hi, I'm Brady, and I am an introvert."

It sounded like an AA meeting at the monthly gathering of 10 pastors in our circuit. We had a new pastor among us, so we decided to start with an icebreaker by asking each pastor to answer: "What is your greatest weakness?" Over the next 15 minutes it became obvious that we were a heavily-introverted circuit. In different ways, most of us described introverted tendencies as our chief problem: "I enjoy time by myself when I should be visiting people"; "I'm not the greatest at presenting myself to new members"; and "I tend to enjoy time studying the Bible as opposed to socializing." Looks of shame and guilt accompanied these statements. The one pastor who knew he was an extrovert was shocked at this reality and gave a 10-minute exhortation on how important it is to be social in this job, placing our differences front and center. Does this mean, then, that introverts are somehow unfit for pastoral ministry?

I have known I was an introvert since I was very young. I remember as early as age three, when people would approach me, I would quickly hide behind my mother. That was the time I heard the three words that I have forever despised: "He is shy!" Those words were like finger nails on a chalkboard. It was like I had a disease, that my inner-feelings were a disability, and the only way to function in this world was to look like an extrovert.

Although I had many friends growing up, I enjoyed watching sports on ESPN (alone), looking at trading cards for hours (alone), and playing basketball (alone!). As I entered junior high, I despised social gatherings where there would be loud noises and many people, such as dances, parties, and Lenten meals at church. My mind would race as I prepared for such fellowship. "Who will be there?" "Whom will I sit by?" "How long will it be?" "Is there any place I can sneak to and be by myself?" Still today I get nervous about any speaking engagement, which makes each Saturday night a particularly anxious time for me; and if I go to a gathering where I do not know many people, I still get butterflies in my stomach.

My natural demeanor and the circuit meeting led me to consider a host of questions. How does the church care for the souls of introverts? What do the church and her shepherds need to consider when we preach, teach, administer the sacraments, and visit God's introverted people? Where do introverts fit in and how can we be mindful of their strengths and weaknesses so that they might receive the gifts of Christ and serve their neighbors? Instead of seeing introversion simply as a weakness, might introverted pastors be particularly suited to care for introverts in their congregations?

## What Is Introversion?

The terms "introvert" and "extrovert" were coined by twentieth-century Swiss psychiatrist Carl Jung. He proposed that although everyone has both extroverted and introverted attributes, each person is at a different place on the continuum. Jung's somewhat cumbersome definitions of introversion and extroversion can be summarized as follows: introversion is an attitude type characterized by focus on things subjective, on one's inner-world; and extroversion is an attitude type characterized by focus on things external, on the outside world.[1]

Central to this topic is the question of where people gain their "energy." Introverts and extroverts differ on the level of outside stimulation they need in order to function well. Introverts feel "just right" with less stimulation, as when they read a book, listen to quiet jazz music, watch a movie, or sit with a close friend over coffee.

---

[1]Carl Gustav Jung, *Memories, Dreams, Reflections* (ed. Aniela Jaffé; trans. Richard and Clara Winston; rev. ed.; London: Fontana, 1995), 414–15.

Extroverts enjoy the extra buzz that comes from activities like meeting new people, attending large gatherings, and listening to loud music. This does not mean an introvert never wants to go to a party or that an extrovert cannot read a novel, but these generalizations help us understand where people are most comfortable.[2]

In our American context, we have many misperceptions of introverts. We assume they are hermits, shy, socially awkward, and bookworms; yet they usually inhabit the workplace, church, neighborhood, and even their own family with none the wiser. Many influential and famous people have publicly admitted that they are on the introvert spectrum, including Rosa Parks, Eleanor Roosevelt, Barbara Streisand, Clint Eastwood, Steve Martin, Albert Einstein, Steven Spielberg, and Meryl Streep.[3] According to a few studies, at least one-third—perhaps up to one-half—of all Americans are introverts.[4]

I remember hearing those negative assumptions when I was in seminary and took the Myers-Briggs Type Indicator, an introspective questionnaire used to determine people's different psychological preferences. When the results indicated I was an introvert, I heard remarks like, "Really? You seem to be so social!" However, many of us are living a double life: the extroverted-introvert! Each day introverts interact with a wide variety of people, go to work, nail sales presentations, energetically greet people in stores, and gather at church socials while appearing to gain energy; but once they leave those settings they are worn out. They come home unprepared to interact with anybody, preferring to escape to their caves alone and read a book, walk their dog, tend their garden, watch sports, or work on some hobby.

These misperceptions of introverts are due to living in an extroverted society. We are highly influenced by Dale Carnegie's 1936 book, *How to Win Friends & Influence People.*[5] Carnegie observed

---

[2]Susan Cain, *Quiet: The Power of Introverts in a World That Can't Stop Talking* (New York: Broadway Books, 2012), 11–12.

[3]Marti Olsen Laney, *The Introvert Advantage: How Quiet People Can Thrive in an Extrovert World* (New York: Workman, 2002), 39.

[4]Roman Bayne, *The Myers-Briggs Indicator: A Critical Review and Practical Guide* (London: Chapman and Hall, 1995), 47.

[5]Dale Carnegie, *How to Win Friends & Influence People* (repr., New York: Pocket Books, 1995).

that students who win campus speaking contests were perceived to be leaders.[6] He began a public speaking course in New York City in the 1920s, leading to a line of widely influential books published throughout the world that rode the wave of the new extroverted ideal. This is the belief that the ideal person is social, independent, motivated, quick-witted, and comfortable in the spot-light. Talkative people are perceived to be smarter, better-looking, more interesting, and more desirable as friends.[7] Even books that address a happy life, like David Myers's *The Pursuit of Happiness*, claim there are three essential ingredients in the recipe for being content: self-esteem, optimism, and extroversion.[8]

We are taught from an early age that if one does not live up to the extroverted ideal then there is some sort of problem. We are told as children: "You have to be more social"; "Look people in the eye"; "You have to stick up for yourself"; and "You need to be more confident." We see those with outgoing social skills become homecoming king and queen, getting promotions and better college placements, selling more books, making more sales, and earning more money. Thus shamed, introverts learn quickly that they need to train themselves to look like an extrovert if they are to survive in today's world.

## Introverts and the Church

So what does this have to do with the church and caring for the souls of her members? Beyond doubt, the church is the place where introverts and extroverts alike can receive cleansing from their guilt, a clear conscience from their shame, and ongoing care for their tarnished souls. But do introverts in particular see the church as a safe place of refuge? Our current challenge is that the church has followed the tide of a culture that exalts extroverted traits and has often pushed her quieter members aside.

It begins with our view of God. In 2004, students at a Christian college were asked to rate the person of Jesus according to the profiles of temperaments in the Myers-Briggs Type Indicator. In

---

[6]Cain, *Quiet*, 20–21.

[7]Cain, *Quiet*, 4.

[8]Laney, *Introvert Advantage*, 6.

most categories the students were divided and often showed a bias toward their own personality type. The truly revealing result was that although 54 percent of the students were considered introverts, *over 97 percent of students said Jesus was an extrovert.* This finding is not all that surprising because we often see Jesus with a large group—though we also see numerous occasions where Jesus went to pray with only a few close friends, if not alone.

> Psychologist Susan Howell made this observation based on the study's results:
> Making an assumption that Jesus was extroverted based on cultural bias might make it difficult for introverts in such a culture to accept and affirm their own behavioral preference as legitimate and valuable; not something to be overcome or even tolerated, but something to be appreciated and blessed.[9]

Reflect on those findings and consider: each week, the church gathers in a large group for worship. Entering often involves cold-call interactions with many people, some who are complete strangers. People are expected to sing publicly to louder-than-normal music. On top of this we ask many, especially children, to make forced public appearances in front of the whole assembly during VBS, children's messages, Sunday School, Christmas programs, and choir. Finally, once worship is over, there is an expectation to join as a large group in an even smaller room to enjoy coffee and treats for fellowship.

One might even get the impression that the church sets out a sign for future leaders: "Introverts need not apply." Indeed, the church often places a high priority on people who are social, confident, and able to serve on boards. Professor of psychology Richard Beck says that "for some churches *spirituality* is equated with *sociability*."[10] Our church bulletins and announcements continually beg people to serve on a board, lead Sunday School, head up VBS, and direct the upcoming church supper. When the introvert hears the word of God say, "Go and make disciples of all nations" and "present your bodies

---

[9]Quoted in Adam McHugh, *Introverts in the Church: Finding Our Place in an Extroverted Culture* (Downers Grove, Ill.: InterVarsity), 16–17.

[10]McHugh, *Introverts in the Church*, 22.

as a living sacrifice," the imperatives have taken on an unintentional extroverted flavor, and it feels like one constantly needs to be on the go and interact with loads of people to be a good Christian (or, for that matter, a good pastor).

These realities present a problem for the introvert, who is sensitive to overstimulation and for whom social interactions can be draining. If the basic structure of the church proclaims a precedent of the value for extroverts and if most people assume that Jesus is an extrovert, are introverts thinking, "What is wrong with me?" If at least one-third of church members are introverts, where is the right fit in the life of the church? How can the church be a place of peace, joy, and encouragement for the introvert without requiring a separate ministry or subgroup in the body of Christ? How does the pastor (who may well be an introvert himself) care for the souls of introverts according to their specific needs, reminding them of their worth in Christ?

## Shame, Guilt, and Healing

In one of my classes at seminary, we were instructed to create a "transition plan" into our first church. It was a wonderful process of evaluating ways to introduce ourselves, learn about the church's history, and find ways to learn about the unique personalities of the congregation. I have always enjoyed these kinds of assignments because they involve researching history, asking individuals or small groups about their stories, and spending unhurried time with people. When I sat down with a few classmates and my professor to discuss my plan, one of my questions to them was, "How do I introduce myself as an introvert?" You could have heard crickets in the background! I instantly felt a sense of guilt and shame for bringing up the subject, transgressing the unwritten rule, "You can be introverted; but make sure you don't tell anyone."

Based upon my reading, research, and interviews, the uncomfortable sense of shame and guilt is widespread among introverts, if not universal. These feelings cut deep for these psyches that are naturally bent toward self-examination,[11] making them feel like they

---

[11]McHugh, *Introverts in the Church*, 49.

are flawed and unable to function in the world like extroverts. These feelings often increase since introverts tend to remember past events more intensely: they remember, for instance, the moments where they failed to connect with people or where they were not the life of a party.[12] This guilt and shame goes with them everywhere, influencing them each time they enter school, work, social gatherings, or church.

Addressing this guilt and shame requires healing and providing a clear conscience with their Lord. John Kleinig describes the conscience as being like a mirror.[13] If it is stained, it does not receive and reflect the light of God; if it is clear, it is filled with the light that enlightens it and gives it insight. Introverts will often have a stained view of themselves as those who are not good with people and thus are unable to fulfill their daily vocations faithfully.

## Listening as Pastoral Care

All spiritual care begins with listening, as James reminds us: be "quick to listen and slow to speak" (Jas 1:19). When we are listening, we consider the conscience and soul of the individual as a child of God that needs care (1 John 3:1). Eugene Peterson perhaps put it best when he said, "The question put to myself is not, 'How many people have you spoken to about Christ this week?' But, 'How many people have you listened to in Christ this week?'"[14] This is especially vital when it comes to the introvert. Typical introverts are rarely heard. They are quick to listen and slow to speak. Ideas do not flow freely from their tongue, and they need time for reflection to answer sufficiently and comfortably.[15] This requires time, patience, and well-placed questions.

To listen attentively to introverts also means respecting their requests not to participate in an activity. In my own congregation,

---

[12]Laney, *Introvert Advantage*, 56.

[13]John W. Kleinig, "Living with a Clear Conscience," https://www.doxology .us/wp-content/uploads/2015/03/30_living.pdf.

[14]Eugene H. Peterson, *The Contemplative Pastor: Returning to the Art of Spiritual Direction* (Grand Rapids: Eerdmans, 1993), 21.

[15]Laney, *Introvert Advantage*, 49.

while guiding numerous families through the Scriptures and Small Catechism for new member instruction, one common question has arisen: "Do we have to go up in front of church and say something as a new member?" I have had a difficult time navigating that question. Part of me wants to respect their wishes, because I know how nerve-wracking it can be to be in front of a large crowd: remember, every Sunday morning still brings me butterflies. Yet part of me wants to force people up front to "prove" how many people are new to the church, that we are growing, that we are having some "success." But I have to remember to listen to their needs. Each family has expressed different reasons why they fear standing in front of church, which has led us to find varying ways to celebrate God bringing them to our congregation, while treating them with dignity and respect.

In addition, it is important to spend unhurried time with those who are more introverted. They appreciate the effort, even if it might not look like it, because many people are unwilling to try.

## Who Am I?

I love teaching confirmation class. The joy of teaching God's word to young people and bringing the assurance of their identity in Christ is one of my favorite parts of being a pastor. Every year I begin class by asking, "Who am I?"

I teach my confirmands to answer this question with two simple words: "A sinner." I have found that this starting point, regardless of whether a student is an introvert or extrovert, levels the playing field. Everywhere we go we are judged based on success, jobs, money, possessions, and social standing; but when we gather as Christians we begin with the same reality of sinfulness in thought, word, and deed (Ps 51:5; Rom 7:24; 1 Tim 1:15) just as we confess in the liturgy. By way of contrast, I remember a handful of worship services at the liberal college I attended where the preacher would continually tell us, "You are fine just the way God made you!" This sounded good for a moment, until I realized the ways I had hurt people and that my thoughts were not something I could excuse as "the way God made me!" He demands holiness (1 Pet 1:16) and we deserve nothing but his wrath due to our sin (Ps 12:1–6; Deut 1:26–46).

Yet the joy of the Christian faith is that we never end our identity with sin, but ask the final question, "Who am I *in Christ*?" and then cling to the answer: "A forgiven sinner!" Forgiven because our sins have been nailed to the cross (Col 2:14) and he will remember them no more (Heb 8:12). Forgiven because he brought that forgiveness to us in the water (1 Pet 3:21) and daily forgives us by his blood (1 John 1:7–9). Our identity is found in Christ's words, "It is finished," reminding us that "Nothing in my hand I bring; Simply to Thy cross I cling."[16]

In the blood of the Lamb (1 Pet 1:18–19), we see clearly that our identity begins and ends with God making us a new creation (2 Cor 5:17). Christians (including pastors!) stand before their Lord as people who are made in his image (Gen 1:27), as people one knitted and formed by God in their mothers' wombs (Ps 139:13–14), and as people created in Christ Jesus for good works (Eph 2:10). This ought to lead many to reconsider their thoughts on introversion and the Lord. Remember the 2004 study: If 97 percent of people view Jesus as an extrovert, does that mean Jesus made a mistake with my introversion? However, as a new creation in Christ, my introversion has been redeemed with all of me. He does not make mistakes; rather, he has prepared good works for me, an introvert, that I might walk in them (Eph 2:10). Being introverted is not a sin one needs to have forgiven, or a brokenness one needs to have fixed; nor is introversion something to be viewed negatively. It is a First Article gift from God and part of his design for us to serve him in his kingdom.

Scientific studies have indicated this as well. Introversion has a strong biological component, according to Jung and others,[17] and Jerome Kagan's study is perhaps the most profound. In 1989, the Harvard developmental psychologist started an ongoing longitudinal study on infants who were most likely to be extroverts or introverts. He exposed the infants to carefully chosen experiences such as balloon popping, different colored mobiles, and inhaling different scents of alcohol, then continued the study when the children were ages 2, 4, 7, and 11, and also into adulthood. Kagan found that what separated the introvert from the extrovert was a stimulation

---

[16]*Lutheran Service Book* (St. Louis: Concordia, 2006), 761:3.

[17]Laney, *Introvert Advantage*, 7–8.

continuum. The infants most reactive to different smells and noises were more likely to be introverts because they were highly sensitive to stimulation. The children who were least reactive to these stimuli were more likely to be extroverts.[18]

## How Does the Introvert Fit into the Christian Life and Community?

During my vicarage I met a man at a fitness center named Merle. Merle was a mild-mannered man over 70 who would sit on his recumbent bike for an hour enjoying the company of whomever would sit by him. Toward the end of my vicarage, I finally mustered up the confidence to invite him to worship. He slowly and politely told me, "I can't. I am not good with people and don't like big crowds." His words hit me like a ton of bricks. This was not a reaction the seminary had prepared me for, and I sympathized with his feelings because I often felt the same.

For Merle, the problem was not as simple as a lack of belief or desire to hear the word of God, but the community itself. I have often heard people explain the church in terms of what we do (programs, meals, activities) or how we are (nice, friendly, compassionate)— things not altogether different from aspects of the local Lions club, Rotary club, fitness center, or bicycle club. We often focus on having social and active congregations, but for some people this may actually be a major factor in why they choose not to come.

Merle's response has led me to focus my attention, when describing the church, on what is received. Kleinig defines the Christian as having a "life of reception. We have been justified by the grace of God the Father, so we now live by faith in His grace. We receive grace upon grace from the fullness of the Incarnate Christ."[19] Everything is passively received from our Lord and is a gift that we do not deserve (Acts 17:28). This is wonderful news for the introvert! To know that our Christian faith is not dependent on our work, our energy, our

---

[18]Cain, *Quiet*, 99–101.

[19]John W. Kleinig, *Grace Upon Grace: Spirituality for Today* (St. Louis: Concordia, 2008), 10.

social skills, our commitment, or our time helps begin the process of realizing that in Christ we are able to live peaceful, receptive lives as his children (1 John 3:1).

This also informs our definition of the church as confessional Lutherans. According to Article VII of the Augsburg Confession, "The Church is the congregation of saints (Ps 149:1) in which the Gospel is purely taught and the Sacraments are correctly administered." Through these simple things, the church is most prominently the place where sinners receive cleansing in the gifts of forgiveness, life, and salvation. Most evidently, of course, this happens in the divine service. The introduction to the *Lutheran Service Book* introduces worship in this way: "Our Lord is the Lord who serves. . . . Our Lord serves us today through His holy Word and Sacraments,"[20] delivering his forgiveness and salvation, both to free us from our sins and also to strengthen us for service to one another and to the world. As Norman Nagel once told us regarding why we should attend chapel during our seminary training, "God has gifts to give."

What we receive in the divine service is closely connected to Jesus' words to his disciples on the day of his resurrection. In fear of the Jews, the disciples locked the door where they had gathered. Jesus appeared in their midst and said, "Peace be with you" (John 20:19). After proving who he really was by showing his hands and side, he repeated the words again, "Peace be with you" (John 20:21). People need these resurrection words because they come to worship exhausted. Typical introverts, especially, have put on a show all week. They may look extroverted, but internally they are worn out. The divine service is where they are cleansed (Ps 51:7), renewed (Titus 3:5), strengthened (Isa 40:28–31) and given rest by our Prince of Peace (Isa 9:6; Matt 11:28).

Here, then, are a few ideas for caring for the introvert in worship:

1) *Emphasize the joy of bringing God's word through the liturgy.* The liturgy is a way to bring God's word in a simple, predictable, and rich way. Kleinig states, "Through the enactment of His Word God provides His people with a

---

[20] *LSB*, viii.

good conscience."[21] Many introverts have found additional freedom and comfort in liturgical churches because there is a lesser expectation to "perform." There is often a greater appreciation for the substantive theology expressed through hymnody and liturgical prayer as well because it can lead one to reflect more deeply on the mercies of God in Christ.[22]

2) *Offer a time of silence for prayer and meditation on God's word before, during, and after worship.* As a child, I still remember coming to church early with my dad and seeing a few older ladies who would always sit near the front of the nave in prayer for at least 30 minutes. Such discipline and dedication is difficult to find, especially in a loud, frenetic world. The church might be the only place that allows for a time of silence to meditate on God's word and to pray. In our congregation, we try to allow people time in quiet prayer before worship, but we also give a time of silence during confession and absolution and during the Prayer of the Church.

3) *Consider the ways you present shaking each other's hands before worship or extending the peace before communion.* I have lost count of how many people tell me they disliked it when the pastor would ask everyone to greet each other in the name of the Lord, before or during the service. It is a salutary, historic practice in preparation for worship and receiving the sacrament together; and it can be a good avenue to challenge introverts to interact with their fellow Christians. However, it can also cause great anxiety for many people.

---

[21]John W. Kleinig, "Liturgy and the Delivery of a Good Conscience: Our Earthly Reception of Heavenly Gifts" (paper presented at the Institute of Liturgy, Preaching and Church Music. Seward, Nebr., July 28, 2014), 12; http://www.johnkleinig.com/files/6014/1376/7379/Liturgy_and_conscience.pdf.

[22]McHugh, *Introverts in the Church*, 190.

## What about Evangelism?

The typical evangelism program puts a high priority on confrontation, quick wit, cold-calls, door-to-door visits, and complex problem-solving conversations—all of which take place within just a few minutes.[23] This is downright scary for an introvert. An introvert needs time to respond to a conversation and does not want a high volume of people stimulation, especially if their job already requires them to deal with this every day.

So how does an introvert fit into evangelism? According to Scripture, they and all baptized believers in Christ are members of "a chosen race, a royal priesthood, a holy nation, a people for his own possession" (1 Pet 2:9). Christ calls us to "love the Lord your God with all your heart and with all your soul and with all your mind and with all your strength" and to "love your neighbor as yourself" (Mark 12:30–31; Rom 13:9). And we are also called to pray for all people (1 Tim 2:1). Whether one is an introvert or extrovert, then, these are callings of the Christian's daily life. As chosen people, we fulfill our priestly duties by loving God and others when we fulfill our callings as spouses, parents, children, co-workers, neighbors, community members, and volunteers. We pray for all people, from our boss to the supermarket cashier. This is the Christian life and within these vocations we proclaim the good news of forgiveness in Christ when God gives us the opportunity.

In my own congregation, I have seen introverts be wonderful witnesses to Christ in their vocations. One man is a salesman for a therapeutic shoe company. He has had multiple conversations about his faith with returning customers because he is a good listener and has been blessed with remembering people's stories. Another—a quiet, mild-mannered woman—was a lunch lady at the public schools for over 30 years. Although she has been retired for almost 20 years, she is still remembered in the community as a selfless, Christian servant.

Each day the members of our congregations serve as witnesses of the Christian faith. They need encouragement to remember that it is the Holy Spirit who will give them an opportunity, and it is he who will convert people to Christ (1 Cor 12:3; 1 Cor 2:14; 1 Pet 3:18).

---

[23]McHugh, *Introverts in the Church*, 174.

Here are a few simple suggestions on how to encourage intro-verted members to be witnesses:

1) *In casual conversation, briefly let others know that you attend church.* For example, when someone asks, "What did you do this weekend?" simply reply, "Mowed the lawn, went to church, and watched the Vikings game." See where the conversation goes. Talking to people you already know can be more effective and far less intimidating than going door-to-door.

2) *Pray for everyone you encounter on any given day.* Just as men brought the paralytic to the feet of Christ (Mark 2), bring everyone whom God has placed in your life to him in prayer. Ask the Lord to bring faith, blessings, and his grace to them all.

   This includes praying for the other members of the con-gregation. For example, one now-sainted member of our congregation was homebound in a local nursing home. Yet he was well-known as a "prayer warrior" because he would take the directory and pray for every one of our members throughout the year.

3) *Memorize simple passages that quickly get to the heart of the gospel.* I prefer John 3:16–17, 1 Timothy 1:15, Romans 3:23–24, and 1 Peter 2:24. This way introverts will not feel like they need to have a laundry list of arguments or have to explain the entire Bible, but can succinctly state what it means to be a follower of Jesus.

4) *Invite members to share the different stories and ques-tions that arise in their vocations.* Team up with your fel-low saints to pray and seek God's wisdom on how best to address any situation, question, or conversation in which they find themselves. To help make this a non-threatening experience for introverts, the importance of listening and further contemplation can be emphasized, as well as allow-ing for two or three individuals to meet up instead having everyone meet together in a large group.

## Spiritual Care for Children

The spiritual care of our children is of interest because many introverts realize there is something "different" about them at a young age. I recently spoke with an adult—a self-proclaimed introvert—about church and when he grew in faith. He said that his growth began when he no longer needed to do anything in front of church such as attend VBS, sing, and participate in the Christmas program. I found this profound because we historically expect our children to do more extroverted activities, while many of our adults would rather die than do these same activities themselves. It is worth asking, then, if we have unintentionally placed heavy burdens on our introverted children by expecting them to behave as extroverts.

Here are a few ideas on ways to help an introverted child feel comfortable in the life of the church:

1) *Allow the child to have an option not to participate in front-of-church activities.* This may be difficult to implement since people equate high participation numbers with success, but some kids will be adversely affected if they are forced to participate. I have learned that many more introverted kids will participate if they are given an opt-out because it will be their choice to serve. One might expect the argument that children need to learn to perform publicly at an early age; but while a congregation may be the most supportive audience possible, turning worship into a high-stress experience may not be the best choice for a child's spiritual development.

2) *Try to not call any child "shy."* To use this word is taboo in our national culture. It contributes to the bombardment of identities given to introverts that cause more shame and guilt. Be patient, giving them more time to join in activities or to speak, as well as individual attention when possible.

3) *Highlight the reflective moments and people in the Bible.* Even Jesus went away by himself to pray (Luke 5:16). Jacob was described as a quiet man (Gen 25:27). Moses was slow of speech (Exod 4:10). Mary was highlighted as one

who pondered in her heart everything that had happened
(Luke 2:51). It is important for children to see such behaviors and personalities in a positive light.

## My Current Context

I have served the blessed saints at Messiah Lutheran in Sartell,
Minnesota, for almost a decade. A few years back I had a theory that
we were a heavily-introverted congregation, so one Sunday I conducted a simple survey during Bible study. I distributed a 20-question
survey from the book *The Introvert Advantage*.[24] The questions centered on an individual's preferences and perceptions, such as "I prefer one-on-one conversations" and "People tell me that I am a good
listener." Thirty people completed the survey and we learned that
introverts outnumbered extroverts 22–8.

These numbers were not surprising to me but they might be to
the casual observer of our congregation. The faithful saints of this
church do all the things one should: attend the divine service, receive
the sacrament, pray, and serve in Christ's name. Although we are full
of introverts and led by an introverted pastor, the members absolutely love being with one another. The narthex is buzzing as people
enter church and again as they leave. After every service we have
food, which leads to an extended period for people to catch up—so
much so that we must give a five-minute warning to wind down for
Bible study. Once a month we hold a potluck fellowship meal, which
is well attended and often requires people to be kicked out before the
Vikings game begins.

Perhaps surprisingly for an introvert-dominant congregation,
we often have 70 to 80 percent of the worshipping community in the
room at one time. Why is the majority not running away in fear of
this room? I have two theories: one is that a majority of the members
has been together for over 10 years. Going to church is first and foremost a place to receive the gifts of Christ; but it is also a familiar place
where "everybody knows your name." The other is that the interaction occurs from the safety of 20 round tables in our fellowship hall.

---

[24]Laney, *Introvert Advantage*, 30–31.

These tables hold a maximum of six people—so even though there might be 100 people in the fellowship hall, no one must interact with more than five people at a time. The fellowship is subdivided into manageable company.

These insights have led me, the elders, and board of directors to consider ways that we as a church can help make church settings easier for all people to hear the word of God and grow in Christ. Indeed, by the grace of God, my own introversion has allowed me to be conscientious and compassionate toward the introverts placed under my care in ways I otherwise might not have been with a different, extroverted personality.

## Encouragement for Introverts and the Church

The church is a place for community (Acts 2:42–47; Heb 10:24–25). In this fellowship of believers, we learn the value of unity in Christ (John 17:21–23) and ways to love, listen, and serve other people.[25] Paul tells us in 1 Corinthians 12 that we are baptized into the body of Christ; and within that body, the so-called introverted eye cannot say to the extroverted leg, "I have no need of you," nor vice versa. We need each other for the uplifting of the kingdom of God. Each has a place to be cleansed by him, to love him, to serve others, and to be served. Therefore, we do not deny large gatherings or social times, but enter them knowing that we each have a place as a child of God with unique abilities and strengths.

Here are five ways[26] introverts can potentially contribute to the life of the church:

1) *A discerning, reflective approach to God's word.* Our church has continually promoted simple reading plans of the Bible and devotionals (such as Portals of Prayer, New Testament in 90 days, and Today's Light Bible two-year reading plan).

---

[25]McHugh, *Introverts in the Church*, 88.

[26]Contributions 3–5 are adapted from Alison Abrams, "Seven Reasons to Be Proud to Be an Introvert," Psychology Today, https://www.psychologytoday.com/blog/nurturing-self-compassion/201706/seven-reasons-be-proud-be-introvert.

Often the introverted individuals follow these formats well and can share deep insights with the congregation as they reflect over his word.

2) *A readiness to do behind-the-scenes jobs.* The church has many jobs that may not seem glorious, but are vital and well-suited to an introvert's strengths. The best example is the altar guild: each time the church is ready to receive the sacrament, a group of people has already carefully prepared for the body and blood of Christ to be distributed. It is the same with administrative assistants, janitors, financial secretaries, grounds crew volunteers and Sunday School teachers. Every congregation continues in word and sacrament ministry because of the important works of these blessed saints.

3) *Uncanny powers of observation.* Because many introverts are often better than extroverts at getting a "feel for the room," they better understand what dynamics are at play when a congregation deals with difficult decisions or situations. They can provide excellent advice and observations—though they might not offer without being asked.

4) *An ability to form genuine connections.* Many introverts see the value of depth over numbers. I have noticed that, many times, the quieter members make the most impact in greeting visitors. They can show a genuine care for newer members because they know what it is like to feel uncomfortable in new situations. Encourage the reserved individuals to build relationships with visitors in just the same way they relate with others.

5) *An ability to lead the church quietly.* Peter Steinke continually promotes the strength of the "non-anxious leader," one who is self-differentiated in the church family.[27] In every congregation there are leaders who rarely say a word. They are often introverts, yet they guide the congregation in powerful ways. They serve as a reminder to all of us to "not

---

[27]Peter L. Steinke, *How Your Church Family Works: Understanding Congregations as Emotional Systems* (repr., Herndon, Va.: The Alban Institute, 2006), 346.

be anxious about your life . . . but seek first the kingdom of God and his righteousness" (Matt 6:25, 33).

## Conclusion

An online satirical website called *The Babylon Bee* posted an article which read, "Local Church Offers 'Introvert Service' Where Nobody Has to Talk to Anyone Else," noting that "this new service allows congregants to enjoy church in silence, without being forced to greet each other in any way, touch each other in any way, or engage in never-ending small talk afterward."[28] While somewhat humorous, these statements feed into the idea that introverts do not like people and are not able to function within the life of today's church. But the contrary can be true: the church can be a refuge in which introverts find rest and also flourish, as they are encouraged to exercise their own strengths that have been purposefully designed by God.

My goal is not to start a mission to introverts, but simply to admit that introverts have unique qualities that are to be considered with care for their souls. In this care, let us focus on what we receive from our Lord: the free gift of repentance (Acts 5:31), free forgiveness in Christ (Col 1:14), free salvation in Christ (Matt 19:25–26; Eph 2:8–9), and a new life in Christ (Rom 6:4) to serve each other in freedom (Gal 5:13). These gifts and a new identity in Christ assure introverts that their standing before God and others is not dependent on their social abilities. Rather, they may serve God and others in the way that God leads. May God cleanse our conscience from shame and lead us into thanksgiving for all that he gives. To him alone be all the glory.

---

[28]The Babylon Bee, https://babylonbee.com/news/local-church-offers -introvert-service-nobody-talk-anyone-else/.

# Ten Reasons to Leave the Ministry and One Reason to Stay

*William M. Cwirla*

*This essay is adapted from a banquet speech delivered at the DOXOLOGY Reunion dinner, August 3, 2013, in Kansas City, Missouri. It is presented here in the spirit of fraternal camaraderie, good humor, and respect for the work of Rev. Harold Senkbeil in supporting the work and life of the pastor as* Seelsorger. *This essay is intended to bring a smile to the pastoral face, encouragement to the pastoral heart, and thanksgiving to God for his manifold grace in Jesus Christ, whose office we have the privilege of holding.—WMC*

As a rule, I don't do banquet speeches. Like a Benedictine monk after sunset, I prefer my food and drink in silence. I don't tell jokes. I can't play the banjo, though I can play a few chords on the guitar. I can't speak like angels or preach like Paul. I can tell the love of Jesus and say he died for all. But you paid me for a speech, not a sermon. That's the problem when you invite a preacher. You always get a sermon.

It's a bit intimidating to be asked to speak by two people whom I greatly love, admire, and have heard speak on many occasions—Hal Senkbeil and Bev Yahnke.

Bev Yahnke is DOXOLOGY's in-house version of Dr. Phil. Tall, stylish, insightful, eloquent, with a silken voice as soothing as a single malt Scotch in front of a warm fireplace on a cold Wisconsin night. Bev has the unique ability to be comforting and disturbing at the same time, like Diane Sawyer reading news of global disaster as though it were a bedtime story read to a little child.

Hal is the epitome of the Lutheran concept of the *Seelsorger*, the physician of the soul—strong, loving, wise, pious, faithful, thrifty, generous, patient, kind, apt to teach, and not given to much strong drink, at least as far as any of us is aware. Whenever I read Bo Giertz's *The Hammer of God*, all the hero pastors in the book look like Hal Senkbeil in my mind's eye.

Last year's DOXOLOGY gathering was at Our Lady of the Snows in Illinois, a location that does little to dispel rumors that DOXOLOGY is a clandestine gathering of crypto-sacerdotalists. The banquet speaker that evening spoke on various "coping strategies" to which we pastors mistakenly flee when things are going off the ministerial rails. He had four or five strategies, but I can only recall strategy number two: taking refuge in food and drink. I recall glancing across the room at some new friends from the Pacific Northwest who shared my obsessive fondness for fine food and drink and exchanging a look of puzzlement and dismay. This was bad? Strategy Two had been working quite nicely for us, thank you. Since that speech, "Strategy Two" has become our own in-house code language, as in "That voters' meeting really needs some Strategy Two." Or "Man, what a day! I think I'm doing Strategy Two early tonight," or "Let's Strategy Two this banquet speech."

A few months ago, I ran across an internet article entitled, "Ten Real Reasons Pastors Quit Too Soon" by Tim Peters.[1] The article sparked my imagination. Is there really a "too soon" when it comes to quitting? What about not soon enough? How does one know when it's too soon or too late? And can you actually quit the ministry or even entertain the notion of quitting?

I recall a lovely morning walk in the estuary of Morro Bay with my wife and saying out loud, "You know, the only vow I've ever made that had the words 'until death us do part' was to you." This moment was a major epiphany in my work in the ministry. I realized for the first time that I was free to quit. I was not abandoning my "second spouse" (a creepy analogy at several levels), my post, the troops in battle, or whatever other guilt-infused metaphor we've laid on one

---

[1]Tim Peters, "10 Real Reasons Pastors Quit Too Soon," Church Leaders, http://www.churchleaders.com/pastors/pastor-articles/161343-tim_peters_10 _common_reasons_pastors_quit_too_soon.html.

another. I was, and am, as free to leave this vocation as I was to leave my former vocation as a scientist. That freedom has kept me going for the last ten years.

Seventeen hundred pastors leave the ministry every month, Tim Peters tells us with the appropriate notes of alarm and urgency. Let's not quibble about what is and what isn't a "minister" here—let's just sort of run with that statistic. There are a number of us pastor-types in the room and someone here is surely eyeing the door, and I don't mean of this banquet hall. Peters cites ten reasons why those pastors are hanging up the stole, assuming they wore one in the first place.

## Ten Reasons to Leave

1. **Discouragement**. "Complaints speak louder than compliments. You can receive fifteen compliments and one complaint, and the complaint will stick"—like a well-placed stiletto between the shoulder blades.

   My pastor from the Berkeley days (that was graduate school in chemistry, in case your mind is wandering), who tried unsuccessfully for two years to discourage me from going to the seminary, warned me in no uncertain terms: "You will have your heart broken in ways you cannot imagine." He was right. You preach, and they don't listen. You catechize, and they become Baptists. You admonish, and they still do whatever they want. You stay up all night with them in the emergency room, and they complain that you missed their kid's first birthday bash. Add to this all the judgments and measurements laid on you by your synod, district president, and congregation reminding you that the congregation isn't growing fast enough, you're letting in too many "outsiders," you're not confessional enough, liturgical enough, missional enough, you don't spend enough time with your family, your sermons are boring, and you have bad breath and a bad haircut. Discouraging? You bet it is!

2. **Failure**. "Many pastors have difficulty recognizing success," Peters reports. Fair enough. But how do you measure success when the finish line is resurrection from the dead?

Here's the problem: Our culture admires winners. The gold medal. The championship ring. "We are the champions." Unfortunately, when it comes to the holy ministry, we are losers among the losers—the least, the lost, the lowly, the dead to this world. We preach Jesus Christ crucified. We boast about unanswered prayer and thorns in the flesh and grace being sufficient and power perfected in weakness. We parade behind a crucifix. Winners don't hang on crosses. Let's face it—failure is built into the system. The church isn't a Tony Robbins seminar where winners teach others to win. It isn't a gymnasium where the spiritually-fit coach others into spiritual fitness, as spiritually catchy as "Cross-Fit" might sound. It isn't even a hospital where the sick go to get better, and you stand a reasonable chance of getting out alive. The church is more like a hospice, a place where the dying care for the dying in the death of Jesus and don't try to cure the disease of sin but instead provide the palliative care of forgiveness, love, and mercy in the name of Jesus. How do you even begin to speak of success when the active agent in our ministry works "when and where it pleases him"? You simply can't under a "theology of the cross."

3. **Loneliness**. "With so many people looking to pastors for guidance, it can be difficult for pastors to let their guards down."

I could not have imagined that a public office could be so devastatingly lonely. We're a bit like chefs, line cooks, and dishwashers in a restaurant. We don't experience the foretaste of the Feast in quite the same way as the diners in the front. For this reason, chefs and line cooks tend to hang out at bars and eateries that understand the idiosyncrasies of their work. It's the same with us. We hang out with our own for a very good reason: We're the only ones who aren't potential "clients and customers." We can actually be ourselves around each other without worrying that someone will cease to worship Jesus Christ as Lord because they heard Pastor Bill drop a juicy expletive while engaging in a Strategy Two session. This, by the way, explains a lot of the behavior that goes on at pastors' conferences.

The problem is that we pastor-types are a notoriously insecure lot. Most of us are first-born sons trying to please their hard-to-please mothers, which means we're always comparing, evaluating, judging, and ultimately justifying ourselves at the expense of our peers. My vicarage supervisor, who had been a district president, once remarked that the reason all pastors' conferences are three days long is because pastors are like a bunch of bulldogs let loose in a yard who have to mark every tree. "It takes three days for them to empty their pastoral bladders," he noted. It takes us about three days to start being honest with each other instead of pissing on each other's shoes.

4. **Moral Failure**. "The moral failures of pastors are magnified more than the average person." No kidding. Nothing messes up a ministry faster than a moral misstep.

Where there is despair, failure, and loneliness there will be problems. We want to feel better, so we push on the whoopee center of our brains. Gambling, porn, sex, drunkenness, gluttony, beer, Monday Night Football. It's all the same thing. As Christians we are all Christ in an Adam suit. *Simul iustus et peccator*. We have the mind of Christ in the flesh of Adam. Being *simul* isn't easy or terribly pretty to look at. And being a paid, professional Christian is even worse.

The church isn't much help these days. Our society's preoccupation with sex seems to have driven the church into the opposite puritanical ditch where the only possible moral failing involves sex. We are constantly inundated by pastors' conferences and pastoral letters oozing deep institutional concern over our sex lives and the contents of our computer hard drives . . . leading me to want a medical emergency bracelet that reads, "In case of medical emergency, please erase my hard drive." When Luther wrote the Small Catechism on the Sixth Commandment, he intentionally did not write any "do nots" because he didn't need to give old Adam any ideas. He already knows more than enough ways to break this commandment.

5. **Financial Pressure**. "Most ministries are non-profits, so pastors are not compensated well."

Wow! Now there's a revelation! What's next? The Pope is Catholic? We didn't go into the ministry for cash and prizes. At least I didn't. I was doing quite well as a chemist. I will admit to being among the thirty percent surveyed that do not feel underpaid. I have a generous congregation, a decent salary, a working wife, a comfortable home, a couple of cars that run, and a well-stocked wine cellar. I consider myself fortunate.

A well-intentioned member came up to me after church one Sunday after having read an article on clergy burnout. He said, "Pastor, I don't understand how you guys can be burned out. You have the best job in the world because you work for the best boss in the world." I said to him, "I receive a paycheck every two weeks. In the past twenty years, I have never once seen the name 'Lord Jesus Christ' on the signature line."

Until we collectively come to grips with the paradox of that simple but obvious observation, we will never understand the financial pressures of the pastor. In our polity, the shepherd is paid by the flock he shepherds. He is obligated to irritate them, and they are obligated to pay him. Conflicted? You bet it is!

The laborer is worthy of his hire; the ox treading out the gospel grain is allowed to munch unmuzzled. Yes, the church is to be busy feeding the hungry, clothing the naked, and sheltering the homeless, but the naked, hungry and homeless shouldn't be the pastor and his family. It wouldn't be bad to recover the notion that it took ten men to have a synagogue, because ten households giving ten percent could support a rabbi at the median income of the community. I have heard of at least one congregation who offered to retire not only the educational debt of their new pastor but also the debt of his wife. May their tribe multiply exponentially!

6. **Anger**. "When things aren't going well, pastors become angry—with others, themselves, or God."

I spent the first ten years of my ministry more or less angry. I was angry at the state of the synod, the state of the world, and the state of our congregations. I was angry at being sent to southern California, a place I vowed I'd never live. We're Missouri Synod Lutherans, after all. We thrive on anger. It's in our DNA. Many of us are German, which means we sound angry even when we're making love. When people left the congregation, I got angry. When people misbehaved, I got angry. In fact, I was angry most of the time, which doesn't exactly make for gospel-centered preaching and compassionate pastoral care.

Sometimes anger is justifiable, though it never works the righteousness of God. Still, turning over a few bake sale tables and swinging a whip of cords can be cathartic if not oodles of fun. I began to realize that I was angry because nearly every hope, dream, and aspiration that I'd ever had about being a pastor had died and gone to dust.

A few years ago, I resolved never to let anyone or anything get in the way of the joy of salvation in Christ or of preaching the outrageous good news of sins forgiven for Jesus' sake. If Paul could pen a joyful epistle from prison to the Philippians, I too could endure all things through him who gives me strength. I ceased to take things personally. If people wanted to leave our congregation for the big-box mega-church with the wide-screen hymns and earwax-clearing praise band, I let them depart in peace. If they found the worship unfulfilling, the preaching uninspiring, the fellowship less than utopian, I knew it was more a reflection on their own spiritual malady than my pastoral means. To be blunt, I ceased to care. Eugene Peterson once wrote this little pastoral prayer: "Lord, teach us to care and not to care."[2] Doctors know this all too well. A little distance and objectivity are not necessarily bad; in fact, they are downright essential. I learned to care without caring—about me.

---

[2] See Eugene H. Peterson, *Subversive Spirituality* (Grand Rapids: Eerdmans, 1997), 154–68.

I think one of the greatest sources of pastoral anger is the death of expectations. We lay expectations on each other and then get angry when others don't live up to our expectations. People expect pastors to be always on their A-game—pious, friendly, serious, content, imminent, transcendent, omnipotent, omnipresent, and omniscient. Pastors expect their people to be in church every Sunday, sing fifteen-stanza Reformation rousers with great gusto, give at least ten percent, bring friends and neighbors to church, eagerly volunteer for VBS and other stuff, and generally not be a pain in the neck at board and voters' meetings.

The solution, I believe, is not to alter or diminish expectations, but not to have any in the first place. Drop dead to those expectations and deal with the person as the *simul* believer he or she is. I think we'd all be a lot happier if we stopped trying to fix people and instead be pastor to them.

7. **Burnout**. "Pastors are put on a treadmill. . . . They just keep running until there's no passion or energy left."

Burnout is caused by mind-numbing sameness, the kind that makes your life resemble the movie *Groundhog Day* where every day is a treadmillish repetition of the day before. Or was it last year? Sunday to Sunday. Advent to Pentecost. Not even the three-year lectionary can break the treadmill cycle. Boredom is the underlying cause of burnout, along with compassion fatigue—that business of internalizing all the emotional ooze that goes on around you.

I don't have much of a prescription, except to say what has worked for me. Create adventures. They say adventures are good for mind and memory, too. Dare to dabble. Write a book, a paper, give a talk, a banquet speech. Travel, teach, cook. I've been to Siberia, been president of Higher Things, given talks, made new friends, learned to scuba dive, work with wood, bake bread, garden, cook. Handle material. We who deal in words, feelings, and abstractions need to get a few splinters in our fingers and dirt under our fingernails to remind us that we are flesh and bone of the earth. Paul made tents. Handling material is a good thing, a First Article gift.

Besides, wood and dirt don't talk back. But do be careful as you book passage on a ship bound for Tarshish when the Lord is pointing you to the nasty Ninevites. And watch out for big fish.

8. **Physical Health**. "Many pastors overwork themselves and simply do not care for their bodies."

There's one that's hard to argue with, especially standing naked in front of a full-length mirror. Ours is a sedentary vocation. We sit a lot. We sit at desks, in chairs, in traffic, living rooms, waiting rooms, in front of the TV, in front of the computer. The best piece of furniture I ever bought was a really good chair. We sit in this adrenalized puddle of pastoral anxiety. If it isn't already, being a pastor should be classified by insurance companies as a "pre-existing medical condition."

About the most exercise we get is standing for the liturgy while the rest of the congregation gets to sit for part of the time. Don't you long for the old days when the rabbi sat down to teach? Some have added some liturgical aerobics to our practice with genuflecting and kneeling in an apparent effort to get at least a modicum of exercise and feel the burn.

There's no other way to say this. We need to reduce the collective clergy BMI. Skip the second trip through the potluck line (no matter who is watching which dish you are eating), eat moderately, get that core in shape, walk, swim, run, bicycle, whatever. You'll feel better, think better, look better, sleep better. Your doctor will stop hounding you, you'll fit into that stylish cassock, and you can go back to wearing cinctures around your waist again. Just don't pose shirtless on Facebook. Please, I'm begging you, keep your shirt on.

9. **Marriage and Family Issues**. "Too often, a pastor's spouse and children end up taking a backseat to the ministry."

As they used to say, "The shoemaker's kids are always barefoot." Think about it. If a man in your congregation spent the vast majority of nights and weekends at work away from his wife and kids, you'd be all over his case preaching about his vocational duties as husband and father. Well, physicians of the soul, it's time to take your own prescription.

Pastors' wives, God bless you. You probably didn't know what you were getting into when you married that seminarian or vicar. Well, now you do. You have come to know what "for better, for worse, for richer, for poorer" actually means. While there are a lot of books on pastoring, there are very few books on pastor-wifeing. In case there are any aspiring authors among you, I'd like to offer a few provocative titles as grist for the mill:

- *Raising Arizona: Picture-Perfect Parenting for the Piously Perfect Parsonage*
- *Cultivating Crazy: Making Those Borderline Personality Issues Work for You*
- *Dodging Dorcas: Avoiding Church Ladies Without Leaving the Country*
- *Bless My Lips: Facial Exercises for that Picture-Perfect Sunday Smile*
- *Fifty Shades of Rose: Homemade Vestments for Your Pastor-Husband*
- *Bless Your Heart: How to Piously Decline Used Furniture, Worn-out Clothing, and Out-of-Date Canned Goods*

If your husband asks you to critique that sermon or Bible class of his, simply smile and decline. You should treat all such requests for feedback precisely the same way as when you ask him, "Does this dress make me look fat?" You and I both know that the correct answer is, "You aren't fat." If you have to ask, you already know the answer anyway. When he asks you, "Honey, how was my sermon this morning?" you should answer, "I always love listening to your sermons," even if you didn't hear a word of it because you were refereeing sibling violence in the pew. There are plenty of other people around who will remind your husband of how bad he is at what he does. Don't be one of them.

Having said that, guys, listen to your wife. In all likelihood, her emotional quotient (that is, her EQ) far eclipses your pastoral obliviousness. She likely knows before you do who is hurting, who is happy, and who wants to ring your collared neck. People often use the pastor's wife as a conduit of communication. It's a lot easier, and safer, than making an appointment. They talk to her so they don't have to talk to you. Good idea? No. Something to be encouraged? Of course not! Useful? Always!

When your wife tells you that the tantrum you threw over the Ladies' Guild decorating the Christmas tree on the first Sunday of Advent may not have been one of your most shining pastoral moments, listen to her. When she tells you that the snarky remark you made about kids shacking up in last Sunday's sermon may have hit a raw nerve with the congregation chairman whose daughter just moved in with her boyfriend, you may want to make a phone call or two. Remember, your wife has a vested interest in happy pastor/congregation relations since she knows better than most who signs the paycheck. Your interests are not exactly the same as hers. You are concerned for doctrinal purity, liturgical integrity, and the salvation of souls. She is concerned for clothing and shoes, food and drink, house and home.

As long as we're talking about pastors and their wives, I don't understand this *Schwaermerei* we Lutheran pastors go through whenever another congregation is attempting to entice us away from doing our duty. We mysteriously receive this divine call, which we have been aware of all along and may have actually interviewed for, then announce it to the congregation as though it had been revealed to us by a man from Macedonia in a vision. Then we piously say, "Pray for me and my family as we decide where God wants us to serve." If God had a plan, he'd tell you in no uncertain terms. He's giving you options and isn't giving you any dew-on-the-fleece signs. Just decide and don't look back.

Should you stay or should you go? All other things being more or less equal, here's an easy way to decide a call.

Ask your wife where she wants to live. She tells you. You go or stay. How much more divinely simple can this be? You know that sooner or later, this is where you are going to end up anyway.

10. **Busyness.** Ninety percent of pastors report working 55 to 75 hours per week. I think I'm a ten percenter. I've never been given to working long hours at anything. I actually don't know how many hours a week I work. I cringe when people begin a conversation with "Pastor, I know you're busy. . . ." I'm not busy, I'm lazy. We're busy because we're trying to justify ourselves with our works, the very thing we preach and teach against. Our people are justified by faith apart from works, but we have gotten it into our clerical heads and pastoral hearts that we are not like other people and are justified by our works and not by faith alone. And we have church leadership and boards all too eager to confirm us in that notion.

We need to cultivate a sense of our own "non-necessity," like John the Baptist who pointed to Jesus and said, "Behold the Lamb of God who takes away the sin of the world," and then got out of the way. We must decrease, Christ must increase. We're the waiters and line cooks at the Feast, not the Chef and certainly not the Food.

Until they issue a set of really cool Mars lamps I can stick on the roof of my car and run through red lights, I will not subscribe to the notion of a "pastoral emergency." Besides, there is no such thing as an emergency in light of Jesus' "It is finished." If it's finished for Jesus, then why are we in such a big hurry?

Being a pastor in collar won't even get you out of speeding tickets where I live. I once got stopped by an officer with a hand-held radar on a side street. He was pulling over one car after another for speeding around a blind corner. I was the fourth in a line of offenders. He looked at my collar, smiled, and said, "Reverend, I assume you're in a hurry to get somewhere." I said, "As a matter of fact, I am." (I was late for a dental appointment.) He said, "Don't worry. I'll write you up first." I thanked him.

I do make one exception to what I just said about "pastoral emergencies." They come in handy when you need a quick exit from a tedious meeting or an endless conversation. Just whip out your cell phone, act as though you are listening to voice mail, assume that constipated look that we pastors have when we're being "pastoral," and then just say, "I'm sorry. I need to go." No explanations necessary. You're important. It's an emergency. Instant Strategy Two.

Seriously, there are true pastoral emergencies, as many as there are tragedies, infidelities, suicides, homicides, fires, floods, earthquakes, tornados, hurricanes, crazy people with guns, distraught parents, troubled spouses. We need to be there, always ready to speak the good news of God's reconciling this world to himself in the death of Jesus, even when everything appears to the contrary. There are plenty of genuine emergencies and eschatological urgencies. But none of them hinge on our absolute necessity.

## And One Reason to Stay

Okay, there you have it. I've given you ten reasons to quit. And I've given you the freedom to do it. But before you pack up the U-Haul, the kids, and the family dog, consider St. Paul's words in 2 Corinthians:

> For the love of Christ controls us, because we have concluded this: that one has died for all, therefore all have died; and he died for all, that those who live might no longer live for themselves but for him who for their sake died and was raised. From now on, therefore, we regard no one according to the flesh. Even though we once regarded Christ according to the flesh, we regard him thus no longer.
>
> Therefore, if anyone is in Christ, he is a new creation. The old has passed away; behold, the new has come. All this is from God, who through Christ reconciled us to himself and gave us the ministry of reconciliation; that is, in Christ God was reconciling the world to himself, not counting their trespasses against them, and entrusting to us the message of reconciliation. Therefore, we are ambassadors for Christ, God making his appeal through us. We implore you on behalf of Christ, be reconciled

*to God. For our sake he made him to be sin who knew no sin, so that in him we might become the righteousness of God* (2 Cor 5:14–21).

We are ambassadors for the King of kings. We work in an embassy of the kingdom of God, a little breaking-in point of God's eternal reign. Embassies and ambassadors are easy targets for terrorists. The devil, the world, and our adamic flesh hate this reign of God, his embassy, and his ambassadors. The world doesn't give out Nobel Prizes for preaching the gospel; it nails you to a cross. It has a track record for doing that.

God was in Christ reconciling the world—all things, every sin and every sinner—to himself in the death of Jesus. He works all things together for good. All things—the good, the bad, the ugly—he weaves into a beautiful tapestry of good. It's not that we're playing with loaded dice in a rigged casino, but God declares every roll a winner in the death of Jesus. Boxcars, snake eyes, winners all. God made his Son to be sin for us. He did not simply bear our sins but became our Sin, the corrupting disease itself, so that in him, baptized and believing in him, we might become the righteousness of God. We are ambassadors and heralds of the sweetest swap there ever was—sin for righteousness. Such a deal!

We are peace-speakers, proclaiming the peace that surpasses understanding into the worst of this world's disorder, where children are gunned down in classrooms, where old men and women lie in nursing homes and hospices waiting to die, where unwanted babies are torn from their mother's wombs, and where a dying infant is baptized in her grieving mother's arms. And we are given something to say to all that: God was in Christ reconciling the world to himself, not counting our sins against us. There is peace.

No one else in the religious world has or gets the outrageous punch line that sinners stand before God justified by grace through faith without so much as a twitch of a good work, all for Jesus' sake. No one else in this world can look at Death and the Grave as a vanquished enemy and say, "O Death, where is your sting? O Grave, where is your victory? Is that the best you've got?" No one else in this world can stare into the accusing mirror of the law and say with all confidence, "There is therefore now no condemnation for those who are in Christ Jesus."

To be honest with you, in 1986 when I packed up my stuff and moved to the seminary in St. Louis, had I known then what I know now, I would not have left my career in science. At least, I seriously doubt it. Yet knowing what I now know these many years later, I would not want things any other way. Our Lord is gracious, and he is good.

My dear brothers and sisters, don't let anyone or anything rob you of the joy and freedom you have in Christ. Not the devil, the world, your sinful flesh. Not church bodies or bureaucrats or boards. Not cranky congregations or pesky parishioners. Not the law or that accusing and excusing conscience of yours. Fix your eyes on Jesus who turns our sorrows to joy, our weeping to laughter, our mourning to dancing, our water into wine. He multiplies our meager loaves and fishes to feed the multitudes, and he makes good out of everything by his dying and rising.

When we take our eyes off of Jesus and his cross, we will always find at least ten reasons to quit the ministry. But with the eyes of faith fixed on Jesus, we will see the one reason to stay.

# Take Courage, Brothers, in the Lord

## An Original Hymn Honoring
## Harold Senkbeil's Service
## to the Lord and His Church

*Stephen P. Starke and Phillip Magness*

"Take Courage, Brothers, in the Lord" was written to the glory of God on the occasion of the 45th anniversary of pastoral ministry for Pastor Hal Senkbeil. The text was written from the standpoint of one who is serving in the pastoral ministry, receiving encouragement for that ministry from the ministry of DOXOLOGY. The work of DOXOLOGY is personified in this hymn text as a speaker addressing and encouraging pastors. Pastors are on the front lines of the spiritual battles that continue to rage on, battles marked by increasing hatred and scorn directed toward the Christian faith.

The first stanza encourages pastors to stand firm, be courageous, and boldly preach Christ crucified, with this gospel message briefly summarized in the second stanza. The third and fourth stanzas remind pastors that they are God's letter sent to the hurting world and that they are to be mirrors that reflect the light of God's grace shining for all in the face of Christ Jesus. The fifth stanza highlights the means God has given pastors for their work, the means of grace. This stanza also encourages pastors to be faithful stewards of these sacred mysteries while lovingly caring for their flock, equipping their flock for service to God. The sixth and seventh stanzas remind pastors that their work in the harvest field is urgent work, done with zeal in the light of the approaching Last Day; they work as those who seek to please their Master. Pastoral ministry is a labor of faith, sowing the seed in the field in which God has placed them, marveling at the fact that God uses unworthy sinners to accomplish his will. Stanza eight is a closing doxological stanza that focuses once more upon God's love in Christ, our Savior.

The music for this hymn uses rhythm and harmony to highlight the themes of vocation and struggle. Rhythmically, the walking bass provides a sense of traveling to underscore the pastor's active work of "going forth" to make Christ known. Harmonically, the music modulates through various tonalities to create a sense of going to different places—just as the pastor preaches faithfully to his flock, visits the sick and the elderly, goes out into the community to make the good confession and to seek and to save the lost. Then, at the end of each stanza, the music resolves harmonically and elongates rhythmically to accompany the stanzas' concluding words of hope, encouragement, and praise. The tune, appropriately named EPISTLE, was inspired by the text.

To God alone be the glory!

Stephen P. Starke
Pastor
St. John Evangelical Lutheran
Church of Amelith
Bay City, Michigan

Phillip Magness
Director of Sanctuary Worship
Concordia Lutheran Church
Kirkwood, Missouri

*To the glory of God on the occasion*
*of the 45th anniversary of Harold L. Senkbeil*
*in the Office of the Holy Ministry*

# Take Courage, Brothers, in the Lord

1 Take cour - age, broth - ers, in the Lord,
2 For on that cross our great High Priest,
3 You are the ones God rec - om - mends,
4 Yours is a min - is - try of grace!

In face of dan - ger, ter - ror, sword, Of
From bonds of sin has us re - leased; Our
The ver - y let - ters that Christ sends; Not
Re - flect God's love with un - veiled face, His

ha - tred, scorn, or strife;
debt He paid in full!
scribed on slabs of stone,
glo - ry to re - veal:

Be not a - fraid to suf - fer loss
For Christ a - lone could sin re - dress
But penned on hearts by hand un - flawed,
God's splen - dor that will nev - er fade,

Text: Stephen P. Starke
Music: Phillip Magness

EPISTLE
886 886

*Acts 20:18–24; Col. 2:13–15;*
*1 Cor. 4:1; 2 Cor. 5:6–9*

As      bold - ly   you   pro - claim   the   cross      That
And     robe    us    in    His   righ - teous - ness,      Like
The     Spir - it    of    the   liv - ing   God—       Go
His     grace   in   Christ,   for   all   dis - played,      In

throned   the   Lord      of   Life.
snow     or   whit - est   wool.
forth    and   make   Christ   known!
Word,    at   Font   and   Meal.

5 These mysteries, God's gracious means,
   By which His Spirit sows and gleans,
   Are trusted to your care;
   Be faithful in your stewardship,
   As saints for service you equip,
   With nurture, love, and prayer.

6 Be strong, beloved, God's dear ward,
   Though parted now from Christ our Lord,
   You walk by faith, not sight.
   Come, make your aim the Lord to please,
   Each timely moment gladly seize,
   To toil while fades the light.

7 Soon comes that Day for which we yearn,
   Our gracious Master's sure return;
   Let zeal your duties fill!
   Unworthy servants all are we,
   And yet through us the Trinity
   Performs His saving will!

8 Praise God the Father's love in Christ.
   Whose plan of rescue sacrificed
   His one and only Son;
   Extol His Son, the Lamb once slain,
   The Spirit's praise be our refrain—
   Thrice Holy Three in One!

*To the glory of God on the occasion*
*of the 45th anniversary of Harold L. Senkbeil*
*in the Office of the Holy Ministry*

# Take Courage, Brothers, in the Lord

1 Take cour - age, broth - ers, in the Lord,
2 For on that cross our great High Priest,
3 You are the ones God rec - om - mends,
4 Yours is a min - is - try of grace!

In face of dan - ger, ter - ror, sword, Of
From bonds of sin has us re - leased; Our
The ver - y let - ters that Christ sends; Not
Re - flect God's love with un - veiled face, His

ha - tred, scorn, or strife;
debt He paid in full!
scribed on slabs of stone,
glo - ry to re - veal:

Be not a - fraid to suf - fer loss
For Christ a - lone could sin re - dress
But penned on hearts by hand un - flawed,
God's splen - dor that will nev - er fade,

As bold - ly you pro - claim the cross That
And robe us in His righ - teous - ness, Like
The Spir - it of the liv - ing God— Go
His grace in Christ, for all dis - played, In

throned the Lord of Life.
snow or whit - est wool.
forth and make Christ known!
Word, at Font and Meal.

Text: Stephen P. Starke
Tune: Phillip Magness

EPISTLE
886 886

*Acts 20:18–24; Col. 2:1⁻*
*1 Cor. 4:1; 2 Co*

5 These mysteries, God's gracious means,
By which His Spirit sows and gleans,
Are trusted to your care;
Be faithful in your stewardship,
As saints for service you equip,
With nurture, love, and prayer.

6 Be strong, beloved, God's dear ward,
Though parted now from Christ our Lord,
You walk by faith, not sight.
Come, make your aim the Lord to please,
Each timely moment gladly seize,
To toil while fades the light.

7 Soon comes that Day for which we yearn,
Our gracious Master's sure return;
Let zeal your duties fill!
Unworthy servants all are we,
And yet through us the Trinity
Performs His saving will!

8 Praise God the Father's love in Christ.
Whose plan of rescue sacrificed
His one and only Son;
Extol His Son, the Lamb once slain,
The Spirit's praise be our refrain—
Thrice Holy Three in One!

–15;
5:6–9
folders.

# Harold L. Senkbeil Bibliography

"Romans 10:8–10, 14–17 in the Systematic Theologies of Franz Pieper, Adolf Hoenecke, and Other Selected Commentators." B.D. Thesis, Concordia Theological Seminary, 1971.

Review of James W. Sire, *The Universe Next Door: A Basic World View Catalog*. *Concordia Theological Quarterly* 44, no. 1 (January 1980): 85–86.

"Lutherans for Life." *The Lutheran Synod Quarterly* 24, no. 4 (December 1984): 70–82.

"Sanctification: The Evangelical Challenge." S.T.M. Thesis, Concordia Theological Seminary, 1986.

"Lutheran and/or Evangelical." *Teachers Interaction* 29, no. 8 (September 1988): 2–4.

*Sanctification: Christ in Action, Evangelical Challenge and Lutheran Response*. Milwaukee: Northwestern, 1989.

*Recharting the Waters: The Middle Years, Part 2*. Study Guide. Life Cycle: Journey in Faith. St. Louis: Concordia, 1990.

"A Lutheran Look at the 'Evangelicals.'" *Lutheran Witness* 110, no. 2 (February 1991): 1–3.

"Liturgy as Mission: A Response to the Challenge Facing Lutheranism from Evangelicals in America Today." *Bride of Christ* 15, no. 3 (Pentecost 1991): 5–16.

"The Liturgy Is the Life of the Church." *Lutheran Forum* 26, no. 1 (February 1992): 26–29.

*When the Crying Stops: Abortion, the Pain and the Healing*, with Kathleen Winkler. Milwaukee: Northwestern, 1992.

"Setting Your Bearings: Teaching Sanctification." *Lutheran Education* 127, no. 5 (May/June 1992): 267–76.

"9.5 Theses for a Continuing Reformation." St. Francis, Minn.: Trinity Lutheran Church, 1993. http://www.ctsfw.net/media/pdfs/Senkbeil9-5Theses.pdf.

*Dying to Live: The Power of Forgiveness*. St. Louis: Concordia, 1994.

> Also translated into Russian as *Смерть ради жизни: сила про-щения*. Sterling Heights, MI, USA: Izd. Fonda "Lîuteranskoe nasledie," 1998. (With Александр. Иншаков, Алексей. Комаров, and Lutheran Heritage Foundation.)

> Also translated into Danish as *At dø for at leve: et liv i gudstjeneste*. [Hillerød]: Luthersk Missionsforeinings Bibelskoles Elevforening, 2007.

> Also translated into Czech as *Cesta k životu v umírajícím světě*. Vyd. 1. Kontext 1; Kontext 1. Praha: Lutherova společnost, 2009.

Review of Fred L. Precht, ed., *Lutheran Worship: History and Practice*. *Logia* 3, no. 4 (October 1994): 61.

"Holiness: God's Work or Ours?" *Modern Reformation* 5, no. 6 (November/December 1996): 9–13. Repr. pages 155–62 in *Justified: Modern Reformation Essays on the Doctrine of Justification*. Edited by Ryan Glomsrud and Michael S. Horton. 2d ed. CreateSpace Independent Publishing Platform, 2013.

"Luther and the Fanatics: The Gospel under Fire." *Lutheran Synod Quarterly* 36, no. 4 (December 1996): 3–12.

"Luther and the Fanatics: The Gospel under Fire II: The Pietistic Threat to the Reformation." *Lutheran Synod Quarterly* 36, no. 4 (December 1996): 13–30.

"Luther and the Fanatics: The Gospel under Fire III: The Evangelical Threat to the Reformation." *Lutheran Synod Quarterly* 36, no. 4 (December 1996): 31–57.

"Dining with the Devil: The Megachurch Movement Flirts with Modernity." *Logia* 7, no. 3 (1998): 65–66.

"Through the Shadowlands: A Christian Handbook on Death and Life." *Logia* 8, no. 3 (1999): 17–19.

*Triumph at the Cross: Lenten Devotions for Repentance and Renewal*. Milwaukee: Northwestern, 1999.

*Where in the World Is God?*, with Beverly K. Yahnke. Milwaukee: Northwestern, 1999.

"Generation X and the Care of the Soul." Pages 287–303 in *Mysteria Dei: Essays in Honor of Kurt Marquart*. Edited by Paul T. McCain and John R. Stephenson. Fort Wayne, Ind.: Concordia Theological Seminary Press, 2000.

"The Art of Spiritual Evaluation: A Framework for Understanding the Health of the Soul and Its Cure." Pages 51–67 in *Christ's Gifts for Healing the Soul: Toward a Lutheran Identity in the New Millennium*. Edited by Daniel Zager. Fort Wayne, Ind.: Concordia Theological Seminary Press, 2001.

*To All Eternity: the Essential Teachings of Christianity*, with Edward A. Engelbrecht et al. St. Louis: Concordia, 2002.

Review of Gilbert Meilaender, *Love Taking Shape: Sermons on the Christian Life*. *Concordia Theological Quarterly* 66, no. 4 (October 2002): 374–75.

"The Cross and Personal Piety." *For the Life of the World* 7, no. 3 (July 2003): 4–6.

Review of Craig A. Parton. *The Defense Never Rests: A Lawyer's Quest for the Gospel*. *Logia* 12, no. 4 (Reformation 2003): 42–43.

*Tunnustakaa syntinne toisillenne: rippi kristityn elämässä*. Aamutähti; nro. 28. Macomb, Mich.: Lutheran Heritage Foundation, 2003. (With Maria. Vähäkangas and Suomen Luther-säätiö.)

"The Holy Life and Thanksgiving." *The British Lutheran* 46, no. 2 (Autumn 2003): 14.

"When Peace Seems Out of Reach." *Modern Reformation* 13, no. 6 (November/December 2004): 23–26.

Review of Mike Graves, ed., *What's the Matter with Preaching Today?* *Concordia Pulpit Resources*, 16 (2005), 13.

"Till the Trumpets Sound: Hold Fast and Hold Forth." *Logia* 15, no. 2 (Eastertide 2006): 17–27.

"When God Takes Aim." *For the Life of the World* 10, no. 2 (April 2006): 4–6.

*Tätä elämää janosin*. Hengen viisaus; nro. 6; Hengen viisaus; nro. 6. [Helsinki]: Suomen Luther-säätiö, 2006. (With Petri. Hiltunen, Maria. Vähäkangas, and Lutheran Heritage Foundation.)

"The Marriage Bed Undefiled: Pastoral Care for Sexual Sins." *Mercy Works* (July 2006).

"The Essence of Legalism: Bewitched and Bedazzled." *Journal of Inter-School Christian Fellowship* (July 2006).

Review of Robert J. Koester, *Gospel Motivation: More than "Jesus Died for My Sins"*. *Concordia Theological Quarterly* 71, no. 3–4 (July/October 2007): 375–77.

"Pastor, Psalms, and Day by Day Life: Visitation, Sickbed, and Deathbed." Pages 81–96 in *Day by Day We Magnify Thee: Psalms in the Life of the Church.* Edited by Daniel Zager. Fort Wayne, Ind.: Concordia Theological Seminary Press, 2007.

"The Cure of Souls: Good for What Ails You." *For the Life of the World* 11, no. 2 (April 2007): 10–12.

*Lamb of God, Pure and Holy: Resources for Lent-Easter Preaching and Worship Based on O Lamm Gottes,* with Kevin Hildebrand et al. St. Louis: Concordia, 2008.

Review of Paul A. Zimmerman, *A Seminary in Crisis: The Inside Story of the Preus Fact Finding Committee. Logia* 17, no. 2 (Eastertide 2008): 47–48.

"Fit for Ministry." *For the Life of the World* 12, no. 1 (January 2008): 15–16.

"Sound Doctrine and Spiritual Health: An Exercise in the Intentional Care of Souls." *Lutheran Theological Journal* 43, no. 2 (August 2009): 118–24.

Review of Kenneth W. Wieting, *The Blessings of Weekly Communion. Concordia Theological Quarterly* 73, no. 4 (October 2009): 374–76.

"Lutheran and/or Evangelical? The Impact of Evangelicalism on Lutheran Church—Missouri Synod Pastors." Pages 20–39 in *Evangelicalism and the Missouri Synod.* Vol. 12 of *The Pieper Lectures.* Edited by John A. Maxfield. St. Louis: Concordia Historical Institute & The Luther Academy, 2011.

Foreword to *Counseling and Confession: The Role of Confession and Absolution in Pastoral Counseling,* by Walter J. Koehler. Repr., St. Louis: Concordia Seminary Press, 2011.

"Lead Us Not into Temptation: Acedia, the Pastoral Pandemic." Pages 263–74 in *You, My People, Shall Be Holy: A Festschrift in Honour of John W. Kleinig.* Edited by John R. Stephenson and Thomas M. Winger. St. Catharines, Ontario, Canada: Concordia Lutheran Theological Seminary, 2013.

Review of Kathryn Ann Hill, *Rich in Grace: The Bible of the Poor for 21st-Century Christians: Meditations in Verse on the Triptychs of the Biblia Pauperum. Logia* 22, no. 1 (2013): 59.

"The Christian Faces Contemporary Challenges." *Lutheran Synod Quarterly* 54, no. 1 (March 2014), 37–69.

"Caring for Body and Soul: Q&A with Harold Senkbeil." *Modern Reformation* 23, no. 4 (July/August 2014): 5–9.

"Engaging Our Culture Faithfully." *Concordia Journal* 40, no. 4 (Fall 2014): 292–314.

"The Means of Grace: The Word and Sacraments." Pages 111–37 in *Where Christ Is Present: A Theology for All Seasons on the 500th Anniversary of the Reformation.* Edited by John Warwick Montgomery and Gene Edward Veith. Irvine, Calif.: NRP Books, 2015.

"Love among the Ruins: How Do We Reclaim Sexual Virtue in a Depraved World." *Lutheran Witness* 134, no. 2 (February, 2015): 10–13.

"*Meditatio*: On the Making of a Pastor." https://www.doxology.us/wp -content/uploads/2015/03/meditatio.pdf.

"Individual Confession: Personalized Forgiveness." https://www .doxology.us/wp-content/uploads/2015/03/25_confession forgiveness.pdf.

"Mission and Ministry Mash Up," with Lucas Woodford. *Lutheran Witness* 134, no. 5 (May 2015): 8–10.

"Pastoral Care and Sex." *Concordia Theological Quarterly* 79, no. 3–4 (July/October 2015): 329–45.

"Contemporary Ministry." *Seelsorger* 2 (2016): 2–3.

"Shepherding God's Flock." *Seelsorger* 3 (2017): 2–3.

"Holiness and the Cure of Souls." *Logia* 27, no. 2 (Eastertide 2018): 7–14.

"The Savior's Right-Hand Men." *Seelsorger* 4 (2018): 2–3.

"What's the Problem with Porn?" https://www.doxology.us/wp -content/uploads/2019/07/what-about-porn.pdf.

"Ambassadors for Christ." *Seelsorger* 5 (2019): 3.

*The Care of Souls: Cultivating a Pastor's Heart.* Bellingham, Wash.: Lexham Press, 2019.

*Church Leadership & Strategy: For the Care of Souls,* with Lucas Woodford. Bellingham, Wash.: Lexham Press, 2019.

*Christ and Calamity: Grace & Gratitude in the Darkest Valley.* Bellingham, Wash.: Lexham Press, 2020.

Made in the USA
Coppell, TX
14 May 2021